Church as Sanctuary

Church as Sanctuary

*Reconstructing Refuge
in an Age of Forced Displacement*

Leo Guardado

Maryknoll, New York 10545

Founded in 1970, Orbis Books endeavors to publish works that enlighten the mind, nourish the spirit, and challenge the conscience. The publishing arm of the Maryknoll Fathers and Brothers, Orbis seeks to explore the global dimensions of the Christian faith and mission, to invite dialogue with diverse cultures and religious traditions, and to serve the cause of reconciliation and peace. The books published reflect the views of their authors and do not represent the official position of the Maryknoll Society. To learn more about Maryknoll and Orbis Books, please visit our website at www.orbisbooks.com.

Copyright © 2023 by Leo Guardado.

Published by Orbis Books, Box 302, Maryknoll, NY 10545-0302.

All rights reserved.

No part of this publication may be reproduced or transmitted in any form or by any means, electronic or mechanical, including photocopying, recording, or any information storage or retrieval system, without prior permission in writing from the publisher.

Queries regarding rights and permissions should be addressed to: Orbis Books, P.O. Box 302, Maryknoll, NY 10545-0302.

Manufactured in the United States of America.

Manuscript editing and typesetting by Joan Weber Laflamme.

Library of Congress Cataloging-in-Publication Data

Names: Guardado, Leo, author.
Title: Church as sanctuary : reconstructing refuge in an age of forced displacement / Leo Guardado.
Description: Maryknoll, NY : Orbis Books, [2023] | Includes bibliographical references and index. | Summary: "Examines ancient and contemporary practices of refuge in the church"— Provided by publisher.
Identifiers: LCCN 2023022732 (print) | LCCN 2023022733 (ebook) | ISBN 9781626985407 | ISBN 9781608339976 (epub)
Subjects: LCSH: Church work with refugees. | Refugees—Religious aspects—Christianity.
Classification: LCC BV4466 .G83 2023 (print) | LCC BV4466 (ebook) | DDC 261.8/32—dc23/eng/20230821
LC record available at https://lccn.loc.gov/2023022732
LC ebook record available at https://lccn.loc.gov/2023022733

Contents

Introduction *vii*

Part I

**1. The Sanctuary of God for the Oppressed
of Central America**   **3**
Laying the Foundation for the Ministry of Sanctuary   7
Spiritual and Theological Discernment of Sanctuary   11
The Ministry of Sanctuary Goes Public   16
Conflicting Visions of Sanctuary   20
Attempts to Classify the Nature and Purpose of
Sanctuary   24

**2. Nonviolent Communion across Borders: The Theology and
Gandhian Philosophy of Sanctuary**   **29**
Theological Horizon of the Sanctuary Church   30
Sanctuary's Capacity to Construct a More Human
Society   37
Sanctuary in a Gandhian Framework for
Social Change   44
Civil Initiative—Gandhi's Method for Social Change
in the Borderlands   53
Sanctuary as Nonviolent Means and Ends   55

Part II

3. Traditions of Refuge for the Persecuted   **63**
Cities of Refuge and Asylum   64
Refuge in the Church   71
Disappearing the Ecclesiastical Right of Asylum   85

Contents

4. **The Sacramental and Humanizing Vision of Vatican II: A Firm Foundation for the Reconstruction of Church Sanctuary**   93

Incarnating the Church in History—Chenu and John XXIII   94

The Nature of the Church as Sacrament, as a People of God   104

The Mission of the People of God   113

A Human and Humanizing Church   120

5. **The Church of the Poor: A Sacrament of and for Christ**   127

Learning to Listen to the Poor   128

A Church of Love Witnesses against Injustice   135

A Church of Peace Witnesses against Violence   137

A Church of the Poor Witnesses against Poverty   141

A True and Mystical Sacrament of Life   150

A Sanctuary for the Body of Christ   157

Part III

6. **Archbishop Óscar Romero: A Living Sanctuary for the Persecuted**   163

Living in the Company of the Poor   165

The Violation of Sanctuary   169

The *Corpus Christi* of Aguilares   173

"You Are the Image of the Divine One Who Has Been Pierced"   176

A Living Sanctuary for the *Corpus Christi*   179

7. **Church as Sanctuary: Refuge, Healing, Holiness, and Salvation**   183

Refuge from Violence   185

Healing of Wounds   196

Dwelling in Holiness   209

Mutual Salvation   217

Conclusion   229

Acknowledgments   233

Index   235

Introduction

For months my mother and the rest of the family tried to convince me to leave. They would say, "Antes de que algo pase"—"before something happens." This "something" referred to the possibility of being taken by the military or the guerrillas to fight for them. My mother had returned from the United States six months prior, after having lived in Los Angeles for four-and-a-half years cleaning houses and working as a nanny in order to provide for the basic needs of life that El Salvador's war economy could not provide. She returned to El Salvador afraid that she would lose her son "sea a la guerra o a la ausencia"—"either to the war or to absence." She promised not to leave again without me, but the rest of our extended family was eager for us to flee together. At the beginning of October 1991 we finally left. Before dawn a bus pulled up in front of my grandparent's adobe house, where my family had gathered the night before. After hugs and attempts to hold back tears, I began to board the colorful bus typical of El Salvador, turning around one last time to gaze upon my grandfather, who, in the absence of a father, had served as a loving and protective presence in my childhood. This would be the last time I would see him.

The bus carried other Salvadorans forced to flee the country, all adults except for a fifteen-year-old girl and me. During the bus ride from my village in Chalatenango to the capital, I counted palm trees. I wanted to commit to memory the sights of my country, not knowing if or when I would return. After one hundred and some palm trees, I lost count and wept as we approached the Guatemalan border. Throughout the journey north my mother kept reciting a prayer that my great grandmother taught her to use in times of danger:

> Detrás de un cedro dichoso estaba Cristo y Francisco. Francisco le dijo a Cristo, "hay vienen los enemigos." "Déjalos que lleguen, Francisco," le dijo Cristo, "que su vista la traen vendada. Tu cuerpo no será tocado, tu alma será santa y salvada."

This prayer, which had been passed from generation to generation, accompanied us in a journey that was as intense and harrowing as the place we had left.

A month later, after terrifying moments and encounters with thieves, deportation by Mexican immigration, a night in jail, and pursuits by US immigration agents at the Tijuana–San Diego border, we finally made it into the United States of America. At that point we became "illegals"—a whole category of forcibly displaced persons set apart for persecution. Soldiers and guerrillas were no longer the danger; it was now a matter of evading and surviving border patrol, police, and other agents of the US government who desired our expulsion.

At that time the only hope of legal protection that we had was to apply for a temporary permit. Such permits were issued to Salvadorans and Guatemalans after churches that were providing sanctuary in the United States successfully sued the government for its discriminatory practices against asylum seekers throughout the 1980s. In the midst of the US government's failure to protect, church communities had become sites of refuge for displaced and persecuted persons. The churches had come to serve as a sanctuary for the poor of Central America, and the creative impact of their faithful actions had opened a way for us to remain temporarily in the United States and not face deportation back to war.

Church and *sanctuary* are two concepts and historical realities that are fundamentally intertwined. By definition, to speak of sanctuary is to speak of both a place of refuge or protection and of a holy place, such as a temple or church. And to speak of church, by definition, implies both a community of people and particular sites, such as a building used for worship. In the coming chapters I bring these multiple meanings together to argue for an understanding of church as sanctuary, as a people and site of refuge in an age of forced displacement. More specifically, I make the case that the ancient and contemporary practice of refuge in the church is a concretization of a church of and for the poor in the United States. In times of unprecedented global displacement, sanctuary is a pillar of what it means to be church.

Since the 1980s, when church sanctuary became a controversial national movement in the United States, various academic works have engaged this concept and practice, mostly from a sociological or anthropological perspective, but an explicit theological analysis of church sanctuary has been lacking. Particularly in the Roman Catholic tradition there has been a theological gap concerning church sanctuary, which has accompanied a widespread ecclesiastical rejection of this practice. This work aims to relocate the tradition of sanctuary in the heart of the church.

As in the 1980s, unbearable violence in Central America continues to displace persons and communities, who then are forced to seek refuge in other countries; many of them attempt to find it in the United States. In addition to Central Americans, there are persons from South America, Africa, China, Haiti, and from many other regions and countries throughout the globe who now cross through Central America and Mexico in order to arrive at the US-Mexico border in search of refuge and asylum. While the specific countries from where people come can change in a given year, the fact that the number of forcibly displaced persons globally has more than doubled in the past decade means that, for the foreseeable future, a vast sector of humanity will be on the move. The United States temporarily allows some communities to enter legally, but the vast majority of the world's displaced are denied legal entry. Unable to live in their places of origin and rejected at the border, an unauthorized entry through the desert wilderness becomes their act of hope and their struggle for life. Those who make it into the United States can begin a complex process of rebuilding fragments of life anew, but under the ever-present threat of deportation. Months and years can go by before a person or family receives an order of deportation or is apprehended in an ICE (Immigration and Customs Enforcement) raid, but once this happens, there are very few options available to stay. In some cases the person or family has no other choice to resist deportation but to seek refuge in a church. This is not technically a legal option, but it can lead to new legal possibilities as the local community gathers in support, unleashing creative responses previously unseen.

In contrast to the 1980s experience of church sanctuary, which focused on transporting and providing refuge and protection to persons and families who were fleeing the violence of Central America and who were arriving in the United States, most of the persons who are now forced to seek sanctuary have already been living in the United States for years and may even have children who are US citizens. This does not mean that there is not a network of active churches and communities who help transport and protect persons in various creative ways across borders today, but this work is not public or at the scale at which it took place in prior decades. Among other factors, such as changed immigration laws and penalties for breaking these laws, the changed political situation in Latin America affects the public's conception of sanctuary.

In the 1980s, the US government was directly supporting the Salvadoran military during El Salvador's civil war. Although homicide rates in El Salvador and across Central America continue to approximate those of a country or region at war, officially there is no armed conflict taking place that fits classical notions of war. At best, one can argue that what Central America lives through now is the aftermath of many decades of direct US neocolonial interests in the region. But without direct US involvement in a Central American war, in the public's consciousness US society does not have direct responsibility for the thousands of people who continue to arrive at the border or who are threatened with deportation back to warlike conditions. Among ecclesiastical leaders in the United States, both in the 1980s and now, there is general opposition to church sanctuary. And yet, when all other options have failed, people still turn to church communities with the hope of refuge, and some churches still become sites of sanctuary, but rarely does this happen in the Roman Catholic Church.

Sanctuary is an emergency response to a situation of persecution, and, in the United States, the nature of the persecution of unauthorized persons is directly connected to the political interests of a given administration. During the Trump presidency, for example, more people sought sanctuary in churches because the risks of deportation were higher as ICE targeted unauthorized persons not only in an attempt to expel them, but also in an attempt to maintain private prisons at full capacity in order to further justify the political need for such private prisons. It is well known that the incarceration of black and brown persons in the United States is very profitable for corporations, and it behooves faith communities and ecclesiastical leaders to take such political and financial interests into account when discerning how they will respond to persons threatened with deportation who seek sanctuary in the church.

The emphasis on church sanctuary may appear too traditional in its scope, too ecclesio-centered, too bound up with church hierarchy and with patriarchal structures that can end up enacting harm upon persons who are forced to seek refuge. Some scholars may legitimately ask whether church sanctuary in the United States is not simply the privileged actions of mostly white communities who can turn refuge on and off depending on how pleased they are with those who seek refuge. Critics of church sanctuary may argue that we need to decouple sanctuary from church and church from sanctuary. After all, refuge can be practiced in any place by any people without any reference to notions of church. While there is truth in these questions and critiques, I maintain that church and sanctuary are fundamentally bound together in theory and in practice. Church sanctuary, despite all of its historical shortcomings and contradictions, complements and ensures that other forms of sanctuary beyond the church are legible as a common heritage of humanity. The endurance of church sanctuary is, has been, and, I trust, will continue to be an efficacious sign of hope that there are, can, and must be sites of refuge in this world where death-dealing violence is resisted and overcome. Until the deportation of forcibly displaced, poor, and persecuted persons is no longer a form of death sentence, the church in the modern world cannot close the door to sanctuary, but must be rebuilt as sanctuary.

This book is divided into three intersecting parts. Part I remembers the enduring ecclesial challenge of the 1980s sanctuary ministry and movement. Part II lays the theological foundation for rethinking the church in an age of forced displacement. Part III envisions the rebuilding of the church as sanctuary, as a people and site of refuge, healing, holiness, and salvation.

Chapter 1 revisits the sanctuary movement of the 1980s and its origin as a faith-based ecumenical and interreligious ministry with refugees who were being sent back to the US-funded war in El Salvador. Communities in southern Arizona, with the initiative of Jim Corbett, a Friend (Quaker), developed a capacious vision of sanctuary that included, yet exceeded, any religious tradition that was willing to stand with those whose humanity the government was violating. The rapid expansion of sanctuary beyond the Arizona borderlands gave rise not only to a national movement, but also to competing visions of the nature of sanctuary and of the role of churches.

Chapter 2 shows that the conflicting visions of sanctuary were marked less by religious and denominational differences and more by philosophical and theological frameworks for social transformation and political engagement. For Corbett, sanctuary was built on a theology of God's dwelling and communion and a Gandhian philosophy of nonviolence for social change. Borderland communities argued that sanctuary churches were enacting civil initiative, not civil disobedience, and that their actions were fundamentally constructive of, and for, humanity. Sanctuary was not seen as a means to an end but as a way of being that already contained within itself the possibility of a humanizing global society and of a borderless church.

Chapter 3 shows how the ancient practice of church sanctuary, akin to biblical cities of refuge, served as a practice for the protection of persecuted life. Beyond its associations as a refuge for criminals, the earliest Christian references to sanctuary from the fourth century reveal that it was also a refuge for the poor and oppressed who sought what bishops called the mercy of the church. Codified as a right within ecclesiastical law from the fifth century on, references to sanctuary were removed in the late twentieth century based on the assumption that sanctuary was no longer needed in the modern nation-state because laws had been "humanized." Today, sanctuary may no longer exist as a legal right in the modern nation-state, but it can exist again as the religious principle that it was before it became a right.

Chapter 4 undertakes an examination of the nature and mission of the church as expressed through key documents of Vatican II and the thinkers that shaped this ecclesial event. The erasure of the tradition of sanctuary from the Roman Catholic Church's canon law in the twentieth century invites a reconsideration of fundamental ecclesiological questions—who and what is the church, and what is it for? The church's theological affirmation that it is a humanizing presence in the world and a sacrament of salvation invites both historical verification and translation in relation to particular contexts of dehumanization and death.

Chapter 5 argues that, if Vatican II opened up the possibility for responding to the pressing signs of the times of modernity, the Latin American church's recommitment to struggle against institutionalized violence allows for a rethinking of the church as the dwelling place of, and for, the poor and persecuted, where the church encounters its own foundation in Christ. A sacramental understanding of Christ's presence in the poor holds the greatest possibility for a people of faith enfleshing sanctuary despite the borders of the church and the state.

Chapter 6 demonstrates how Archbishop Óscar Romero, like the bishops of the fourth century who lived into their sacramental responsibility to protect persons forced to seek sanctuary, risked his life in defense of the poor and persecuted of El Salvador, especially in the town of Aguilares in 1977. His embodied witness and sacramental insights about the nature and mission of the church in the midst of the idolatry of national security illustrate a fundamental aspect of the tradition of church sanctuary: a people in communion with one another constructs sanctuary. His martyrdom remains a piercing challenge for ecclesiastical leaders and for Christian churches in the United States who hold on to their own security at the cost of those who are persecuted for seeking life.

Chapter 7, the final chapter, develops an understanding of church as sanctuary in relation to four key categories: refuge, healing, holiness, and salvation. Refuge within church communities resists deportation and the way that these state practices become naturalized within a society and church that are being psychologically trained to be indifferent to killing. The sustained encounter that takes place through church sanctuary can give rise to a dynamic process of social healing capable of locating and touching the deepest identities of both the church and of persecuted persons as each becomes an echo of the other. Sanctuary is the practice of holiness, the invocation of the uncontainable presence of God who dwells in the midst of persons and communities who commit their life for the life of others, sanctifying what has been deemed illegal and making of it a sacrament of the Holy. Lastly, where the Holy is practiced, there is salvation. The historicization of salvation incorporates a people into a borderless body that is both marked by the wounds of violence yet transfigured into a sign of peace. In an age of forced displacement, to be church is to be sanctuary.

Part I

1

The Sanctuary of God
for the Oppressed of Central America

From an interview with Óscar, a Salvadoran refugee:

> When I was arrested, I first realized the brutality they used. They don't respect the rights of people, or the fact that they're coming from an oppressive situation. At the beginning they didn't hit me, but asked me absurd questions like "where was I from." When I said I was from El Salvador, they asked if I was a guerrilla. I don't know why. I observed some cooperation between the police and immigration officers because the police first arrested me. It was in Tucson. For no reason, they stopped the vehicle I was in, asking for papers. They called the Immigration Service, who came in five minutes and questioned me. They said I had to tell the truth because I was in a country where lies weren't told. . . . I said I wasn't a guerrilla when they asked about this. They asked when I left El Salvador and I said eight days ago. "Why did you come?" "Because there is repression and war there." Questions like that.
>
> They said if I wanted to get out, I'd have to pay a bond. They said I'd be sent to El Centro [detention center] and took me there in a bus. It was very hard; it smelled like urine and excrement; they weren't very clean—very bad conditions. . . . The camp is about the size of an orchard. The place they kept us was meant for 100–200 people, but there were 400–500 there. We were crowded, exchanging diseases, as many were sick. The structure had a roof and floor but was open, and small. In the summer we were very hot, and couldn't escape the sun—it seemed to be 136°F.
>
> There was psychological torture from the moment I was arrested. Over the loudspeakers they always used to say, "All you Salvadorans

are going to be deported, and they're going to kill you." This is psychological warfare.

I was at [El Centro] from May 14, 1981, until near the end of July. The [Tucson Ecumenical Council] paid my $2,000 bond at this time, and helped me file my political asylum application. They [immigration officials] say they send them to Washington, but I think they just themselves mark them "denied." They just leave you hanging. Once released, one is just a different kind of refugee, without work or anything, and it's pretty difficult to live.

Q: Can you talk about why you left El Salvador?

Besides the persecution of students, the church, and the unemployment, which all together make one want to leave, there's the fact that there is martial law. At any time the military can come and take a person and kill them; no one feels secure, most of the people are intimidated and just want to find somewhere safe to go. The governments of Guatemala and Honduras are helping to massacre the people. Mexico is deporting Salvadorans to the Guatemala border, where they are killed there. Then we are deported from the US, too. . . . I think I'd be killed if I arrived at the airport without a passport, which I no longer have. I'd be suspicious and be killed.[1]

On July 4, 1980, a year before Óscar was bailed out from the immigrant detention center, a group of twenty-six Salvadorans fleeing the US-sponsored social, political, and economic crisis of their country was attempting to cross southern Arizona with the hope of finding refuge in the United States. The previous day two Mexican coyotes had left most of the group stranded in an isolated and arid region of the Organ Pipe Cactus National Monument desert, where summer temperatures easily surpass 120 degrees. As it became clear that the Mexican coyotes were not coming back, some of the men decided to venture forth in search of water, leaving about ten of the women behind with the Salvadoran

---

[1] Excerpt from an interview with Óscar, a Salvadoran refugee who was released from El Centro detention center in July 1981. He was interviewed in Tucson, Arizona, in November 1981. See "Conversations with Refugees from El Salvador, 1982," University of Arizona Special Collections, MS 362, Box 30, Folder 24.

coyote who had organized the trip. On the evening of July 5, Border Patrol discovered the men who left to find water, but three of them had already died of thirst. The rest of the group who had remained behind was not found until the morning of July 6. Seven of those ten were dead. In total, thirteen of the original twenty-six survived, three were never found, and the rest perished in the desert wilderness.

According to reports and further research conducted on this tragedy, the group comprised Salvadorans from various walks of life that included students, factory workers, a shoemaker, a bus driver, and others who could be considered middle class.[2] A Border Patrol agent who was interviewed days later stated with a sense of surprise that some of the Salvadorans who were recently coming across the desert were not "riffraff" but rather included merchants, teachers, lawyers, and even a judge.[3] Another Border Patrol agent, emphasizing the contrast between the group's expectations of the journey and the reality of the desert wilderness said that "instead of loading up with water, they were carrying luggage with winter clothes and books in it" and that the "women were wearing high heels."[4] While these comments reveal that some Salvadorans were not prepared for the desert terrain, more fundamentally they reveal the disconnected reality under which most US citizens lived in regards to the violence engulfing El Salvador—a violence that cut across socioeconomic status or profession.

When this tragedy took place in July 1980, some US Americans may have known that, four months prior, the Catholic archbishop of El Salvador—Óscar Romero—had been assassinated. However, the violent rape and murder of the four churchwomen from the United States—Sr. Dorothy Kazel, Sr. Ita Ford, Sr. Maura Clarke, and Jean Donovan—an event that would bring the effects of the war closer to home for most US Americans, would not take place for another six months. In between these two piercing moments of the early days of the war, when

---

[2] See Miriam Davidson, *Convictions of the Heart* (Tucson: University of Arizona Press, 1988), 7; Aron Spilken, *Escape! A True Story of Betrayal and Survival* (New York: Penguin Group, 1984); Al Senia, "13 Smuggled Salvadorans Found Dead in U.S. Desert," *Washington Post*, July 7, 1980.

[3] Mart Starr, "Salvadorans Risked Death to Escape It," *Chicago Tribune* online, July 13, 1980.

[4] Starr.

an average of one thousand Salvadoran civilians were killed per month,[5] the US population began to awaken to the displacement of Salvadorans who were now reaching the US border. The erroneous expectation that only the economically poor fled El Salvador to survive was giving way to the puzzling reality that even middle-class professionals had to flee with their books and high heels. A newspaper reporter summarized the impact of the asylum seekers' deaths: "The American public will be left with a grim memory of a desert disaster in which human beings were forced to drink cologne, deodorant, and finally their own urine and to try and eat dry cactus in a desperate attempt to survive."[6] The reporter failed to emphasize that those who survived were immediately placed under house arrest while they recuperated. Later, they were transferred to a jail in Tucson, Arizona, to await the deportation processes that would attempt to send them back to the very violence from which they had fled.[7]

By the time Óscar was bailed out a year later, many more Salvadorans had tried to leave the country, giving rise to the first major phenomenon of forcibly displaced persons and refugees from El Salvador,[8] a phenomenon that still continues decades later. In the midst of the transnational violence that was forcing people to flee north only to be sent back into the abyss of war, the concept and practice of sanctuary became a creative and faithful response that resisted their dehumanization. A sanctuary ministry developed in the borderlands, grounded on a theological understanding of humanizing presence and communion. This communal ministry simultaneously affirmed the dignity and life of displaced Salvadorans while challenging ecclesial communities in the United States to imagine their potential for the construction of a more human society.

This chapter analyzes the discernment process that led to the creation of a sanctuary ministry and network that became public in 1982. I show how a group of ecumenical faith leaders in Tucson, Arizona, began to develop the theoretical and theological frameworks that would provide

---

[5] Paul Almeida, *Waves of Protest* (Minneapolis: University of Minnesota Press, 2008), 151.

[6] Starr, "Salvadorans Risked Death to Escape It."

[7] Al Senia, "13 Smuggled Salvadorans Found Dead in US Desert," *Washington Post,* July 7, 1980.

[8] Segundo Montes, et al., *Desplazados y refugiados salvadoreños: investigación* (San Salvador: Instituto de Investigaciones de la Universidad Centroamericana de El Salvador José Simeon Cañas (UCA)), 1985.

the religious and legal grounding for sanctuary practices in the years to come. Remembering the foundations of the 1980s sanctuary ministry is part of imagining future possibilities that go beyond the existing scholarly categorizations of the nature and purpose of sanctuary.

Laying the Foundation for the Ministry of Sanctuary

The thirteen Salvadoran survivors who were arrested by the Immigration and Naturalization Service (INS) for illegally entering the United States through the desert wilderness became the unexpected catalyst that prepared the foundation for what the media eventually called the sanctuary movement. In July 1980, the legal representative of the thirteen survivors approached the Tucson Ecumenical Council (TEC) with a request for financial assistance in order to bail out the Salvadorans.[9] If the thirteen could be bailed out, then they would also need social services until the law made an appropriate decision about their future. Members of the TEC, especially St. Mark's Presbyterian Church and the Catholic Diocese of Tucson, helped raise the funds for bail, and Southside Presbyterian Church assisted with food, clothing, and other social and pastoral services. This became the initial point of contact and involvement between member churches of the TEC and Salvadorans fleeing war.[10]

Rev. John Fife, the pastor of Southside Presbyterian Church in South Tucson, along with Fr. Ricardo Elford, a Roman Catholic priest in the Redemptorist Order and member of the TEC, began a process of discernment on how to educate the Tucson community on the violence and persecution of the church that was taking place in El Salvador. By January 1981, it was decided that a weekly prayer vigil, combined with

---

[9] William Walker, "Memorandum to Sanctuary Defense Lawyers," September 18, 1985, University of Arizona Special Collections, MS 362, Series 01, Box 01, Folder 02. The chronology of events that William Walker developed in preparation for the Tucson Sanctuary Trials of 1985 are helpful for analyzing the roots of the sanctuary movement between 1980 and 1982.

[10] Although individual members of these churches, especially lawyers, had previously assisted Salvadorans fleeing violence as early as 1979, churches as communal institutions were not directly involved. However, some churches like St. Mark's Presbyterian had previously assisted Chilean refugees in the mid-1970s. See Lane Van Ham, *A Common Humanity* (Tucson: University of Arizona Press, 2011), 46.

information and education, could serve as a gathering place for the community. The prayer service consisted of a public demonstration in front of the federal courthouse during rush hour on Thursday afternoons, followed by prayers and the sharing of news about the war and violence in Central America.[11] The event informed the wider community (religious and nonreligious) on the effects of war and US policy in Central America while also forming those who participated in the vigil into an increasingly committed group. In the context of this weekly vigil, many sustainable networks and relationships began to form among faith leaders, lawyers, social workers, students, and others who began to understand more intimately the stories that refugees were bringing with them into the jails of southern Arizona.

As the wider community became more informed, the TEC developed the Task Force on Central America (TECTF), which focused on a more systematic response to the ongoing arrival of Salvadorans, and increasingly Guatemalans, who were also fleeing war in their country. The task force began to raise necessary funds to bail out refugees who would otherwise remain in detention centers during their legal asylum proceedings. This initiative was also a response to the fact that, by January 1981, Salvadoran refugees in the INS detention center in El Centro, California, located about three hundred miles west of Tucson, had begun a hunger strike to protest the US government's practice of ignoring their asylum claims and deporting them back to war, where they feared they would be killed. News had begun to spread about Salvadorans who were deported from El Centro on Christmas Eve of 1980 and who had been killed within days of arrival.[12] Since it was protocol that INS provide the names of detained Salvadorans to the Salvadoran consulate in Los Angeles, the Salvadoran government knew which deportees arrived on a given day and could intercept them upon arrival. Those who were not deported immediately stayed in detention centers for a year or more.

---

[11] Hilary Cunningham, *God and Caesar at the Rio Grande* (Minneapolis: University of Minnesota Press, 1995), 16. According to Cunningham, the first of these prayer services was held on February 19, 1981. The vigil/public demonstration continues to this day in different forms, often at the El Tiradito shrine in the Barrio Viejo section of Tucson.

[12] John Crewdson, "US Returns Illegal Immigrants Who Are Fleeing Salvador War," *New York Times*, March 2, 1981.

In July 1981, task force and community members who had put up their homes and property as collateral to raise bond money were able to bail out over 115 asylum seekers from El Centro and from other INS facilities at a cost of two to three thousand dollars a person.[13] Once released from the detention centers, these asylum seekers were relocated to churches throughout Tucson and Los Angeles.[14] Unfortunately, in less than two months there were another two hundred Salvadoran asylum seekers at El Centro, and the sheer amount of money required for bail forced the Tucson community to rethink its efforts. As one of the Tucson lawyers wrote in a memo, "By concentrating on aiding the refugees to fight deportation, they were only delaying the deportation and not preventing it."[15] Statistically, the lawyer was right. Of the seven thousand asylum applications submitted by Central Americans in 1980, none had been granted; only two had been approved by the first months of 1981.[16] Actually preventing refugees from being sent back to their possible death required the development of a new approach that went beyond temporarily bailing them out of detention.

Jim Corbett was a goatherder, Friend (Quaker), and philosopher by training. By the summer of 1981, he was involved with Fr. Ricardo Elford, Rev. John Fife, the TECTF, and other community members working to assist refugees. He suggested a more direct but uncertain strategy that could protect refugees from deportation. In brief, Corbett argued that "in order to save lives, the group needed to aid Central American refugees to avoid capture."[17] Corbett had already been assisting refugees avoid capture and had been providing his own house as a temporary place of refuge. An initial effort to help one detained refugee had quickly evolved into more direct assistance to others on their journey.

---

[13] Between April and May 1981, bail bonds to release Salvadorans from INS detention centers increased from less than five hundred dollars to over two thousand dollars. Miriam Davidson, *Convictions of the Heart* (Tucson: University of Arizona Press, 1988), 25.

[14] For one perspective on the origins of the sanctuary ministry and movement in Los Angeles, see Mario Garcia, *Father Luis Olivares* (Chapel Hill: University of North Carolina Press, 2018).

[15] William Walker, "Memorandum to Sanctuary Defense Lawyers," September 18, 1985, University of Arizona Special Collections, MS 362, Series 01, Box 01, Folder 02, 4.

[16] Walker, 4.

[17] Walker, 5.

Through his encounters with refugees Corbett had personally learned of the ways in which INS appeared to be violating international protocols on the protection of refugees by sending them back to El Salvador before they could secure legal representation in the United States. For example, in late June 1981, he personally accompanied three refugees to the federal court in Tucson where they could apply for asylum, only to watch them be arrested and taken away to jail to begin deportation proceedings. Around the same time Corbett asked one of the detention center employees if she knew about the war taking place in El Salvador, to which she simply responded: "How could I be with these people every day and not know? But you can't get involved or relate to them personally or you'd lose your mind. I'm not responsible for what's happening to them, I just do my job."[18] Reflecting on the jailer's words, Corbett later wrote, "She's quite young and doesn't realize it's been said before."[19] The allusion was clearly to the Nazi deportation of Jews and to the officers' self-defense during the Nuremberg Trials where they argued that they were just following orders.

Corbett realized that the work of concerned citizens could not stop with helping refugees apply for asylum, but that citizens needed to help refugees avoid the very legal structures that were supposed to protect them but which had become what he termed "internal US branches of [El Salvador's] reign of terror."[20] In the first of a series of "Dear Friends" letters written to other Quaker communities, Corbett wrote:

> If Central American refugees' rights to political asylum are decisively rejected by the US government or if the US legal system insists on ransom that exceeds our ability to pay, active resistance will be the only alternative to abandoning the refugees to their fate. The creation of a network of actively concerned, mutually supporting people in the US and Mexico may be the best preparation for an adequate response. A network? Quakers will know what I mean.[21]

---

[18] Jim Corbett, "Dear Friends" letter, July 6, 1981, University of Arizona Special Collections, MS 362, Series 01, Box 01, Folder 09, 1.

[19] Corbett, 1.

[20] Corbett, 1.

[21] Jim Corbett, "Dear Friends" letter, May 12, 1981, University of Arizona Special Collections, MS 362, Series 01, Box 01, Folder 09, 2.

The development and justification of a transnational network that would actively resist the deportation of refugees became Corbett's conceptual and practical concern in the months to come. Corbett is considered one of the founders of the 1980s sanctuary ministry, and his philosophical and theological reflections on refugees and sanctuary became guideposts for the Tucson community's ongoing discernment of responsibility.

The practical foundations for such a transnational network were established with the initial trust and participation of Roman Catholic priests such as Fr. Ricardo Elford in Tucson; Fr. Arnie Noriega in Nogales, Arizona; and Fr. Ramon Quiñones in Nogales, Mexico. Through Fr. Ricardo, Corbett learned that Sacred Heart Catholic Church, located just a few blocks away from the Mexico border, could serve as a relatively safe place to pick up Salvadorans who could make it across the border. On the Mexican side, the Santuario de Nuestra Señora de Guadalupe was already a church where Salvadorans had found shelter and protection. The local prison also became a site for developing the network. Fr. Quiñones' pastoral visits to the prison in Nogales, Mexico, had exposed him to the large number of Salvadorans who were regularly apprehended by the Mexican government and were being sent back to the Guatemala-Mexico border. On his own, Fr. Quiñones could not possibly see all of the apprehended Salvadorans, so he asked Corbett for help. Corbett accepted Fr. Quiñones' invitation to assist with the pastoral care of these Salvadorans, who needed both someone with whom they could speak and information about the dangers of crossing into the United States, knowledge of refugee rights, and a means of getting messages back to their families in Central America and the United States. So, once a week for the next two years, Jim Corbett, who was neither Roman Catholic nor an ordained minister, became "Padre Jaime" in order to pastorally accompany Salvadoran refugees imprisoned on the Mexico side of the US-Mexico border.[22]

Spiritual and Theological Discernment of Sanctuary

The network for displaced Salvadorans that Corbett had begun to establish reached a critical stage toward the end of September 1981,

---

[22] Davidson, *Convictions of the Heart*, 38–41.

when he asked Rev. John Fife at Southside Presbyterian Church for assistance with places of refuge. By this time Corbett's home had reached maximum refuge capacity. According to William Walker, a lawyer who would go on to defend the sanctuary workers in the years to come, there were twenty-one Salvadorans living in Corbett's house, and the constant arguments among refugees were creating problems for his family.[23] Fife brought the matter to the elders at Southside Presbyterian Church for approval, and, after a 7–0 vote, the church quietly began to shelter refugees and to assist directly with their transportation from the border to Tucson. This action marked the beginning of the "quiet" phase of church sanctuary. During later months of 1981, Corbett, Fife, and other Tucson leaders found themselves in the crucible of spiritual and theological discernment about their degree of responsibility toward refugees. Corbett's "Dear Friends" letter of July 6, 1981, which Fife and others in the church had read, captured the agony of discernment, but it also began to envision sanctuary as a way of working toward "a kingdom of peace." The construction of such peace would require their willingness to sacrifice and suffer for the life and dignity of the forcibly displaced communities who kept arriving at the border.

In his letter Corbett explicitly located the war against Salvadorans as taking place not only in El Salvador, but also simultaneously in the United States. "Yet," he writes, "because the refugees are among us, the basic communities capable of waging the peace can also emerge here."[24] The peacemaking basic communities Corbett imagined seemed to resemble the ecclesial base communities of Latin America that he believed were "determined to live the freedom, peace, and justice of the Kingdom into actuality."[25] Through the unauthorized arrival of refugees, and especially through the sharing of their "joys," "hopes," and "griefs,"[26] Corbett

---

[23] Walker, "Memorandum to Sanctuary Defense Lawyers."

[24] Corbett, "Dear Friends" letter, July 6, 1981, 3.

[25] Corbett, 3. His exact words are: "The refugees themselves bring strength and renewal. They share their joys and their hopes as well as their griefs, and one soon learns that a new religious awareness has been spreading through Latin America, a revolutionary religious consciousness taking root in basic communities that are determined to live the freedom, peace, and justice of the Kingdom into actuality. There is, indeed, a force at work that threatens to sweep away the established powers of this hemisphere, and it is far more radical than the state capitalism of Cuba or Russia."

[26] Corbett, 3.

discerned a "strength and renewal" that was reaching those who were involved in their struggle for survival.

Although Corbett did not explicitly reference the Catholic Church's Vatican II document on the church in the modern world (*Gaudium et Spes*), to which I turn in a later chapter, his use of its iconic opening words is a veiled reference to that document's vision of the followers of Christ as sharing the same fate as the poor: "The joys and hopes, the grief and anguish of the people of our time, especially of those who are poor or afflicted, are the joys and hopes, the grief and anguish of the followers of Christ as well."[27] Sharing in the depths of the joy and suffering of the poor and persecuted from Latin America had to lead faith communities to more than just "another petition addressed to those who command the war machine."[28] At the core of his discernment, Corbett encountered the radical invitation not simply to assist refugees, but to enter into an incarnate communion with them.

According to Corbett, a community of peace that chooses to enter into communion with refugees would have to forfeit privileges and immunities:

> [In] choosing to serve the poor and powerless—not just as an intellectual posture or as a charitable gesture, but in spirit and truth—we will soon be stripped of our wealth and position. And, just as the refugees are outlawed, hunted down, and imprisoned, if we do choose to serve them in spirit and truth, we will also be outlawed by the Kingdom of Money.[29]

As he continued to discern the spirit required of a community that would enter into communion with refugees, the biblical echoes of his reflections became more pronounced. His use of the phrase "in spirit and truth" in the context of serving the poor and powerless is arguably a reference to John 4:23–24, where the phrase is used to point out a future reality that was already present, and how this influenced the authentic worship of God. In the gospel text, the eschatological element adds an

---

[27] Paul VI, *Pastoral Constitution on the Church in the Modern World*, December 7, 1965, preface. Older translations begin: "The joys and the hopes, the griefs and the anxieties," whereas more recent translations change "anxieties" to "anguish."

[28] Corbett, "Dear Friends" letter, July 6, 1981, 3.

[29] Corbett, 3.

urgency of discernment and discipleship, and such urgency is also present in Corbett's strategic use of the phrase to refer to the possibility of living in communion with the poor and persecuted.

In the midst of the scale of the situation affecting forcibly displaced communities, Corbett began to sketch out a vision of a community of faith that was broader and deeper than any one tradition or denomination. He called such a community "a catholic church that is a people rather than creed or rite, a living Church of many cultures that must be met to be known."[30] This was a community that was willing to live the way of the cross by being outlawed, hunted down, and imprisoned in order to unmask the dehumanizing violence that was killing Central Americans.

Becoming a "peripheral witness" to what Corbett called the "crucifixion of the Salvadoran people" meant that there was no neutral space upon which he or the borderland community could stand. The choice between serving a kingdom of money or a kingdom of peace was at the core of their communal discernment. He writes:

> The kingdom of money is selling us an alternative theology of violence that must come under the shadow of the Cross to be adequately exposed, [for] we are being tempted to dismiss the Salvadoran refugees among us as mere "economic refugees" who are looking for better jobs and to accept the growing reign of terror in Latin America as no more than a historic-cultural curse which this hemisphere's non-Anglos inherit from their ancestors.[31]

In the possibility of the US community sharing the cross of those Latin Americans who were being crucified, the violence of the nation could be revealed and exposed as the worship of money. Idolatrous worship makes the lives of persons fleeing terror into an economic factor and renders a whole people in Latin America as the unfortunate byproduct of a history for which the United States claimed to bear no direct responsibility.

Corbett foresaw an all-too-common temptation in the process of communities discerning responsibility across borders. US citizens would seek to charitably serve "economic refugees" while continuing to worship

---

[30] Corbett, 3.
[31] Corbett, 4.

The Sanctuary of God for the Oppressed of Central America 15

the economic frameworks that had funded their torture and forced their displacement. Against this temptation to remain distant from the suffering of the poor and persecuted, Corbett argued that "the way of the cross is communicated by being lived, [and] it is met in those who point the way with their lives."[32] To understand the sacrifice and the suffering that was required for communion with Salvadorans who had been displaced by the war and who were being persecuted by the US government, one had to accompany and be led by them.

Corbett closed his July 1981 letter by referencing Archbishop Óscar Romero's struggle against the ideology of violence in El Salvador: "Systematically stripped of their humanity and fashioned into instruments of violence, soldiers are among the most victimized, [but] Monseñor reached out in fellowship to win them from the way of violence."[33] Romero's attempt to reach the heart and consciousness of soldiers made him a powerful threat to the military elite who needed soldiers that could carry out violence and killing without questions. To the government's command to kill, Romero reminded soldiers of the commandment "Thou shalt not kill."[34]

By invoking Romero's appeal to Salvadoran soldiers to cease their cooperation with violence, Corbett also sought to extend Romero's exhortation to the United States, where the young jailer's words, "I just do my job," crystallized the dehumanization of US citizens. The parallel between Salvadoran soldiers and US immigration officers fashioned into instruments of violence gave rise to the question of who or which

---

[32] Corbett, 4.

[33] Corbett, 5. Although Corbett is speaking about the dehumanization of Salvadoran soldiers, the phrase "fashioned into instruments of violence" also echoes the words of Adolf Eichmann, who in a 1962 letter argued that Nazi soldiers were "forced to serve as mere instruments in the hands of the leaders." The point is that violence dehumanizes both the perpetrators and the victims. For a translation of Eichmann's letter, see "Letter by Adolf Eichmann to President Yitzhak Ben-Zvi of Israel," *New York Times*, January 27, 2016.

[34] Óscar Romero, *Homilies*, March 23, 1980, in *A Prophetic Bishop Speaks to His People: The Complete Homilies of Archbishop Óscar Arnulfo Romero*, vol. 6, trans. Joseph Owens (Miami, FL: Convivium Press, 2017). The English translation is based on the authoritative Spanish six volumes of homilies published in 2005. For the original Spanish, see Óscar Romero, *Homilías*, vol. 6 (San Salvador: UCA Editores, 2005). All references to Óscar Romero's homilies will be drawn from the Spanish text; translations are my own.

communities in the United States could enter into communion with the spirit of Monseñor Romero and declare to the people and church: "thou shalt not kill." This fundamental question and response against violence became the bedrock for the ongoing discernment of what responsibility churches had for refugees who were now in their midst. Corbett ended his letter with a prayer that was recited by the community the following year, during the public declaration of sanctuary. It conveyed the sufferings, but also the sacramental grace of accompanying persecuted Salvadorans:

> Give us, then, our share of pain, survivor's grief and
> unnamed ills, the slow decay that yet may maim
> and torture years before it kills.
> Burn us with their mark of Cain, the outlaw brand
> the powers despise, and freeze us with the misfit
> shame that touches ice in knowing eyes.
> Bind us with the pauper's chain, here where life and
> health are sold by those who play the money
> game and fashion God of Mammon's gold. And
> let our sense be clear and sane, unnumbed by
> drugs or pious lies, unpoisoned by the urge to
> blame, undrained into self-pity's sighs.
> Let it be that this, our fate, reveals the working of
> Your grace, that we can bear the hurt and hate,
> to grow love's realm, in this pain's place.[35]

The Ministry of Sanctuary Goes Public

The quiet phase of church sanctuary that had been approved by the elders at Southside Presbyterian continued through the fall of 1981. By January of 1982, a congregation-wide discernment about the church's participation had to take place. The public discernment process forced congregants to decide whether they were willing to endure the consequences of becoming a public sanctuary church. Perhaps contrary to expectations, continuing to keep the sanctuary ministry quiet and hidden from the public made it vulnerable to government shutdown.

---

[35] Corbett, "Dear Friends" letter, July 6, 1981, 5.

In December of 1981, an INS lawyer informed Margo Cowan, a lead TEC lawyer, that Jim Corbett's phone number was being found with arrested refugees.[36] Since INS knew that Corbett and other community members were helping transport Salvadorans into Tucson and to other cities like Los Angeles, it was a matter either of waiting until the ministry was terminated through their arrest or of going public, hoping that the broader civil society—especially churches—would join in solidarity.

In the weeks leading up to Southside's annual general meeting in January 1982, information sessions on immigration law were held, and Bible studies provided parishioners with the tools necessary to discern their position on the concept and practice of sanctuary.[37] After a half-day of deliberations on the day of the annual meeting, a secret ballot yielded seventy-nine votes in support and two against becoming a church that provided public refuge to Central Americans arriving across the border. One of the congregants who was opposed to the decision wrote to the FBI the following day to inform them of the church's actions.[38] Nonetheless, most of the community had decided to become a sanctuary church. The second anniversary of the assassination of Archbishop Óscar Romero was chosen as the symbolic date for the public announcement.

At the ecumenical religious service on March 24, 1982, two banners captured the essence of how the community understood sanctuary. On one banner was written, "La migra no profana el santuario" (immigration [agents] do not profane the sanctuary), and on the other, "Este es el santuario de Dios para los oprimidos de Centro América" (This is the sanctuary of God for the oppressed of Central America).[39] By invoking the church as consecrated and belonging to God, and by declaring that it was a site for the oppressed of Central America, immigration agents were placed in the contentious position of having to choose whether they would desecrate the church through their deportation actions or would accept and respect the affirmation of the church's nature and mission—that it was God's church, and particularly, God's dwelling place for the oppressed. Placing the deportation orders of immigration officials in direct opposition to the work of God in and through the

---

[36] Davidson, *Convictions of the Heart*, 65.

[37] Cunningham, *God and Caesar at the Rio Grande*, 32.

[38] Cunningham, 32.

[39] See photographs in Davidson, *Convictions of the Heart*, 83ff.

church echoèd Romero's March 23, 1980, homily, when he ordered soldiers not to kill.

Southside Presbyterian's declaration of sanctuary served as the beginning of a formation process to raise the public's consciousness about Central American refugees and the responsibility of US citizens to prevent these forcibly displaced communities from being sent back to war. In an effort of good faith, the Rev. John Fife sent a letter to the attorney general of the United States a day before declaring sanctuary. In the letter, which was also read in front of the press on March 24, 1982, Rev. Fife explained the reasons for providing sanctuary:

> We take this action because we believe the current policy and practice of the United States Government with regard to Central American refugees to be illegal and immoral. We believe our government is in violation of the 1980 Refugee Act and international law by continuing to arrest, detain, and forcibly return refugees to the terror, persecution, and murder in El Salvador and Guatemala.[40]

From the beginning of public sanctuary, the Tucson sanctuary community argued that the government's actions were illegal because they violated not only its own domestic laws, but also the accepted norms of international law. For Fife and others, helping refugees avoid capture and providing them with refuge was both moral and legal before the general norms and laws of humanity. Corbett and Fife believed that what they were doing through sanctuary was "civil initiative"—taking initiative to uphold the fundamental norms of a human society, even against government threats. For the press and for the government, however, faith communities were breaking the law rather than upholding the law. This led to the public misunderstanding that these faith communities were simply practicing civil disobedience.

Alfredo (pseudonym), a refugee from El Salvador who entered sanctuary at Southside, became the symbolic voice during the press conference for the thousands of refugees who had to avoid the US government lest they be sent back to their death. He said:

---

[40] John Fife, "Letter to Honorable William French Smith," March 23, 1982, University of Arizona Special Collections, MS 362, Series 01, Box 01, Folder 01.

"I come fleeing from the government of my country, El Salvador, because I was condemned to death if I remained any longer in El Salvador, and the only reason is that I was on the side of the Salvadoran people; that is, I am aware of the condition of poverty, repression, exploitation and misery inflicted upon us during more than 50 years of opprobrious military tyranny."[41]

Alfredo also spoke of the Mexican government's collusion with the US government to keep Salvadorans from reaching the US border so that they could not ask for asylum.[42] Although some Salvadorans could get Mexican visas in order to escape to Mexico instead of fleeing by land, they were not allowed to travel north of Guadalajara; otherwise, Mexico would deport them back to El Salvador. In light of these transnational government efforts to contain Salvadorans and keep them from reaching the US border, it was critical to develop a network of sanctuary communities that could protect and transport Salvadorans like Alfredo and other Central Americans to safe refuge in the United States.[43]

Alfredo's declaration would be the first time that many US citizens would learn that churches were not only providing refuge to Central Americans, but also helping them get to that refuge. Jim Corbett attempted to clarify what was already being labeled "an underground railroad." In his public remarks he warned "Anglo America" not to become entranced with the romantic images of an underground railroad at the expense of actually addressing the fundamental issue of why it was even necessary to have such "evasion services." He said: "As a result of US refugee policy, terror now reaches up through Mexico and into the United States itself in pursuit of Salvadorans and Guatemalans who are

---

[41] "Vengo huyendo del gobierno de mi país, El Salvador, porque yo estaba condenado a muerte si permanecía unos días más en El Salvador; y la única razón es que yo estaba al lado del pueblo salvadoreño. Es decir, soy consciente de la situación de pobreza, represión, explotación y miseria por la que hemos venido atravesando por más de 50 años de oprobiosas tiranías militares." Press conference statement, March 24, 1982, University of Arizona Special Collections, MS 362, Series 01, Box 01, Folder 01.

[42] For an analysis of how the US continues to contain Central Americans using Mexico as a buffer country, see David Scott Fitzgerald, *Refuge beyond Reach: How Rich Democracies Repel Asylum Seekers* (New York: Oxford University Press, 2019).

[43] Press Conference statement.

hunted down and shipped back."[44] The reach of terror made it necessary that people of goodwill in Mexico and the US accompany refugees on their journey north.

As of March 1982, the ministry of sanctuary in Tucson had helped approximately two hundred Salvadorans and Guatemalans avoid capture.[45] With the goal to move these refugees away from the border region and into other communities across the country where they would be safer, the network grew rapidly in the weeks and months after the public declaration of sanctuary. By August 1982, the Tucson community needed assistance coordinating the growing network in the United States, and Corbett turned to a recently founded group in Chicago for assistance. The involvement of the Chicago Religious Task Force on Central America (CRTFCA) allowed the network to expand, but it also gave rise to different conceptions of the nature of sanctuary.

Conflicting Visions of Sanctuary

In mid-July 1982, Rev. John Fife was visiting the University of Notre Dame in Indiana with Alicia, a Salvadoran catechist who had fled death threats from the Salvadoran security forces.[46] Aware that the Wellington Avenue United Church of Christ in nearby Chicago was in the midst of discerning whether it would become a church that provided sanctuary, Alicia and Fife spoke at the church to share their respective experiences. The church voted overwhelmingly to become a site of refuge, and a few days later Jim Corbett accompanied the Vargas family from Tucson to Chicago.

While in Chicago, Corbett shared with the CRTFCA the growing need to have an organization coordinate the transportation and placement of refugees so that they would not accumulate close to the border in Tucson. Although initially reluctant, the CRTFCA agreed a few

---

[44] Jim Corbett, "Some Comments on the Underground Railroad for Central American Refugees," March 24, 1982, University of Arizona Special Collections, MS 362, Series 01, Box 01, Folder 01.

[45] Corbett.

[46] Robert Tomsho, *The American Sanctuary Movement* (Austin: Texas Monthly Press, 1987), 89. To read Alicia's story of persecution, see Renny Golden and Michael McConnell, *Sanctuary: The New Underground Railroad* (Maryknoll, NY: Orbis Books, 1986), 159–62.

months later to become the coordinating body for the expansion of the sanctuary network.[47]

Renny Golden and Michael McConnell, who were closely involved with the CRTFCA, write:

> Task force members put their hands to telephone receivers, beginning a project that would open more than two hundred sanctuaries in churches, synagogues, and Quaker meetings in the next few years . . . [and that] published over thirty thousand copies of sanctuary manuals and booklets that were sent across the country.[48]

Through the work of the CRTFCA, the US sanctuary network expanded from Tucson to the border with Canada, and from San Francisco to Boston.

For the first two years the CRTFCA coordinated a simultaneous declaration of sanctuary status for churches across the country either on March 24 or on December 2, the former commemorating Archbishop Óscar Romero, and the latter commemorating the assassination of the four US churchwomen killed in El Salvador in 1980. However, by 1984 there were so many communities wishing to declare publicly that they were a sanctuary that, instead of the CRTFCA directly coordinating the announcement twice a year, communities declared themselves a sanctuary when they had discerned that they were ready to take such a stand.[49] Once a community declared sanctuary and had agreed to receive a person or family who had requested refuge, it was the responsibility of the CRTFCA to connect that person or family with the sanctuary

---

[47] Corbett provides the following narrative of the events: "While in Chicago [I] asked members of the CRTF to take on the chore of being a clearinghouse for sanctuary inquiries. They explained that the CRTF, concentrates all its efforts on political action against US intervention in Central America and has no wish to divert any energy into refugee work, but I pointed out that they could do the job precisely because their office in downtown Chicago is far from the border and isolated from daily refugee crises, and that, as far as political impact was concerned, in allowing the refugees themselves to be heard, sanctuary fuses faith commitment, humanitarian concern, and political awakening in a way that the CRTF was unlikely to equal with any other activity." Jim Corbett, "Dear Friends letter," December 26, 1984, University of Arizona Special Collections, MS 362, Box 47, Folder 18, 2.

[48] Golden and McConnell, *Sanctuary*, 52.

[49] Golden and McConnell, 53.

community and to facilitate the journey through the so-called underground railroad.

Connecting Central American refugees with US sanctuary communities complemented the work of the Tucson Ecumenical Council (TEC), which focused on coordinating the immediate needs of refugees that made it to Tucson. Corbett increasingly turned his attention to developing more effective ways of protecting refugees crossing Guatemala and Mexico so that they could make it to the US border. As of November 1981, Corbett had been traveling to Guatemala and Mexico to learn firsthand about "la situación" (the situation) and to build relationships with churches that were already serving displaced Salvadorans fleeing the war. In a January 24, 1982, "Dear Friends" letter, he wrote: "Channels of communication with refugees at the Mexican-Guatemalan border—including refugees deported from Sonora and other parts of Mexico—are now open. A co-operative effort to provide needed services for Central American refugees has been initiated."[50] Corbett was establishing this south-of-the-border network before US churches started declaring themselves sanctuaries. By 1983, the network had adopted screening procedures drawn from the United Nations High Commissioner for Refugees.[51] The procedures allowed members of the Tucson refugee support group (Trsg—a subgroup of the TEC that focused on getting refugees to, and across, the US-Mexico border) to prioritize urgent cases of persecuted persons who needed to make it to sanctuary in the United States.

For Corbett and the Tucson community, the network south and north of the US border was a means of preventing the government from capturing refugees and sending them back to war. Sanctuaries in the United States were part of a long procession of faith communities that extended from El Salvador to Canada, actively participating and celebrating the life and refuge of Central Americans. But, as the US network of sanctuary churches grew, differences in priorities and objectives between the Tucson community and the CRTFCA began to emerge.

One of the first moments that foreshadowed a deeper conflict occurred just a few months after the CRTFCA started coordinating refugee

---

[50] Jim Corbett, "Dear Friends" letter, January 24, 1982, University of Arizona Special Collections, MS 362, Series 02, Box 01, Folder 07.

[51] Davidson, *Convictions of the Heart*, 81.

placements. At the end of October 1982, two young indigenous Guatemalans who were fleeing the bombings in their village and whom the Tucson community considered high-priority refugees were sent from Tucson to Chicago along with a Salvadoran man who was a deserter from the Treasury Police in El Salvador. The Salvadoran man who had fled because he feared for his life was already scheduled to enter sanctuary at a Presbyterian church in Minnesota, but the two Guatemalans did not have pre-arranged provisions for sanctuary. Because a trip (underground railroad) was already scheduled to take place from Tucson to Chicago, and because it was dangerous for the Guatemalans to remain near the border where apprehensions were more likely, the Tucson leaders notified the CRTFCA about their case and sent them to Chicago.

Tragically, instead of finding a sanctuary community for the two Guatemalans, the CRTFCA sent them back to Arizona. The young couple from the mountains of Huehuetenango did not make it back to the Tucson community. Since they were traveling alone and spoke very little Spanish and no English, they were likely apprehended by immigration agents en route, or at one of the bus stations on the way south. In a strongly worded letter to the CRTFCA, Jim Corbett wrote:

> We obviously misunderstood the rigor with which you are assessing refugees in relation to their use . . . [and] at this point we need to get a better idea of what you intend to do with refugees who flunk out of the sanctuary program. . . . I'm confident that you don't intend simply to discard those who flunk, but at some point you'll need to decide what else you're willing to do when prospective sanctuary participants fail to meet expectations.[52]

Corbett's November 1982 letter would be one of the first of many letters between the Tucson community and the CRTFCA that tried to discern their fundamental mis/understandings of the nature and purpose of sanctuary and of the role of refugees in the growing network and movement. Scholars who have researched the 1980s sanctuary movement and the growing conflict within the network generally distinguish between a more humanitarian approach and a more political approach to sanctuary.

---

[52] Jim Corbett, "Letter to Chicago Religious Task Force," November 28, 1982, University of Arizona Special Collections, MS 362, Box 26, Folder 17.

Attempts to Classify the Nature and Purpose of Sanctuary

In his work on the US Central American peace movement, sociologist Christian Smith studied sanctuary through the lens of social movement activism. He has framed the key struggle in sanctuary as one between its roots in humanitarian hospitality and its evolution into a political movement.[53] When he analyzes how internal social movement forces can lead to disintegration, fracturing, or outright failure, he categorizes the main differences in the movement as a discrepancy of primary objectives. "The Tucson camp," he writes, "viewed sanctuary primarily as a humanitarian endeavor to assist the victims of war. That mission necessarily demanded that the movement help all refugees whose lives appeared to be at risk, regardless of their personal or political commitments and abilities."[54] This position was clearly illustrated in the letter that Corbett sent to the CRTFCA questioning the notion that refugees had to be useful to a movement. For the Tucson leaders, even right-wing military deserters with whom they did not politically agree could be protected and given refuge if their lives were under direct threat.

According to Smith, if the Tucson community's primary objective was humanitarian hospitality, then the primary objective of the CRTFCA was political. Smith argues that the Chicago leaders "viewed Sanctuary as a fundamentally political movement aimed at ending US support for the war in Central America by employing refugees' stories to raise the political consciousness of middle-class US Citizens." Additionally, he writes, "that vision dictated that the entire movement be united nationally under a centralized organization that could set policies, coordinate political actions, and speak for the movement with one voice."[55] If stopping US support for Latin America's repressive governments was the primary objective of the CRTFCA, providing sanctuary to refugees was certainly part of that larger vision. However, who in fact could enter into sanctuary was determined by the degree to which they could contribute to the broader objectives of the movement. The sanctuary network coordinated by the CRTFCA prioritized refugees who were willing to speak

---

[53] Christian Smith, *Resisting Reagan: The US Central American Peace Movement* (Chicago: University of Chicago Press, 1996), 69.

[54] Smith, 337.

[55] Smith, 337.

publicly about their experience, who could speak against the Salvadoran or Guatemalan governments, and who were informed about politics in the region. The indigenous couple from the mountains of Guatemala who could barely speak Spanish did not fit the criteria.

Different understandings of objectives and perhaps of the very nature of sanctuary existed across the transnational sanctuary network. Although scholars of the sanctuary movement employ some version of this humanitarian-political dichotomy to categorize the differences within the movement, their particular conceptualizations nonetheless reveal nuances. For example, Ann Crittenden has written, "By the end of its first year sanctuary had in effect become two movements, living in an uneasy alliance."[56] While the notion that there were two separate movements points to the deep differences that emerged between the Tucson community and the CRTFCA, speaking of two movements would actually necessitate speaking of multiple sanctuary movements across the country, for different regions that provided sanctuary were marked by the particularities of their local history.

The East Bay Sanctuary Covenant communities in Berkeley, California, for example, had been active sanctuary communities that declared their sanctuary status along with Southside Presbyterian on March 24, 1982. One of the Salvadoran survivors of the July 1980 tragedy in Organ Pipe National Monument eventually took sanctuary in one of the Berkeley churches.[57] These East Bay communities had their own organizational structures, objectives, and conceptualizations of sanctuary and were not a clear-cut reflection of either the Tucson community's approach or of the approach of CRTFCA. At most, one can argue that the East Bay Covenant communities were a hybrid of Tucson and the CRTFCA, reflecting the former's focus on independent churches and faith communities covenanting together to protect refugees, and the latter's desire for more hierarchical organizational frameworks that could sustain a political movement. Sociocultural anthropologist Susan Bibler Coutin, whose sanctuary research focused on the Bay Area communities, has categorized the differences in the following manner:

---

[56] Ann Crittenden, *Sanctuary: A Story of American Conscience and the Law in Collision* (New York: Weidenfeld and Nicolson, 1988), 92.

[57] Susan Bibler Coutin, *Culture of Protest: Religious Activism and the US Sanctuary Movement* (Boulder, CO: Westview Press, 1993), 30.

In general, Tucson sanctuary workers saw the movement's goal as saving refugees' lives, East Bay volunteers compared sanctuary to the anti–Vietnam War protests, and those whom I met at national meetings argued that to be successful, sanctuary had to challenge institutionalized imperialism. The refugee rights perspective focused on direct services, the structural change position confronted the root cause of oppression in Central America, and the antiwar contingent tried to do both.[58]

The attempt of the East Bay sanctuary communities to do both direct service or humanitarian work as well as political work that addressed root causes was an outgrowth of their own local and historical context. Long before sanctuary was declared in 1982 for Salvadoran and Guatemalan refugees, these communities had invoked the concept of sanctuary for conscientious objectors[59] and had deep roots in Latin America's social and ecclesial movements.[60]

For Gregory Leffel, who has researched the relationship between missiology and social movements, the tensions within the sanctuary movement were a difference of protest strategy. Leffel writes, "Unlike Chicago's CRTFCA, which was founded as a direct action coalition, the Tucson network was more pastoral in nature and grew from its encounter with refugees in flight. . . . Their public witness was first of all the result of faithful action to protect refugees, and only then a denunciation of injustice."[61] Understanding that the political dimension of Tucson's sanctuary work emerged from or followed the primary task of pastoral accompaniment with refugees is key in Leffel's categorization of the conflict. Given his more theological focus on missiology, Leffel distinguishes a prophetic task from direct political action.

Anthropologist Hilary Cunningham provides one of the most nuanced categorizations of the tensions in the movement. Cunningham argues

---

[58] Coutin, 176.

[59] Coutin, 28.

[60] For oral histories of the participants in the East Bay sanctuary communities and their prior involvement with invocations of sanctuary and involvement with Latin America, see the *Sanctuary Oral History Project* compiled and edited by Eileen Purcell and archived at the Graduate Theological Union in Berkeley, California.

[61] Gregory Leffel, *Faith Seeking Action: Mission, Social Movements, and the Church in Motion* (Lanham, MD: Scarecrow Press, 2007), 128.

that at the core of the conflict were not only matters of structure, strategy, or objectives, but theological and ecclesiological differences. She argues that "differences between 'Catholic' and 'Quaker/congregationalist-Protestant' cultures may have played an important role in dividing the movement. Each group possessed a different set of cultural values about what a church movement was and how it should be organized."[62] Cunningham points out that the CRTFCA was dominated by "Catholic clerics, nuns, and laypersons," and that their national vision for sanctuary in some ways resembled that of a Catholic Church's understanding of centralized structures and membership. On the other hand, she argues, the Tucson community to some degree resembled a "congregational paradigm" that resisted a "hierarchical, bureaucratic 'superstructure.'"[63] Cunningham's emphasis on the different denominational cultures somewhat shifts attention from the humanitarian or political objectives categories to the question of the religious frameworks that may have deepened already existing differences in the understanding of sanctuary.

Cunningham's insights into the denominational cultures that were present in the leadership bodies of the sanctuary movement merit further research, especially for an in-depth comparison between the Tucson community and the CRTFCA. However, it is important to note that both communities were already denominationally diverse. For example, the first church to participate in the sanctuary network with the CRTFCA in Chicago was not Roman Catholic, but from the United Church of Christ tradition (Wellington Avenue Church). In Tucson, the Roman Catholic diocese and Catholic parishes and priests were involved with developing the sanctuary network from the very beginning, even before the public declaration at Southside Presbyterian Church. Catholic clergy and diocesan representatives were part of the planning for the public declaration on the feast of the martyrdom of Archbishop Óscar Romero and continued to serve as key members of the TEC, which worked closely with the sanctuary ministry. Furthermore, although Jim Corbett, a Quaker, emerged as one of the key intellectual and logistical coordinators of the sanctuary ministry in Tucson and beyond, his deep knowledge of Catholic theology and encyclicals, of Jewish and Christian scriptures, and of other religious and philosophical systems makes

---

[62] Cunningham, *God and Caesar at the Rio Grande,* 42.

[63] Cunningham, 42.

it difficult to categorize his influence on sanctuary as simply a Quaker influence. While the impact of Corbett's Quaker background upon the Tucson community's understanding of sanctuary cannot be denied, denominational cultures still do not sufficiently account for the differing understandings of the nature and purpose of sanctuary between the CRTFCA and the Tucson community.

Refugees arriving at the border—some with bullets still lodged in them—directed the discernment and creative response of the community. The ongoing personal encounter in the borderlands with displaced Salvadorans and Guatemalans, systematically stripped of their humanity in their home countries and on the journey north, were the fertile ground from which theological insights and a commitment to sociopolitical transformation emerged. The categorizations of humanitarian vs. political, or of Catholic vs. Quaker, Congregationalist, or Protestant, while important, were not the key differences. The borderland community's understanding of the nature and purpose of sanctuary was fundamentally based on a vision of rehumanization as a response to dehumanizing violence.

Most scholarship engages with the concept of sanctuary based on the ways in which sanctuary was practiced and developed as a mass social movement. However, to understand the depth and vision of the tradition of sanctuary and the ways in which it transcends the above categorizations, one must come to understand sanctuary as a nonviolent ecclesial ministry. The next chapter enters into the inner logic of the sanctuary ministry at the border and examines its theological foundations as well as its philosophical underpinnings in a Gandhian conception of social change that resists and overcomes distinctions between what is humanitarian, religious, or political.

2

Nonviolent Communion across Borders

The Theology and Gandhian Philosophy of Sanctuary

Upon James A. Corbett's death in 2001, the *New York Times* obituary described him as a "rancher and Harvard educated philosopher,"[1] and *The Economist* wrote: "In Europe, the widespread hostility to those seeking asylum from countries as far away as China and Afghanistan has touched some consciences, perhaps presaging another sanctuary movement. But a new Jim Corbett has yet to emerge to speak of the unity of humanity."[2] Those who knew Corbett considered him a brilliant thinker and a quiet theologian who had an uncanny ability to analyze the world as it was and as it could be, while remaining grounded in the local lived reality of the desert borderlands. As the words from *The Economist* imply, for Corbett and the sanctuary communities with which he worked, the practice of sanctuary was sustained by a transformed vision of human relationships across borders.

At the root of the sanctuary ministry was the belief that local communities binding themselves together in communion with persons seeking refuge had the potential to transform society and politics. This vision was informed by a biblical understanding of the responsibility to continue making present in history a people's covenant with God and by Mahatma Gandhi's insights that genuine power, including political power, ultimately resides in responding to the immediate needs of humanity. To address the transnational violence of a political system, society had to be reconstructed at the local level through humanizing

---

[1] Douglas Martin, "James A. Corbett, 67, Is Dead; A Champion of Movement to Safeguard Illegal Refugees," *New York Times*, August 12, 2001.

[2] "Jim Corbett," *The Economist,* August 16, 2001.

encounters with displaced and persecuted Central Americans. Corbett's theological, nonviolent, and political understandings of the nature and purpose of sanctuary remain a challenge for imagining and constructing what he called "the sanctuary church."[3] This chapter illuminates the contours of how Corbett and the borderland communities envisioned the foundation and future of sanctuary.

Theological Horizon of the Sanctuary Church

In the previous chapter I analyzed briefly Corbett's letter of July 1981, written two months after his initial encounter with Salvadoran refugees in the desert. There, he reflected on the notion of a catholic (universal) church as a people who choose to live under the cross and in service to what he termed the kingdom of peace.[4] That letter was one of Corbett's first formulations of his theological perspectives regarding refugees and the possibility of sanctuary. He wrote:

> Each week we must turn our backs on refugees who desperately need help but for whom there's just not enough time or money. And there are hundreds of thousands in El Salvador whose agonies far exceed the sufferings of those reaching the US. "If a man has enough to live on and yet when he sees his brother in need shuts up his heart against him, how can it be said that the divine love dwells in him?"[5]

---

[3] Jim Corbett, *The Sanctuary Church* (Wallingford, PA: Pendle Hill Publications, 1986).

[4] Although Jim Corbett's understanding of *church* does not as a whole reflect the dominant ecclesiological models of Roman Catholicism, his emphasis on the *universal* nature of the church highlights one of the fundamental attributes or marks of the church. For these attributes in ecclesiology, see Avery Dulles, *Models of the Church* (New York: Image Books, 1978), chap. 8.

[5] Jim Corbett, "Dear Friends" letter, July 6, 1981, University of Arizona Special Collections, MS 362, Series 01, Box 01, Folder 09, 3. While some of Corbett's letters were included in his published books (*Goatwalking*, 1991; *Sanctuary for All Life*, 2005), I will follow the organizational structure of the *Sanctuary Movement Trial Papers* archive at the University of Arizona. Additional material relating to Corbett can be found in the *Miriam Davidson Papers*, MS 433, and in the *Jim Corbett Collection 1960–1995*, MS 502, all at the University of Arizona.

The verse from the First Letter of John (1 Jn 3:17) is a key biblical reference for grasping the theological density present in refugees who placed an existential and religious claim upon Corbett and on the community's resources. Instead of recoiling from the scale of the situation, and contrary to any temptation to become a passive bystander, Corbett directly tied the necessity of responding to refugees with a theology of God's dwelling in the human person by invoking 1 John 3:17. Responding to the embodied claims of refugees incarnated the presence of God in history, and theologically affirming the dynamic presence and dwelling of God in particular places, persons, and communities who committed themselves to the needs of those fleeing across borders became foundational for the borderland communities' conceptualization of what constituted church.[6]

Through the provision of sanctuary for Central American refugees, Corbett saw a "recombinant church," which he also called "the sanctuary church," coming into existence.[7] Typically used in a technical manner in the field of genetic modification to refer to the re-combination of genetic matter in the formation of a new or different organism, *recombinant* befits the creation of what he described as "a living church of many cultures."[8] By the mid-1980s Corbett had already seen and experienced the ecumenical, interreligious, and intercultural recombination of traditions among those communities committed to providing sanctuary, and those experiences pointed toward the emergence of a church that was a people of peoples, a community of communities, united across

---

[6] Corbett's insights echo Pope John XXIII, who in a similar manner used this same scriptural passage in his 1961 encyclical, *Mater et Magistra,* which deals with the role of the church in the midst of international challenges and relationships. In a section titled "The Mystical Body of Christ," located between the section "Obligation of Wealthy Nations" and the section "International Aid," John XXIII wrote: "The Church has always emphasized that this obligation of helping those who are in misery and want should be felt most strongly by Catholics, in view of the fact that they are members of the Mystical Body of Christ. 'In this we have known the charity of God,' says St. John, 'because he has laid down his life for us; and we ought to lay down our lives for the brethren. He that hath the substance of this world and shall see his brother in need and shall shut up his bowels [of compassion] from him; how doth the charity of God abide in him?'" (no. 159).

[7] Corbett, *The Sanctuary Church*, 4.

[8] Corbett, 4.

differences in sanctuary. Two vignettes from Corbett's writings illustrate the recombination of traditions that he was witnessing: the 1984 Freedom Seder at Temple Emanu-El in Tucson, and the hanging of an icon-styled poster in a Tucson Quaker house.

The tradition of Freedom Seders arose in 1969, when Passover coincided with the first anniversary of the assassination of Rev. Martin Luther King Jr. In 1968, Martin Luther King Jr. had planned to celebrate the Passover seder with Rabbi Abraham Joshua Heschel and his family, but he was killed before Passover. Since then, the struggle against racism, poverty, sexism, militarism, and other forms of injustice has been ritually celebrated in partnership with Jewish communities across the country. Arthur Waskow, who modified the Passover service to develop the text for the Freedom Seder, explains that the Freedom Seder blends "traditional passages from the Haggadah with the words of Martin Luther King, Gandhi, Nat Turner, and others" and that it creatively mines the Jewish tradition to address contemporary issues.[9]

In 1984, refugees and community volunteers in Tucson were encouraged to participate in the local celebration of Passover through the Freedom Seder that would take place on April 18, linking one people's historical and religious experience of liberation with another people's struggle for survival. Because refugee participation in the Freedom Seder risked their apprehension by federal immigration officials, a "nonviolent protective response" that consisted of a caravan of vehicles was planned from Southside Presbyterian Church to Temple Emanu-El for those who decided that they wanted to attend. A week earlier, Jack Elder, director of Casa Óscar Romero, a part of the refugee aid program of the Roman Catholic Diocese of Brownsville in Texas, was arrested and charged with providing transportation for three unauthorized Salvadorans, so there was a real possibility of arrests in Tucson.[10] However, over seventy Salvadorans and Guatemalans chose to participate and received transportation the evening of the Freedom Seder. The protective caravan that accompanied them through the city to Temple Emanu-El was two

---

[9] Arthur Waskow, "The Freedom Seder," *The Jewish Americans: Three Centuries of Jewish Voices in America* (New York: Doubleday, 2007), 355. For the Freedom Seder text, see Arthur Waskow, *The Freedom Seder: A New Haggadah for Passover* (Washington, DC: Micah Press, 1969).

[10] Mack Sisk, "Sanctuary Movement Leader Jack Elder Pleaded Innocent Friday To . . ." *United Press International*, April 13, 1984.

miles long.[11] Reflecting theologically on the experience, Corbett made the following comments:

> The Freedom Seder has become a holy day in the Tucson sanctuary congregations' liturgical year, a formal assembly and communion to renew the sanctuary covenant that gathers us into a people of peoples. It is a remembrance of Passover that weaves the present experience of refugees and sanctuary congregations into an awareness of more than three millennia of exile, oppression, and liberation. In the Arizona-Sonoran borderlands where the First and Third Worlds meet, sanctuary for Central American refugees is—in a limited but decisively practical way—weaving Isaiah's prophecy of the gathering of peoples into history, as a fulfillment. Whatever else this gathering of peoples may be or become, as a communion it *is* sanctuary for the violated.[12]

Corbett's description of a simple scene in a Tucson Quaker house further highlights how traditions were being recombined through sanctuary: "A Guatemalan woman devoutly hanging a large, icon-styled poster of St. Romero of the Americas in the Pima Friends Meeting House for the Central American masses Father Ricardo celebrated there."[13] In both vignettes we find an encounter between traditions that exceeds facile demarcation. In this latter scene the encounter is between a Quaker worship space, a Roman Catholic liturgy and priest, a Guatemalan woman, and a revered Salvadoran saint who serves as an icon of the faith of the poor. The spiritual presence of Óscar Romero, whose image the Guatemalan woman was hanging, gathered geographical, cultural, and religious difference into a human and humanizing community—into a universal sanctuary church that was forging a communion with Central Americans who were being violently displaced to the United States.

The recombinant or sanctuary church that was coming into being was a glimpse of the eschatological vision in Isaiah 56, where the prophet announces that all who keep God's covenant will be welcome in the presence of the Lord and where God proclaims through the prophet:

---

[11] Jim Corbett, *Goatwalking: A Quest for the Peaceable Kingdom* (New York: Penguin Books, 1991), 157.

[12] Corbett, *Goatwalking*, 157. Emphasis in the original.

[13] Corbett, *The Sanctuary Church*, 4.

"My house shall be called a house of prayer for all peoples" (v. 7). At the heart of what was taking place through sanctuary communities was the *doing* of the covenant at Sinai, a gathering of the "people of peoples that covenant to serve the Kingdom."[14]

Corbett hesitated using the term *church* for a community that extended beyond the Christian tradition. On the other hand, he considered church as a living reality, a container that could hold together the encounter and diversity of traditions and practices embedded into the affirmation that there truly could exist a fully *catholic*—universal—church, which was being gathered together to provide protection to those whom "the security state" was hunting down.[15] Not unlike the ecumenical insights of liberation theologians like Jon Sobrino, Corbett's notion of church as a people of peoples transcended conventional borders of faith and religious difference.[16] This capacious ecclesial vision was grounded in communities' boundless covenanting with the violated, the persecuted, the displaced poor, those whose very existence was threatened.

The possibility of a church that was not wedded to political power, or what Corbett referred to as post-Constantinian, resided within the emergence of the communion that was the sanctuary church. While it may appear simplistic to speak of a Constantinian church in the late twentieth century, the fact that Christian churches continued to up-hold nationalistic tendencies at the expense of the suffering of Central Americans arriving at the border in the 1980s—and continue in the

---

[14] Corbett, 5.

[15] Corbett, 5.

[16] Corbett's vision of a church as communities covenanting together across different traditions in communion with poor and persecuted refugees has direct parallels with Jon Sobrino's theological reflections on solidarity as a way of rethinking ecumenism. Sobrino says that in thinking about the catholicity (universality) of the church, solidarity is a way of historically constructing the universal church made up of many faith experiences and traditions. Sobrino argues that an interconfessional convergence upon the poor will displace other divisions or differences among churches and traditions and will clarify that the greatest division in humanity and in the churches is between those who are oppressors and oppressed; between those who die because of oppression and those who live because of it. Essentially, the poor present a greater alterity than ecclesial differences. Sobrino argues that Óscar Romero unleashed an immense process of solidarity, and that once unleashed, Romero grew into a way of living his ecclesial reality and faith in solidarity with others—all focused on the reality of the poor. See Jon Sobrino, *The Principle of Mercy* (Maryknoll, NY: Orbis Books, 1994), 144–72.

present—pointed to an ecclesial identity that was, and is, too closely tied to the nation-state. "That government disapproval makes the observance of minimal standards of decency a major issue for the church," he wrote, "indicates how urgently it needs to free itself from its seventeen centuries of Constantinian captivity."[17] The question was not whether individual persons had the capacity to embrace a post-Constantinian freedom, but whether faith communities—the church—could break free of their binding and religious servitude to established power. In 1982, at the beginning of the sanctuary ministry, Corbett reflected on the freedom that was emerging within Roman Catholicism:

> Pope John XXIII called the Church to liberate itself from the Constantinian captivity; Vatican II opened the way; and the Latin American Church's declaration of sanctuary for undocumented refugees incorporates Anglo-American communities of faith into this liberation from the Constantinian captivity, and in the process we are forming a truly catholic, ecumenical Church. A year ago we did not recognize this consequence of declared sanctuary. We don't yet know the full consequences, although we do realize, of course, that the post-Constantinian Church that frees itself to stand with the oppressed is also bound to resemble the pre-Constantinian Church in being vitalized by the blood of its martyrs.[18]

The Latin American church, including the refugees themselves, who constitute a living church, had truly invoked and declared sanctuary before God. Anglo-American communities were providing a response to the embodied invitation that was present in the presence of displaced Salvadorans and Guatemalans, for they were, as Corbett emphasized, "the church on the move."[19]

This church on the move from Central America was a catalyst for learning to unbind from institutionalized violence. "A religious awakening

---

[17] Corbett, *The Sanctuary Church*, 7.

[18] "Jim Corbett, "BASTA Nuts and Bolts supplement #1," 1982, University of Arizona Special Collections, MS 362, Box 03, Folder 11, 30. As will be shown in the coming chapters, such liberation is a dream deferred within the Roman Catholic Church, but where it is attempted, Corbett rightly states that, like the early church, it becomes a church of martyrs.

[19] Corbett, *The Sanctuary Church*, 8.

dawned across Latin America and is now reaching Anglo-America," Corbett wrote. "It is not arriving as a new theology,[20] creed or ritual, but in person, as a refugee who confronts congregations in the United States with the pivotal choice that faced the bishops at Medellin."[21] The invitation was to accompany the displaced poor and persecuted, and to pay the price for doing so, even if it meant a new age of martyrs. The church could not simply serve the poor and powerless, for it had to become itself poor and powerless. In the former, the church remained the agent of empowerment, whereas, in the latter, the shared communion became the source of boundless power.

Through the practice of sanctuary with refugees, the church in the United States was faced with the challenge and possibility of entering into communion with the poor of Central America and of divesting itself of entrapments with a security state that desired to make such communion illegal. Corbett argued that "through the corporate practice of love and service, we are to enter into the full community with the violated that heals humanity into one body"[22] and makes the church "a people that hallows the earth."[23] These theological convictions echo Isaiah 58, where the prophet declared the service that God desires and that constitutes true worship: "to loose the bonds of injustice," to "bring the homeless poor into your house," to "not to hide yourself from your own kin" (vv. 6–7). Through such practices of love, that are themselves worship, the prophet declared that "healing shall spring up quickly" (v. 8). In the wilderness of the borderlands, as in the biblical wilderness, sanctuary was conceived as the means through which God could heal the wounds of humanity. Sanctuary bore the possibilities of addressing the dehumanization of displaced Central Americans and of healing the church in the

---

[20] The reference to "new theology" is a veiled commentary on liberation theology. Corbett valued liberation theology positively. However, he was critical of certain appropriations and deformations of this theology that were used as a cover to incite hatred and violence toward an opponent. Also, he was aware of the ways in which liberation theology was used in the United States by some groups who wanted to politically, and in his view simplistically, pit the church against the state through civil disobedience. See Jim Corbett, "Dear Friends" letter, January 24, 1982, 6–7.

[21] Corbett, *The Sanctuary Church*, 9. The pivotal role of Medellín in the Latin American church's transformation, and the ways that half a century later it is a challenge for the church in the United States, will be analyzed in Chapter 5.

[22] Corbett, 12.

[23] Corbett, 11.

United States from its complicity with the institutions of violence. In becoming one church across borders, in making communion historically present through sanctuary, mutual healing could spring up even in the unlikeliest of arid circumstances. To this day, sanctuary churches serve as a sign and instrument of this prophetic and holy vision.

Sanctuary's Capacity to Construct a More Human Society

As an expression of communion with the poor and a covenant with God, sanctuary exists always within the dynamic and contentious relationship between the church and the state. The shifting nature of this relationship influences the historically possible forms of sanctuary. For example, when empire and church were mutually reinforcing, the practice of sanctuary existed as a codified right that churches could legally invoke within the boundaries of their church space. Corbett refers to this kind of sanctuary associated only with church buildings as a "static sanctuary," which, although limited, offered persecuted persons a place of protection. In contemporary societies, where the church is more explicitly demarcated by the nation-state's exercise of power, sanctuary typically does not have legal recognition. Its unauthorized practice, however, can alter the state and its affairs. Corbett writes, "As a people of peoples that covenant to do justice and to love mercy (that is, to do justice nonviolently),[24] the church has an enormous potential for checking and balancing the state's use and abuse of coercive force."[25] Through the practice of sanctuary, the church resists and contains the overflow of violence in society.

The sanctuary church's protective actions can thrust it directly into the realms of national legal affairs and into those of the international community, for it can serve as an implementer of global norms, such as the norms of asylum, within the nation-state. Whereas the state apparatus depends on police powers to carry out orders that may be legal within

---

[24] The reference here is to Micah 6:8. Corbett associates mercy with nonviolence, a connection that finds support in Pope Francis's writings and initiatives. During the Year of Mercy that took place in 2016, Francis developed a brief document on nonviolence titled *Nonviolence: A Style of Politics for Peace*, and a historic conference on gospel nonviolence also took place at the Vatican. See Pope Francis, "Message of His Holiness Pope Francis for the Celebration of the Fiftieth World Day of Peace—January 1, 2017."

[25] Corbett, *The Sanctuary Church*, 13.

the domestic legal sphere, but that may violate international norms, the church that is a people does not depend on police powers for its legitimacy, but rather on its binding relationship with the victims of violence. The convictions that a more just domestic and global society is possible and that the church's historical responsibility to do love and mercy is not dependent on or ultimately limited by the nation-state are at the core of the profound responsibility toward those whose humanity is violated. In its practice of sanctuary, however, the church seeks to hold the nation-state accountable to already-binding international norms of humanity rather than dismiss or bypass it. The church becomes a mediator of the rights of humanity within the nation-state that it also inhabits: "Just as the legal order enforced by the state presupposes an underlying social order established by the communities that form the state, the evolution of the rule of law among nations depends on the prior development of an international social order rooted in local community practice."[26] The church, by its international presence, is key for integrating notions of global responsibility within the immediate local context. The sanctuary church's capacity to become a transnational catalyst was an expression of what Corbett and the borderland communities named "civil initiative."

The concept of civil initiative was directly tied to the principles set forth by the Nuremberg Trials that began to codify crimes against humanity. Perhaps one of the most widely known principles is principle IV, which states, "The fact that a person acted pursuant to order of his government or of a superior does not relieve him from responsibility under international law, provided a moral choice was in fact possible to him."[27] This principle was in response to the well-known practice of Nazi soldiers disavowing responsibility for their crimes by stating that they were only following a superior's orders. As pointed out in the previous chapter, Corbett encountered similar words from a young jailer at the detention center in El Centro, California, in July 1981. Corbett's fundamental belief that the Nuremberg principles depended on local communities for their implementation led him to argue for the practice of sanctuary as a practice of civil initiative—literally, a practice of civilians taking initiative for upholding international norms of the rights of, and to, humanity as

---

[26] Corbett, *The Sanctuary Church*, 14.

[27] United Nations, *Principles of International Law Recognized in the Charter of the Nürnberg Tribunal and in the Judgment of the Tribunal*, 1950.

the law, norms that theoretically expand beyond codified human rights. He wrote: "Implementing the Nuremberg mandate is the task of civil initiative. The sanctuary movement is building the institutional foundations—it is mobilizing the church—to fulfill this task."[28] He added that "civil initiative is designed to claim and incorporate these disputed frontier territories of codified law into our country's accepted social standards."[29] Corbett was aware of the disputed nature of the Nuremburg principles, the degree to which they were legally binding, and the very concept of international legal norms and frameworks in relation to theoretical impingement on notions of national sovereignty. Nonetheless, he believed that, in their grassroots practice, universal norms of humanity could be woven into the social fabric. Civil initiative was a socially constructive means that could organically build a more just and nonviolent society by uniting the global and the local through the practice of sanctuary for refugees who were being sent back into the violence of war.

In the immediate context, civil initiative sought to uphold codified laws on the protection of refugees, including the UN Refugee Protocol, the US 1980 Refugee Act, and the Geneva Conventions on War and War Victims, which theoretically prevent a government from sending persons back to a war zone.[30] Already by 1981 a team of researchers from the United Nations Refugee Agency (UNHCR) had carried out an investigation in Tucson about the Immigration and Naturalization Service's (INS) practices toward Salvadorans, and the team concluded that the UNHCR "should continue to express its concern to the US government that its apparent failure to grant asylum to any significant numbers of Salvadorans, coupled with the continuing large scale forcible and voluntary return to El Salvador, would appear to represent a negation of its responsibilities assumed upon its adherence to the Protocol."[31] The

---

[28] Corbett, *The Sanctuary Church*, 18.

[29] Corbett, 18.

[30] For a detailed analysis of refugee law up to 1985 and the ways in which the government systematically failed to comply with international protocols, see Ignatius Bau, *This Ground Is Holy: Church Sanctuary and Central American Refugees* (Mahwah, NJ: Paulist Press, 1985), 38–74.

[31] UNHCR, "United Nations High Commissioner for Refugees Mission to Monitor INS Asylum Processing of Salvadoran Illegal Entrants—September 13–18, 1981," reprinted in *Congressional Record*, vol. 128 (February 11, 1982), 1698. Also see Bau, *This Ground Is Holy*, 70.

conclusion of the UNHCR and of other investigative organizations that were also documenting human rights violations in El Salvador further catalyzed local church communities in the United States to take responsibility and uphold international norms by preventing the deportation of refugees back to war.[32] "In the face of massive disobedience by federal administrators," Corbett wrote, "the sanctuary church is complying with our country's refugee laws."[33] Naturally, the US government's argument was that the Salvadorans and Guatemalans arriving in the United States were not refugees but simply economic migrants seeking a better life, and thus, legally, they could be sent back.[34]

Since the concept of civil initiative was conceived in relation to the fulfillment or protection of basic rights of humanity that the government was failing to uphold, Corbett and those who worked closely with him in the "evasion services" of the sanctuary network attempted to carry out such norms with genuine integrity and transparency. He wrote:

> The sanctuary network's screening, placement, and protection of Central American refugees is an emergency alternative to the INS. . . . [Thus], to preserve the laws at issue, our sanctuary procedures must integrate our protection of refugees into the legal order, establishing an accountability that prevents sanctuary from degenerating into a kind of do-gooder vigilantism.[35]

Corbett was invested in clarifying that the practice of sanctuary was intimately bound up with fulfilling and enacting existing legal frameworks that theoretically protect humanity. The common rhetoric of a clash between "divine law" and "civil law," or the notion that sanctuary

---

[32] Of more than two thousand asylum applications for Salvadorans that the legal services of the Tucson Ecumenical Council (TEC) submitted starting in 1981, not even one was approved until after September 1985. See Jim Corbett, "Sanctuary on the Fault Line," 1988, MS 502, University of Arizona Special Collections, Box 01, Folder 21, 3.

[33] Corbett, *The Sanctuary Church*, 18.

[34] The US government continues to make similar arguments despite the UNHCR's acknowledgments that there is an ongoing refugee crisis in Central America. See, for example, UNHCR, "Eligibility Guidelines for Assessing the International Protection Needs of Asylum-Seekers from El Salvador," March 2016, The UN Refugee Agency.

[35] Corbett, *The Sanctuary Church*, 23.

practices were simply civil disobedience rather than civil initiative, was problematic for Corbett because such rhetoric failed to recognize that there were laws that existed to protect the poor and persecuted, and that it was the government that was failing to live into the law.

Although Corbett placed a strong emphasis on sanctuary as a form of civil initiative that sought locally to uphold a global sense of the rule of law, he recognized that there could exist situations when appealing to legal frameworks was no longer possible. For example, he wrote, "When a Hitler or Stalin destroys a society's legal order, only a residual rule of law may remain in the church or other institutions . . . so there is no absolute or conclusive formulation of the way to tailor sanctuary as civil initiative."[36] Every historical iteration of church sanctuary, and the degree to which it can live into or fulfill existing laws, depends on any given number of local circumstances, but it always aspires to uphold the good in laws that may already exist. As a way of remaining accountable to legal frameworks that protected the rights of humanity, seven principles guided civil initiative. Civil initiative had to be nonviolent, truthful, catholic, dialogical, germane, volunteer based, and community centered.

The principle of *nonviolence* was more than an expression of particular religious commitments. It expressed the conviction that nonviolence checks vigilantism by emphasizing (nonviolent) means rather than particular objectives, goals, or ends. In the practice of sanctuary as a form of civil initiative, communities were not seeking to become the government or to primarily oppose the government. Rather, they were practicing basic humanizing norms that could protect the life of refugees. Since the government challenged such actions and persecuted those involved with sanctuary, it was also important that sanctuary communities not resist arrest and that they insist on a trial by jury.[37] Theoretically, trial by jury could offer an opportunity for sanctuary communities to defend themselves by appealing to the disputed laws they were attempting to uphold, enact, and weave into the social fabric through their embodied actions.

The second principle, *truthfulness,* emphasized that the actions being carried out were to illuminate the underlying issue, or truth, that was at stake rather than to deceive society. Truthfulness provided an opportunity

---

[36] Corbett, "Sanctuary, Basic Rights, and Humanity's Fault Lines," April 23, 1987, MS 502, Series 8, Box 26, Folder 21, 6.

[37] Corbett, *The Sanctuary Church*, 23.

to forge genuine social cohesion through accountability and transparency. More will be said about truthfulness in the coming pages.

The principle of *catholicity* specifically pointed to the commitment that civil initiative would not become factional. In terms of sanctuary practices it meant that the refugees' political positions would not be a determining factor for sanctuary. In contrast, the US government generally accepted the refugee claims of those Salvadorans fleeing from the guerrillas ("right-wing refugees") because it was politically beneficial for the government, but it rejected the claims of the vast majority who were fleeing from the Salvadoran government and military ("left-wing refugees") because it was politically disastrous—after all, the United States was funding the Salvadoran government and military. Catholicity encouraged sanctuary not to become an inverse mirror image of the government's politics, where only those fleeing from the military would be helped and those fleeing from the guerrillas would be abandoned. Corbett argued that, "everywhere along the border, sanctuary services are provided by religious rather than political groups, and the religious groups respond according to refugees' needs rather than their political alignments or usefulness."[38] Although border communities tried to practice this catholic or non-factional approach to sanctuary, the Chicago Religious Task Force on Central America (CRTFCA) did not agree that the sanctuary network could also protect refugees fleeing from guerrillas, a view that Corbett referred to as "politicized sanctuary."[39]

The fourth principle emphasized that civil initiative was *dialogical*. The primary dialogue partners were the sanctuary communities and the government. If genuine dialogue was to take place, then those in the government had to be treated as persons and not as the enemy. Corbett argued that "any genuine reconciliation of civil initiative with bureaucratic practice—the discovery of an accommodation that does not compromise human rights—is a joint achievement."[40] Dialogue also meant that a willingness to negotiate, and if necessary to compromise on nonessential aspects of the ministry, was essential for sanctuary communities.

---

[38] Corbett, "Sanctuary, Basic Rights, and Humanity's Fault Lines," 10.
[39] Corbett, *Goatwalking*, 160.
[40] Corbett, *The Sanctuary Church*, 23.

The fifth principle asserted that civil initiative actions had to be *germane* to the issue at hand. For sanctuary communities, the "victim's need for protection" had to guide their actions rather than a desire for symbolic protests or political gestures. Corbett added that "media coverage and public opinion are of secondary importance when our central concern is to do justice rather than to petition others to do it."[41] The notion of germane actions further critiqued protest actions that did not actually contribute to refugees' immediate needs for protection from deportation.

Civil initiative was *volunteer based*. This principle recognized the legitimate role of government and that citizens freely entrust their responsibilities to the government. In times of emergency, communities, as the basic building blocks of society, could and must exercise the functions of government. Any government functions that were temporarily subsumed by sanctuary communities had to be forfeited and returned to the government once it was abiding by the legal frameworks to which it was fundamentally obliged.

Last, the principle that civil initiative was *community centered* referred to the belief that individual acts, however important, were not enough. A community of communities was necessary to sustain the transformation of society and the resistance to regimes that failed to uphold the basic rights of humanity. A community and its cohesion were required to live into the kind of protective social responsibility that was envisioned by frameworks such as the Nuremberg Principles.

These seven guiding principles undergirding civil initiative were, fundamentally, a version of Gandhi's conceptualization and practice of Satyagraha, a method for addressing social conflict. The close link between sanctuary and Gandhian philosophy is generally overlooked, even though Corbett himself acknowledges that civil initiative is a form of Satyagraha.[42] Entering into the logic of Satyagraha provides further insights into the complex and nuanced frameworks at the root of the Tucson community's vision of sanctuary as a faithful response to dehumanizing violence. Illuminating how Gandhi was present at the border shows that sanctuary was—and is—more capacious than the popularized acts of civil disobedience, or the bifurcated categories

---

[41] Corbett, 24.
[42] Corbett, *Goatwalking*, 106.

of direct political action and humanitarianism that are typically associated with sanctuary.

Sanctuary in a Gandhian Framework for Social Change

Satyagraha is a method of social construction and transformation that is often reduced to civil disobedience. Even in India, some scholars argue, Satyagraha devolved into civil disobedience after Gandhi's death and the gaining of the country's independence.[43] The temptation to reduce Gandhi's philosophy of nonviolence and conflict transformation simply to what is commonly referred to as "breaking the law" is thus not unique to the US context. Joan Bondurant, one of the early interpreters of Gandhi's method within the US context, distills Gandhi's political philosophy and the challenge of Satyagraha for US democracy in her classic work *Conquest of Violence: The Gandhian Philosophy of Conflict* (1958). Bondurant met and studied Gandhi while serving as a US spy in India before going on to teach political science at the University of California, Berkeley, and at the University of the Pacific. Although she retired to Tucson and lived there until her death in 2006, living there throughout the sanctuary movement, it is unclear whether she and Jim Corbett ever met, though her work on Satyagraha arguably influenced Corbett.[44]

Bondurant argued that, while Satyagraha emerged from Gandhi's initial practice of civil disobedience, it extended beyond this earlier concept. She wrote, "Satyagraha became something more than a method of resistance to particular legal norms; it became an instrument of struggle for positive objectives and for fundamental change—a technique more widely used than understood and one which yet called for testing in the field of social and political action."[45] The conceptual shift from resisting

---

[43] Jagannath Swaroop Mathur, *Contemporary Society: A Gandhian Appraisal* (New Delhi: Gyan Publishing House, 2010), 127; see chap. 11.

[44] Although it's unclear whether Bondurant and Corbett knew each other personally, Corbett briefly references Bondurant's classic book in his own reflections on Satyagraha. See Jim Corbett, *Goatwalking*, 107.

[45] Joan Bondurant, *Conquest of Violence: The Gandhian Philosophy of Conflict* (Princeton, NJ: Princeton University Press, 1958), 4.

to enacting, or more precisely, from opposing certain legal norms to practicing positive norms, legal or otherwise, opens a much wider conceptual horizon of the possibilities inherent in Satyagraha.

The meaning of the word *Satyagraha* already points toward the positive social effect it seeks to enact, for it is composed of *Satya* (truth) and *Agraha* (holding fast, firmness, love). Gandhi called it "the Force which is born of Truth and Love or non-violence."[46] Tragically, before Gandhi could better systematize Satyagraha as a method, he was killed by three bullets during a prayer ceremony on January 30, 1948. In the absence of specific rules for what constitutes this method, Satyagraha became a loosely applied label for a wide variety of social actions, even if they did not cohere with Gandhi's previous practices, or if they stopped just short of outright violence. There are, however, core pillars to Satyagraha, including truth, nonviolence, and self-suffering.

Truth, Nonviolence, Self-Suffering

Satyagraha was a movement based entirely on truth that was intended to replace methods of violence. Thus one can also translate *Satyagraha* as "truth force." Gandhi's high regard for truth led him to claim that "the more truthful we are, the nearer we are to God. We *are* only to the extent that we are truthful."[47] The correlation between God and truth means that to approximate one was to approximate the other. It is not surprising that he preferred the phrase "Truth is God" rather than "God is Truth," for the former emphasized more adequately the ontology of truth.[48] Satya (truth) was, for Gandhi, an all-encompassing reality from which universal values could be derived. According to John Chathanatt,

---

[46] M. K. Gandhi, "Satyagraha in South Africa," in *The Collected Works of Mahatma Gandhi*, vol. 34 (New Delhi, Publications Division Government of India, 1999, 98 volumes), 93. See also, Bondurant, *Conquest of Violence*, 8.

[47] M. K. Gandhi, "Letter to P. G. Matthew," July 9, 1932, in *The Collected Works of Mahatma Gandhi* 56:128. See also Bondurant, *Conquest of Violence*, 19.

[48] M. K. Gandhi, "History of the Satyagraha Ashram," II Prayer (iv), July 11, 1932, in *The Collected Works of Mahatma Gandhi* 56:158. See also David Cortright, *Gandhi and Beyond: Nonviolence for a New Political Age* (Boulder, CO: Paradigm Publishers, 2009), 16.

"Truth as truth (veracity) in the epistemological realm is only a part of its wider meaning"; other values like "righteousness (in the sphere of conduct), and justice (in the domain of social relations) derive their origin from Satya, which itself is derived from *Sat*, the One omnipotent Reality."[49] Gandhi's search for absolute truth (God) led him to pay particular attention to the means for reaching that truth, and, since he had the conviction that the human person could not fully know absolute truth, persons had to be open to the possibility of being wrong, or only partially right. This led to the conclusion that the search for truth is an inherently communal process in which one could not legitimately resort to violence toward an opponent. Rather, the opponent had to be "weaned from error by patience and sympathy"[50] so as not to give rise to cycles of hatred or violence. Through the community's practice of the nonviolent search for truth, the opponent could become a genuine co-searcher. Truth, ultimately, is inseparable from nonviolence.

Gandhi understood nonviolence as the means—the way—in the search for truth. The Sanskrit word for nonviolence, *ahimsa,* is composed of *a* and *himsa*, which at its most basic level refers to not harming or doing injury. However, in the same manner that the word *Satyagraha* points toward a positive vision and not just the resistance of a negative reality, ahimsa refers more fully to a humanizing action in its refusal to do harm. Bondurant emphasized that ahimsa is "not merely a negative state of harmlessness but it is a positive state of love, of doing good even to the evil doer," while yet resisting the evil doer.[51] The way of love is the only way to move forward in the search for truth, and any possibility of reaching deeper truths is inseparable from the means of love/nonviolence. Stated differently, to give in to violence is to forfeit a legitimate and honest search for that which is true in self and society. This leads to

---

[49] John Chathanatt, SJ, *Two Paradigms of Liberative Transformation: Approaches to Social Action in the Theological Ethics of Gandhi and Gutiérrez,* PhD diss., University of Chicago, 1991, 156. For the book version of this work, see John Chathanatt SJ, *Gandhi and Gutiérrez: Two Paradigms of Liberative Transformation* (New Delhi, India: Decent Books, 2004).

[50] M. K. Gandhi, "Statement to Disorders Inquiry Committee," January 5, 1920, in *The Collected Works of Mahatma Gandhi* 19:206. See also Bondurant, *Conquest of Violence,* 16.

[51] Bondurant, *Conquest of Violence*, 24.

the realization that the standard for judging what is actually true in our relative and contested truths is the practice of nonviolence/love. Gandhi's commitment to nonviolence as the means for working out conflicting truths was so central to his philosophy that Bondurant wrote, "The one principle to which he adhered to the end was this theme of ahimsa—the supreme and only means to the discovery of social truths."[52] One way of summarizing the relationship between ahimsa and truth is to say that truth is the end, and ahimsa is the means, or simply, that nonviolence/love leads to truth. David Cortright, a scholar of theories of nonviolence, explains that "conventional philosophy attempts to analyze ends and means separately, but Gandhi reconciled the two. To say that truth is the end and nonviolence the means is to link the two in a continuous process of striving toward truth and higher being."[53] The search for deeper truth is always ongoing, because society is always in a constant process of change. Any objectives or goals for society are always contingent and in flux and, in the Gandhian vision, always secondary to the means that may or may not bring them about.

Conceptually and practically, the means are fundamentally more important than the ends. Or, in Cortright's words, "the means are the end."[54] To make the means the end in social processes entails a radical focus on the moral qualities of present actions and an honest assessment of the violence that may undergird them. To be "present centered" inevitably leads to a certain sacrifice of fixed goals or objectives. The just society one envisions can be reached only by living into that just way of being in the present moment. The ends become subject to the means; goals and objectives begin their fulfillment in the present. However, none of this becomes a reality without a willingness to suffer.

Self-suffering, in Gandhi's thinking, was not taken up as an end in itself but was bound with the process of resisting and persuading the opponent (person, community, society) in the nonviolent search for truth. Self-suffering must not be confused with passive resistance, with cowardice, or with an inability to use violence. Rather, as Gandhi wrote, self-suffering "is the chosen substitute for violence to others," and "it results in the long run in the least loss of life, and, what is more,

---

[52] Bondurant, *Conquest of Violence*, 25.
[53] Cortright, *Gandhi and Beyond*, 17.
[54] Cortright, 18.

it ennobles those who lose their lives and morally enriches the world for their sacrifice."[55] It is no surprise that Gandhi referred to the early Christians who nonviolently endured the violent persecution of the Roman Empire as satyagrahis.[56] To understand Gandhi's conviction that self-suffering in the midst of a social struggle ennobles and enriches, a community must grasp that self-suffering serves as a strategic force of positive and active resistance that, paradoxically, holds more power than violence. To choose and accept self-suffering is to understand that it is a step along the way toward the embodiment of ahimsa—love for the truth (God) and one's neighbor.

One of Gandhi's most piercing statements about the role of self-suffering is that "just as one must learn the art of killing in the training for violence, so one must learn the art of dying in the training for non-violence."[57] To learn the art of dying is to overcome the fear of death or suffering, and, in doing so, to overcome the temptation to use violence against an opponent in the midst of struggle. At no point does the rejection of violence or injury to the other imply passivity or aimless suffering. Self-suffering is always actively directed toward one's opponent in love. Bondurant summarizes it thus: "The element of self-suffering in satyagraha is, perhaps, of all three fundamentals, the least acceptable to a Western mind. Yet, such sacrifice may well provide the ultimate means of realizing that characteristic so eminent in Western moral philosophy: the dignity of the individual."[58] Self-suffering is indeed paradoxical as a force for social action, but a liberation unto the power and freedom dwelling within oneself for the sake of others is embedded in its willful and courageous practice: the power and freedom to love even one's enemies in the struggle for social transformation. In the awareness and the awakening to the power of self-suffering and in the humanizing

---

[55] M. K. Gandhi, "From Europe," October 8, 1925, in *The Collected Works of Mahatma Gandhi* 33:73. See also Bondurant, *Conquest of Violence*, 27.

[56] M. K. Gandhi, "Satyagraha in South Africa," in *The Collected Works of Mahatma Gandhi* 34:97. See also Ignatius Jesudasan, SJ, "Gandhi's Way of the Cross," in *Lead, Kindly Light: Gandhi on Christianity*, ed. Robert Ellsberg (Maryknoll, NY: Orbis Books, 2021), 103–12.

[57] M. K. Gandhi, "Non-Violence of the Brave," August 27, 1940, in *The Collected Works of Mahatma Gandhi* 79:153. See also Bondurant, *Conquest of Violence*, 29.

[58] Bondurant, *Conquest of Violence,* 29.

dignity that it reveals reside the potential for seeing the human person in community as the fundamental agent of change in the construction of a more truthful society.

Gandhi's Constructive Program

In addition to the three pillars—truth, nonviolence, and self-suffering—there is an additional aspect of Satyagraha that is often forgotten, though it is at the core of Gandhi's approach to social transformation: the constructive program. The constructive program, also called social program or social reform program, was envisioned as an element of nonviolent action—such as noncooperation and civil disobedience—that sought to enact a positive "constructive" dynamic into society. Whereas noncooperation was seen as "the refusal to cooperate with a requirement which is taken to violate fundamental 'truths' or refusal to cooperate with those responsible for such violations," and civil disobedience as "the direct contravention of specific laws,"[59] the constructive program was based on community-led initiatives that began to incarnate in history ways of structuring a nonviolent society. In a critique of the public's fascination with civil disobedience at the expense of constructive work, Gandhi wrote in 1939: "So much for those who are in prison, what about those outside? They must engage in constructive work as the embodiment of the active principle of ahimsa. If it does not appeal to them, it will only betray their lack of faith in ahimsa."[60] It may be tempting to qualify or categorize Gandhi's constructive program as apolitical, or as a reprieve from the intense political work that brought him into direct confrontation with the authorities of the British Empire. Yet, if the constructive program is in fact the embodiment of nonviolence/love (ahimsa), as Gandhi claims, then the constructive program is also at the very heart of sociopolitical transformation.

In Gandhi's own campaigns the constructive program focused on the immediate concerns that were present in a community. Generally, a constructive program entailed volunteer work that responded to needs around basic education, communal unity, village sanitation and hygiene,

---

[59] Bondurant, 36.

[60] M. K. Gandhi, *"Discussion with Jaipur Satyagrahis,"* March 20, 1939, in *The Collected Works of Mahatma Gandhi* 75:202.

recognizing and uplifting the role of women, developing village industries that promoted economic equality, and other initiatives that had the potential to rebuild Indian society from the ground up.[61] However, the most iconic constructive work, which came to symbolize the Gandhian experiment of social transformation, was the spinning wheel. Of this practice Gandhi stated: "In the centre of the programme is the spinning wheel—no haphazard programme of spinning, but scientific understanding of every detail, including the mechanics and the mathematics of it, study of cotton and its varieties, and so on."[62] The intensity with which volunteer workers were to give themselves to the craft communicated that such work was not meant to fill time as though it were a distraction. Rather, it was conceived as essential work that formed individuals and communities into self-sustained local societies that served as the foundation for a broader transformation. Gandhi argued that "all this constructive work should be for its own sake. And yet be sure that it will develop the quality required for non-violent responsible government."[63] The very practical and constructive work of spinning cloth became a means of weaving together a society whose independence from economic and imperial powers was bound to basic community-building initiatives that generated social cohesion. .

By going deep into the formation of the self and of the local community, the constructive program made it possible to form and transform humanity itself. Allwyn Tellis has summarized the vision of Gandhi's constructive program in the following words: "Through it, he sought to transform not only the material lives of the impoverished masses, but wanted to outline a new paradigm of development (opposed to that of modernity) that would result in a radical (albeit nonviolent) transformation of all aspects of lived experience—material, social, political, psychological, and spiritual."[64] If Satyagraha was conceived as a method of addressing conflict in the pursuit of truth through nonviolent means such as noncooperation or civil disobedience, the constructive program that had to accompany these other practices was understood as the

---

[61] Bondurant, *Conquest of Violence,* 180.

[62] M. K. Gandhi, "Talks with Co-workers, Rajkot," May 17, 1939, in *The Collected Works of Mahatma Gandhi* 75:401.

[63] Gandhi, 75:401.

[64] Allwyn Tellis, "Mahatma Gandhi's Constructive Programme: Building a New India," PhD diss., University of Illinois at Urbana-Champaign, 2006, 241.

animating soul-force of the whole method.[65] Civil disobedience without a constructive program failed to embody nonviolence:

> Many congressmen are playing at non-violence. They think in terms of civil disobedience anyhow, meaning the filling of jails. This is a childish interpretation of the great force that civil disobedience is. . . . Those, therefore, who wish to see India realize her destiny through non-violence should devote every ounce of their energy towards the fulfillment of the constructive program in right earnest without any thought of civil disobedience.[66]

Because Gandhi considered the practice of civil disobedience such a great force, it was always necessary to bind it to the constructive program so that its genuine power of noncooperation with specific laws would not be cheapened by its symbolic allure, or worse, become itself violent. Anuradha Veeravalli argues that "the constructive program was, according to Gandhi, the prime and necessary weapon of civil disobedience. . . . One without the other would be powerless and directionless."[67] And in Gandhi's own

---

[65] The constructive program was also at the heart of Martin Luther King Jr.'s vision during the civil rights era. He wrote in 1961: "Then there is a factor that may have escaped public notice. So much attention has been given to the movement's emphasis on non-cooperation with evil, that is, with Jim Crow laws and customs, that not much light has been shed on its cooperation with good, that is, its constructive program. This constructive program is a basic part of any genuine non-violent movement, for non-violence is essentially a positive concept. Its corollary must always be growth. Without this broad range of positive goals, non-cooperation ends where it begins. The students have revealed an amazing degree of understanding concerning the needs for such a constructive program. So, on the one hand, they apply non-violent resistance to all forms of racial injustice, including state and local laws and practices, even when it means going to jail. On the other hand, they see the need for imaginative, bold, constructive action to end the demoralization caused by the legacy of slavery and segregation, inferior schools, slums, and second-class citizenship. Certainly the creative thrust of the student's non-violent struggle will in itself help end the demoralization; but they realize that a new frontal assault on the poverty, disease, and ignorance of a people too long ignored by America's conscience will make the victory more certain." Martin Luther King Jr., *The Papers of Martin Luther King, Jr.: To Save the Soul of America, January 1961–August 1962,* vol. 7 (Berkeley, CA: University of California Press, 2014), 212–13.

[66] M. K. Gandhi, "Not Yet," May 28, 1940, in *The Collected Works of Mahatma Gandhi* 78:257–58.

[67] Anuradha Veeravalli, *Gandhi in Political Theory: Truth, Law and Experiment* (New York: Routledge, 2016), 44.

words: "Civil disobedience, mass or individual, is an aid to constructive effort. . . . Just as military training is necessary for armed revolt, training in constructive effort is equally necessary for civil resistance."[68] The point was not to locate civil disobedience hierarchically under the constructive program or vice versa, but to understand their integral relationship. The constructive program and civil disobedience were seen as complementary and inseparable, and it could be argued that, within Satyagraha, one is the mode of the other. Through the constructive program, persons and communities began to prefigure in history their desired social change, simultaneously unlocking a whole social imaginary of what was possible through the disciplined and nonviolent work of local communities.

Both Gandhi and Jim Corbett had great respect for the legal systems they inhabited, perhaps because they were both closely associated with the law—Gandhi a lawyer and Corbett the son of a lawyer—or, more important, because they understood that legal systems have the potential to create either just social structures that humanize or violent structures that subjugate and kill.[69] Because they clearly perceived the power of law in the ordering of society, and thus the power of civil disobedience, they resisted any facile and superficial use of the concept and practice. Their respect for the law certainly did not mean that they subjugated themselves uncritically to the law, but it also did not mean that they spoke lightly or symbolically about breaking the law. Corbett was clear in his critique of popularized versions of civil disobedience:

> The profession of respect for the law often means "I don't want to get in trouble for civil disobedience," but I have no comfort to offer those burdened with this scruple. The symbolic varieties of civil disobedience that are now prevalent can be compartmentalized into scheduled happenings, but violated humanity sets a full-time agenda for civil initiative by base communities.[70]

---

[68] M. K. Gandhi, "Hints for Constructive Workers," October 22, 1944, in *The Collected Works of Mahatma Gandhi* 85:77.

[69] Corbett's father was for a time the chairman of the judiciary committee of the Wyoming House of Representatives, and Corbett grew up learning about the law (including the Nuremberg Trials) over dinnertime discussions. See Corbett, *Goatwalking*, 91, 103.

[70] Jim Corbett, "Sanctuary on the Fault Line," 1988, University of Arizona Special Collections, MS 502, Box 01, Folder 21, 15.

For Corbett, as for Gandhi, civil disobedience as ordinarily understood had become mostly symbolic in nature and detached from constructive forces. Because of this conviction, he insisted that sanctuary was not civil disobedience, for it was not an action that was primarily symbolic or of short term. Rather, sanctuary was a way of being in the world, constructing community anew in communion with those whose humanity was being violated.

Civil Initiative—
Gandhi's Method for Social Change
in the Borderlands

Having examined fundamental elements of Satyagraha, it becomes more evident how Jim Corbett's principles for civil initiative are a form of Gandhi's philosophy for social change. For example, Corbett's emphasis that civil initiative was *dialogical* and should strive for a "joint achievement" with government officials resonates with Gandhi's insistence that the goal of a Satyagraha campaign was not to vilify or condemn an opponent, but rather to convert the opponent to one's truth of the matter.[71] As Gandhi wrote when speaking of love and noncooperation, "I would co-operate a thousand times with this Government to wean it from its career of crime, but I will not for a single moment co-operate with it to continue that career."[72] A commitment to nonviolence as an expression of love challenges the temptation to demonize and make of adversaries intractable enemies beyond the possibility for conversion and some form of reconciliation or social healing.

Another of Corbett's principles was that civil initiative needed to be *germane* to victims' needs for protection rather than focused on reactionary symbolic or expressive actions. This principle echoes Gandhi's warnings about engaging in civil disobedience at the expense of actually meeting community needs through the constructive program. For Corbett, the urgency of protecting human lives demanded the embodi-

---

[71] For Corbett's critique of Saul Alinsky's method for community organizing in contrast to Gandhi's nonviolent approach, see Corbett, *Goatwalking*, 106.

[72] M. K. Gandhi, "Religious Authority for Non-Co-Operation," August 25, 1920, in *The Collected Works of Mahatma Gandhi* 21:200.

ment of nonviolence toward the Salvadoran and Guatemalan refugees already in the borderlands, which meant resisting the violence of the state by preventing their immediate capture and deportation. Corbett's emphasis on germane actions is powerfully captured in the following words from 1982:

> Actively asserting the right to aid fugitives from terror means doing it—not just preaching at a government that is capturing and deporting them, not just urging legislation that might help future refugees. With people in our midst being hunted down and shipped back, denouncing the terror while ignoring the victims simply teaches the public how to live with atrocity.[73]

His words are a reminder of the Nuremberg laws that made it possible to capture and deport Jews under Hitler's administration, as well as the Nuremberg principles that seek to resist such laws that violate the rights of, and to, humanity.

As demonstrated, there was a profound convergence between Gandhi's philosophical frameworks and civil initiative at the border. In order to understand the nature and purpose of sanctuary beyond categories that reduce it simply to "humanitarian" or to "political" actions, it is essential to grasp the more complex theological and philosophical underpinnings that were operative in Corbett's efforts to do justice—to do truth—through sanctuary. The vision of sanctuary that arose in the borderlands of Arizona in the early 1980s was a form of Gandhi's constructive program, and more broadly, of Satyagraha. Sanctuary served as a prefigurative paradigm of the critical role and power that local church communities had in the process of transforming social, political, and legal norms. Gandhi was clear about the direct relationship between the constructive program and political power:

> The capacity of the [Indian] Congress to take political power has increased in exact proportion to its ability to achieve success in the constructive effort. That is to me the substance of political power.

---

[73] Corbett, "National Council of Churches of Christ Consultation on Immigration," January 28–30, 1982, University of Arizona Special Collections, MS 362, Series 02, Box 01, Folder 07.

Actual taking over of the government machinery is but a shadow, an emblem. . . . We have everywhere emphasized the necessity of carrying on the constructive activities as being the means of attaining Swaraj [independence].[74]

For Gandhi and for Corbett the constructive program, which in the borderlands became the practice of sanctuary, was the fundamental basis for a more humanizing society. Through this generative force, persons and communities were liberated unto a microcosm of what society could become as a communion of humanity across borders.

The constructive work of sanctuary was the nonviolent means for local church communities to encounter both a prophetic and civil power that could transform the violence of a political system. However, it was essential that sanctuary not become subjugated to broader political objectives that could sacrifice the non-factional (nonpartisan) dimension of sanctuary. As Corbett wrote in a letter to the CRTFCA, "If we were to try to construct sanctuary on a political platform instead of allowing the political consequences to flow from covenant-based sanctuary, we would be engaged in propaganda rather than prophetic witness."[75] Returning to the question of means and ends and its relation to political power further clarifies how the Tucson borderland community understood the nature and purpose of sanctuary.

Sanctuary as Nonviolent Means and Ends

To grasp sanctuary as both the nonviolent means and ends for transforming society amid the challenge of refugee arrivals in the 1980s, one must venture further into the inner logic of this mode of addressing social conflict. As presented earlier in this chapter, for Gandhi the means are already ends in the making, and there can be no separation between the two. Future political objectives can never be conceived apart from the means used in the present moment, and surrendering to the means

---

[74] M. K. Gandhi, "Power Not an End," July 2, 1931, in *The Collected Works of Mahatma Gandhi* 53:4.

[75] Corbett, "Letter to !BASTA!," September 25, 1984, University of Arizona Special Collections, MS 362, Series 02, Box 01, Folder 08.

inevitably leads to detachment from particular political objectives, which may or may not be achieved in the future.

The challenge of detachment from particular objectives is acutely difficult in western conceptions of the political, where achievement of the ends too often qualifies and justifies the means, as is expressed in the often-used phrase, "by whatever means necessary." Joan Bondurant argues that "if the dichotomy between ends and means is logically tenable, the most acute problem for social and political thought is their reconciliation in the field of action,"[76] for, in action, the means overwhelmingly become subservient to the ends. To put it in terms of a linear time metaphor, the present time that is already here is made subservient and subjugated to a future time that has not yet arrived. Bondurant goes on to say that "it is only when means themselves are understood to be—and designed to be—more than instrumental, to be, in fine, *creative* that the next step will be taken in the evolvement of a constructive philosophy of conflict."[77]

Corbett and the Tucson community's conception and practice of sanctuary was indeed a creative and constructive response to the social conflict in which they found themselves—the arrival of persons fleeing dehumanizing violence and the US government's attempts to apprehend them and return them to that violence. Perhaps it is too paradoxical to claim that by entering deeply into the practice of sanctuary as a covenant communion with displaced Salvadorans and Guatemalans, US policy would change. Yet, that and more was the conviction embedded into the Gandhian framework that undergirded Corbett and the borderland sanctuary communities. Corbett's quixotic[78] conviction in the possibility for a radical change of the violence that structures society resided in the

---

[76] Bondurant, *Conquest of Violence*, 230.

[77] Bondurant, 232.

[78] Jim Corbett had a profound fascination with Miguel de Cervantes's *Don Quixote*, and in many ways Corbett saw his own life as one of "errantry," of "sallying out beyond a society's established ways, to live according to one's inner leadings." He followed his own version of Quixote's madness. The following excerpt from his writings captures what he called the Quixotic Principle: "In its quest of full communion, errantry neither waits for recruits nor compromises to gain allies. It shrugs off the arguments of all theological or political parties, each of which claims to have discovered the right way to fracture time and the world into good ends and effective means. It is therefore an insecure, impolitic, minority way of life. Errantry disdains adaptive pretense, majoritarian morality, and all politic forms of solidarity because it is based on the Quixotic Principle: *To open the way, a cultural breakthrough*

local practice of nonviolent, constructive, and creative forms of active resistance.

The Gandhian relationship of means and ends also informed Corbett's theological insights into sanctuary as presence-centered and present-centered communion. Through presence-centered communion with the displaced poor and persecuted, a covenant from the past (echoing Isaiah 56) was being actualized in the present, and a future community was being prefigured in the now. Eschatologically speaking, through sanctuary a catholic (universal) church was becoming in the present, though not completed. Of this church, a people of peoples, Corbett said: "The church as many of us have come to know it through the sanctuary movement includes all who covenant as primal societies to treat no one as violable enemy, alien, or inferior."[79] The sanctuary church was enacting in time and place the transhistorical reality that God's people are a pilgrim people of peoples called to hallow—to sanctify—the earth, and to participate creatively with the Spirit of the Holy One who is boundless presence in and beyond the present of our history.

In the previous chapter I traced the intricate process that led members of the Tucson community to reflect on their responsibility to protect those who were fleeing the US-financed wars in Central America and who were arriving in the American Southwest. In this chapter I focused on Jim Corbett and the Tucson community's theoretical frameworks for sanctuary. Corbett deftly wove sanctuary into scripture, theology, theories of Gandhian nonviolence, international norms of law and the rights of humanity, sociopolitical and religious history, and, by the end of his life, into a mystical vision of communion with all creation.[80] Certainly, as one scholar writes, Corbett was sanctuary's "philosophical architect."[81] Although this chapter has focused more on the theoretical underpinnings

---

need not involve masses of people but must be done decisively by someone." Corbett, *Goatwalking*, 14.

[79] Corbett, 187.

[80] See Jim Corbett, *Sanctuary for All Life* (Berthoud, CO: Howling Dog Press, 2005). These writings were published posthumously.

[81] Lane Van Ham, *A Common Humanity: Ritual, Religion, and Immigrant Advocacy in Tucson, Arizona* (Tucson: University of Arizona Press, 2011), 48.

of sanctuary than on the practical dimensions of its existence from the early 1980s until the early 1990s, it is nonetheless fitting to ask what sanctuary accomplished during that decade.

On a practical level, in 1990, sanctuary communities effectively won a lawsuit against the US Immigration and Naturalization Services (INS). This lawsuit, known as *American Baptist Churches (ABC) v. Thornburgh*, was filed in 1985 in response to government persecution of persons involved with sanctuary in the borderlands. By 1990, the Department of Justice decided to settle with the plaintiffs (known as the ABC Agreement), and sanctuary communities and their supporters were vindicated in the *truth* of their arguments and practices. This major legal accomplishment provided temporary protected status to at least 500,000 Salvadorans[82] and Guatemalans, and over 100,000 asylum cases could be reviewed under different and reformed procedures from those that had previously discriminated against them throughout the 1980s.[83] For Corbett however, the greater accomplishment resided in establishing the concept and practice of sanctuary within communities, especially communities of faith. He wrote:

> The ABC agreement was a notable victory for the sanctuary movement—yet, just an agreement signed by a government that continues to sponsor gross violators of human rights in Central America and that routinely violates its own statutes and treaties. The sanctuary movement's real victory during the decade had been the development of sanctuary as an enduring institution within the fully catholic church. Particularly in the borderlands, sanctuary congregations now have the experience and networks to continue, regardless of government countermeasures. For these churches, synagogues, and meetings, providing sanctuary has become integral to being faithful.[84]

---

[82] In order to qualify for ABC protections and benefits, Salvadorans had to register for Temporary Protected Status (TPS) by October 31, 1991. My mother and I arrived in the United States around October 26, 1991, after a month-long journey by land in an attempt to flee the war in El Salvador. She applied for TPS a day or two after arrival, and since I was nine years old, her temporary protected status also protected me. The prophetic witness of sanctuary communities and their willingness to suffer the persecution of the state has saved countless lives.

[83] Corbett, *Goatwalking*, 181.

[84] Corbett, 182.

To some degree, Corbett's assessment rings true, especially since Tucson communities continue to practice sanctuary and serve as a resource for other communities across the United States and the world as they discern sanctuary with displaced and persecuted persons in their midst.

In past years the Australian organization Love Makes a Way has reached out to the sanctuary network in the borderlands to learn from its experience. In 2016, the organization's strong focus on nonviolence led it to play a key role in organizing over eighty cathedrals, churches, and convents who were willing to provide sanctuary to 267 asylum seekers threatened with deportation.[85] Sanctuary communities from the borderlands are also in communication with communities in Europe, especially Germany,[86] as they continue to respond to refugees who have fled the violence in Syria, Afghanistan, Iraq, and elsewhere.[87] In the Netherlands, sanctuary practices reached a global audience in 2019 when a church carried out a creative and protective liturgical service that lasted over three months, until the government reconsidered the cases of the persons threatened with deportation.[88]

As a concept and practice, sanctuary continues to have a creative presence across the world, but Corbett's conviction that sanctuary had become "an enduring institution within the fully catholic church" remains a living challenge. To this day sanctuary is often reduced to a political tactic of civil disobedience rather than conceived as a truth-seeking constructive process of "interweaving persons and groups into a communion."[89] The prophetic vision of a world where communities are healed through a shared commitment to, and with, the displaced and persecuted poor will require nothing less than the reconstruction of the church.

---

[85] Paul Farrell, "Churches Offer Sanctuary to Asylum Seekers Facing Deportation to Nauru," *The Guardian* online, February 3, 2016.

[86] Asyl in der Kirche is the major sanctuary organization in Germany. More information can be found at kirchenasyl.de.

[87] See, for example, the signatories of the International Sanctuary Principles Statement, which seeks to respond to the global escalation of displacement. Available online.

[88] Patrick Kingsley, "96 Days Later, Nonstop Church Service to Protect Refugees Finally Ends," *New York Times* online, January 30, 2019.

[89] Corbett, *Goatwalking*, 197.

The words of the First Letter of John, which Corbett echoed, still ask, "If a man has enough to live on and yet when he sees his brother in need shuts up his heart against him, how can it be said that the divine love dwells in him?"[90] Communities who claim a covenant with God must continually ask themselves what faithfulness requires in a world of forced displacement. There is an indelible relationship between the dwelling of the presence of God and a community's response to persecuted life. In the coming chapters, I turn to this theological affirmation as I enter more deeply into the historical and sacramental relationship between sanctuary and the nature and mission of the church.

---

[90] Corbett, "Dear Friends" letter, July 6, 1981, 3.

Part II

3

Traditions of Refuge for the Persecuted

It is fitting that bishops should provide help to those who suffer from any violence, or any widow who is harmed, or orphans who are defrauded—if these persons do indeed have honorable petitions. . . . And since worthy persons frequently come fleeing to the mercy of the Church, whether exiled for their offenses or condemned to islands, or subject to any punishment, such [persons] are not to be denied protection, but without hindrance or delay this protection is to be granted. If this therefore is pleasing, let this also be decreed.

—Council of Serdica, 343 CE

Part I established the theological and philosophical frameworks of the 1980s sanctuary ministry that emerged in the US-Mexico borderlands. A diverse group of faith communities in Tucson, Arizona, developed a network that responded to the US government's failure to protect persons fleeing violence and war in Central America. Sanctuary churches became a means of nonviolent sociopolitical transformation and of reimagined relationships across borders. At the root of the sanctuary ministry was a theological vision of communion with refugees through a response to their embodied invocation of refuge, which led to the persecution of those who provided it as well. More than a humanitarian or political act, sanctuary was a practice that manifested the church and its faith.

To invoke sanctuary in modernity is to echo, consciously or not, ancient traditions of refuge. In this chapter I analyze the tradition of cities of refuge and of early church conceptions of sanctuary, focusing particularly on the theological and sacramental logics that they communicate. These traditions were a means for addressing cycles of violence and persecution in their particular contexts, and, although they were bound by their particular codifications in history, they point to the fundamental relationship between the presence of God and the protection of persecuted life. In turning to these ancient traditions the point is not to retrieve and apply ancient practices uncritically. Rather, the hope is to enter deep into the spirit out of which they operated in order to think about new contexts of persecution. The chapter ends with an analysis of how, in the 1970s and 1980s, the Roman Catholic Church expelled any reference to the tradition of sanctuary or church asylum from its Code of Canon Law. Refuge in the church, however, has continued in new forms, reminding humanity that living traditions always exceed legal or ecclesiastical codifications.

Cities of Refuge and Asylum

Cities of refuge or cities of asylum are part of the deposit of biblical concepts that continue to influence religious imaginaries for responding to deadly persecution and violence. In the Hebrew Scriptures, God is portrayed as explicitly commanding Moses to build such cities for those who have committed manslaughter. The cities were to serve all members of the community, regardless of whether they were Israelites or "aliens." Toward the end of the Book of Numbers, one reads: "These six cities shall serve as refuge for the Israelites, for the resident or transient alien among them, so that anyone who kills a person without intent may flee there" (v. 15). This mandate for the cities of refuge, three of which were to be built beyond the Jordan and three within Canaan, would help delineate the boundaries of the land they were to enter and occupy.

Like an urban planner, God makes provisions for the majority of persons whose lives would theoretically be marked by right relationships and for those who could find themselves in an ambivalent relationship to the laws and norms of the community. The scriptural verses in the Book of Numbers tell us that the cities were for those who kill a person "without intent," but there is much ambiguity as to what constitutes intent. The diversity of passages that ordain the building of these cities intensifies this ambiguity, for there are at least three other references to them in Exodus (21:12–14), Deuteronomy (19:1–6), and Joshua (20:1–9).[1]

In each of the references the mandate and the criteria for who can flee to and inhabit the cities are expressed with a slightly different focus. Whereas, in Numbers, the ambiguity centers simply on lack of intent in the killing, Deuteronomy qualifies lack of intent by focusing on any past enmity that may or may not have existed between the victim and the perpetrator (Deut 19:4). Furthermore, even though the texts provide scenarios to qualify the lack of intentionality—such as accidentally killing someone with an ax (Deut 19:5) or hitting someone with a stone (Num 35:17)—the examples tend to obscure rather than clarify what in fact constitutes intentionality. Craig Stern captures this ambiguity when he asks: "Does meeting any one test or resembling any one scenario describing a capital killing render a killing capital? Or must all tests be met, all scenarios be matched or surpassed?"[2] Thinking about the intersection of biblical law and Anglo-American law, Stern concludes that, although common interpretations of who does *not* qualify for the cities of refuge depends on "intentional" or "deliberate" killing, these standards are never fully explained in the aforementioned passages.

Despite the ambiguity regarding the criteria that qualified a person for refuge, it is clear that these places were meant to interrupt cycles of killing.

---

[1] One way of categorizing the diversity of passages pertaining to cities of refuge is to locate them in relation to the various legal codes that undergird the Torah. The Exodus passage (21:12–14), for example, falls within the Covenant Code that typically ranges from Exodus 20—23. The passage in Deuteronomy (19:1–6) falls within the Deuteronomic Code that typically ranges from Deuteronomy 12—26. The third major legal code is the Holiness Code in Leviticus 17—26. While the references to cities of refuge in Numbers and Joshua do not fall within this code, they are nonetheless references to Levitical cities and are influenced by what some have called the Holiness School. Pamela Barmash, *Homicide in the Biblical World* (Cambridge, UK: Cambridge University Press, 2005), 71–93; Israel Knohl, *The Sanctuary of Silence: The Priestly Torah and the Holiness School* (Minneapolis, MN: Fortress Press, 1995), 99–100; Michael Walzer, "The Legal Codes of Ancient Israel," *Yale Journal of Law and the Humanities* 4 (1992): 335–50; Jeffrey Stackert, "Why Does Deuteronomy Legislate Cities of Refuge? Asylum in the Covenant Collection (Exodus 21:12–14) and Deuteronomy (19:1–13)," *Journal of Biblical Literature* 125, no. 1 (2006): 23–49; Norbert Lohfink, SJ, "Poverty in the Laws of the Ancient Near East and of the Bible," *Theological Studies* 52 (1991): 34–50.

[2] Craig Stern, "Torah and Murder: The Cities of Refuge and Anglo-American Law," *Valparaiso University Law Review* 35 (2001): 477.

Embedded within the concept of the cities of asylum was a due-process mechanism, for the elders of the community had to hold a trial to ascertain intentionality and punishment. During the process the surrounding community was obliged to protect the accused from anyone who might attempt to avenge the life that had been taken (Num 35:24–25). If the community deemed that the killing was intentional, the punishment was paid with the life of the accused and could not be ransomed in any other way (Deut 19:12–13).[3] Paradoxically, this transaction conveys the fundamental value of life, for only life could pay for life, but without giving rise to ongoing cycles of revenge killing. If the killing was deemed not to have been intentional, the accused was innocent but still bore guilt and had to spend the rest of their life in exile in a city of refuge. There, the community could protect their life from those who would have exacted life in return (the *go'el hadam*—"redeemer of spilt blood"), avenging or redeeming the spilt blood. Because the innocent person nonetheless bore the guilt of taking a life, and because the relatives of the slain were prevented from taking life in return, the only mechanism for expiating such guilt was through the death of the high priest. Moshe Greenberg writes that "a religious guilt such as bloodguilt can be expiated only in religious terms. . . . The sole personage whose religious-cultic importance might endow his death with expiatory value for the people at large is the high priest."[4] Upon the high priest's death, those in exile for accidental or innocent killing could return to their previous communities without fear of retribution, for the death of the high priest broke the cycle of requiring a life for a life.[5] An indelible connection existed between the high priest and those who had to flee to live in the cities of refuge, for

---

[3] Moshe Greenberg emphasizes the incommunicability of the purposeful taking of life into other expiatory mechanisms: "Punishment of homicide, as has been said, was not subject to human decision. The kinsman of the slain is not allowed to come to terms with the slayer, either in a monetary or any other fashion. He cannot pardon his act and expunge his sin. This is the explicit law of Numbers 35, but it is not a late idea of the priestly writer; it is a principle informing all of biblical law." Moshe Greenberg, "The Biblical Conception of Asylum," *Journal of Biblical Literature* 78 (1959): 128.

[4] Greenberg, 129–30.

[5] The expiatory role of the high priest is most present in descriptions of cities of refuge in the Book of Numbers. Greenberg argues that this text followed in the Levitical (priestly) tradition and presents an older and less "secularized" notion of cities of refuge when compared to Deuteronomy. In this sense, cities of refuge in

the cities were not simply an example of biblical humanitarianism. At their core, they pointed to a conception of communal life bound with the holy.[6]

The concept of cities of refuge and the contours of its practice as expressed in scripture are a source of contention in contemporary invocations of refuge for persecuted persons. For supporters of sanctuary practices, for example, cities of refuge signify the fundamental biblical exhortation to protect threatened life. For those opposed, invocations of cities of refuge illustrate a misuse of scripture in politics. As one biblical scholar argues: "American cities, counties and universities that offer sanctuary for foreigners who have broken American laws regulating entry to our country cannot claim to be following the practice described in the Bible. Rather, they are twisting biblical statutes to political ends and subverting federal law."[7] The accusation of employing biblical or religious concepts for political ends that break the law was commonplace during the sanctuary movement of the 1980s and becomes commonplace whenever churches, synagogues, and other communities of faith turn to scripture for theological insights and resources on how to respond to the persecution of displaced communities. Those who oppose using the concept of cities of refuge for contemporary sanctuary practices emphasize that the biblical cities of refuge were only for those who had already been subjected to the due process mechanisms of the religious system of the time. As such, they had obeyed the law. In this perspective, the mechanisms by which these cities of refuge operated becomes central, and the telos for which they were ordained—protection of innocent-yet-guilty life—becomes secondary. Such critiques also assume a clear-cut

---

Numbers were imbued with a deep sense of their status as religious sanctuaries and not simply as humanitarian sites of protection. See Greenberg, 131.

[6] Greenberg, 127. In later Christian exegesis in the early church and in the Middle Ages, the death of the high priest who expiates the guilt of those in cities of refuge will be read in relation to the figure of Christ, who advocates or intercedes for all. Ambrose of Milan, "Flight from the World," in *Seven Exegetical Works, The Fathers of the Church,* vol. 65 (Washington, DC: Catholic University of America Press, 1973), 290; Karl Shoemaker, *Sanctuary and Crime in the Middle Ages* (New York: Fordham University Press, 2011), 54.

[7] James Hoffmeier, "Does the Bible Really Advocate Sanctuary Cities?" *Religion News Service* online, February 15, 2017; James Hoffmeier, *The Immigration Crisis: Immigrants, Aliens, and the Bible* (Wheaton, IL: Crossway Books, 2009).

delineation between what constitutes innocence and guilt, a point that the biblical texts themselves problematize.

How one reads the multiple iterations of cities of refuge found in the various texts of the Hebrew Scriptures to a great degree determines whether these passages have any relevance to contemporary situations. After all, it could be argued that these cities were only for those accused of unintended manslaughter, thus having nothing to do with displaced and persecuted persons fleeing violence and war in Latin America or in any other part of the world unless the reason for their persecution is that they have unintentionally killed and are now being threatened with death. The problem with a literal adaptation of cities of refuge to contemporary issues of displacement and persecution is that those fleeing violence and war are conceptually framed as persons who have killed and who are now in need of protection. In order to move beyond these binary framings and into the spirit that inhabits the biblical verses regarding cities of refuge, Emmanuel Levinas's reflections on their contemporary relevance is instructive.

Levinas's insights combine the wisdom of his own Jewish tradition, his location within a dominant Western society, and his experience as a prisoner of war in a German labor camp during World War II.[8] Using the questions and teachings of the Talmud on cities of refuge,[9] he nuances the question of intentionality in killing rather than assuming a clear-cut distinction between innocence and guilt. He asks: "In Western society—free and civilized, but without social equality and a rigorous social justice—is it absurd to wonder whether the advantages available to the rich in relation to the poor . . . are not the cause, somewhere, of someone's agony? Are there not, somewhere in the world, wars and

---

[8] Starting in the early 1960s, Levinas systematically began to engage the Talmud and his Jewish tradition in his ongoing development of a philosophy that was inseparable from ethical commitment. His reflections on cities of refuge are an example of this scriptural engagement. Emmanuel Levinas, *Nine Talmudic Readings* (Bloomington: Indiana University Press, 1990). Nelson Maldonado-Torres, *Against War: Views from the Underside of Modernity* (Durham, NC: Duke University Press, 2008).

[9] The Talmud's tractate that deals with cities of refuge is Makkot 10a. For an online version with the Hebrew text and the English translation, see www.sefaria.org/Makkot.10a.

carnage which result from these advantages?"[10] The shift from an individual to a collective lens of analysis, and from direct killing to the endless forms of both slow and swift death that modern societies and systems inflict upon others, problematizes what it now means to commit manslaughter. Levinas recognizes both the complex and globalized set of relationships of modernity, and the accompanying culpability and innocence, or as he says, "subjective innocence" and "objective guilt," that mark all persons and communities.[11] The notion that we are all already implicated in the taking of life somewhere in the world, that, in some ways, we, too, meet the criteria for cities of refuge, leads him to ask, "Does not all this make our cities cities of refuge or cities of exiles?"[12] By challenging assumptions of innocence, especially those of Western societies, Levinas forces a rethinking of every person's need for refuge. The blurry boundaries of innocence and guilt in the taking of life lead to all places as bearing possibility and responsibility for the protection of life, lest cycles of killing, which on a societal level become war, continue to define the human condition.

In his analysis Levinas accounts for the justice that is desired by the avengers of the death of kin, the redeemers of spilt blood. He writes, "Does not the avenger or the redeemer of blood 'with heated heart' [Deut 19:6] lurk around us, in the form of people's anger, of the spirit of revolt or even of delinquency in our suburbs, the result of the social imbalance in which we are placed?"[13] However, despite the hypocrisy of "civilization" that he critiques, the anger and passion carried by the kin of the slain—by oppressed communities, we could say—cannot justify revenge killing, for the innocent-yet-guilty condition in which all already live exceeds humanity's limited conception of justice.[14] If anything, the anger of a people and the spirit of revolt further emphasize the need to continue wrestling with the spirit of the cities of refuge so as to envision in history the "humanist urbanism" to which they point.[15]

---

[10] Emmanuel Levinas, *Beyond the Verse: Talmudic Readings and Lectures* (Bloomington: Indiana University Press, 1994), 40.

[11] Levinas, 39–40.

[12] Levinas, 40.

[13] Levinas, 40.

[14] Levinas, 46.

[15] Levinas, 38.

The questionable moral status of humanity, the difficulty in ascertaining innocence and guilt, and the possibility that all are already in need of refuge makes cities of refuge a necessary, albeit ambiguous, concept in the modern world.[16] Despite its ambiguity, the concept points most fundamentally to the unambiguous value of life, the life of a subjectively innocent and objectively guilty humanity who otherwise must face death. Within Jewish tradition the Talmudic tractate Makkoth 10a prescribes that these cities be medium-sized boroughs, not a small settlement or a large city, presumably emphasizing the communal spirit that is to guide them. They were to have access to water (a spring), but, if there was no water, then it had to be brought in through a canal as necessary. The cities were to have an abundant population and could not have weapons or materials for traps so that the blood-avenger, persecuting the life of another, could not take a life.[17] If the population of these cities reached a low point, then other people were to move into these cities in order to keep them in existence.[18] The justification for such cities of refuge was ultimately God's command as expressed in the scriptures, that a person who kills without intent be able to "flee to one of these cities and live" (Deut 4:42). Reflecting further about what it can mean to live in such cities, Levinas writes: "Life can thus mean only life worthy of the name; life in the full sense of the term: exile, of course, but no prison, no hard labor, and no concentration camp."[19] The exile of an innocent-yet-guilty humanity

---

[16] Oona Eisenstadt points to this moral ambiguity around the concept of cities of refuge and the way in which the concept illuminates certain realities yet obscures others: "We're aware that responsibility is not limited by negligence, that it is not really adequate to say 'I made a mistake.' But we do make mistakes and we have to forgive each other. Though we understand full responsibility and may assume it deep down, we cannot impose it on others or ourselves. For this reason, says Levinas, all our liberal cities are organized as cities of refuge. The original cities of refuge provided sanctuary because the manslaughterer was innocent, and exile because he was guilty. Our cities too provide sanctuary from radical violence, sanctuary we deserve in our innocence. At the same time they perpetuate unwitting oppression—economic, social, and political—and in this way allow or encourage their citizens to stand in exile from the truth, in sleep's exile from waking." Oona Eisenstadt, "The Problem of the Promise: Derrida on Levinas on the Cities of Refuge," *Cross Currents* 52, no. 4 (2003): 475.

[17] Levinas, *Beyond the Verse*, 34.

[18] Levinas, 34.

[19] Levinas, 42.

cannot lead further into death but rather toward the fullness of communal life, aware that the demand for justice cannot be silenced.[20]

In the wounded histories that we inhabit, cities of refuge are not an ideal but a necessary contradiction for thinking beyond the societal arrangements of modernity that too easily demarcate between innocence and guilt. As Levinas argues: "There are cities of refuge because we have enough conscience to have good intentions, but not enough not to betray them by our acts. Hence the manslaughters. Reality is not transparent to us; we take a confusion of feelings for a conscience and hatreds for fraternity."[21] Only when there is no longer killing, when there isn't, somewhere in the world, wars and carnage because of the advantages of some over others, will cities of refuge cease to exist in their necessity. This is nothing less than the biblical vision of a new humanity, of a society that is, in the words of Levinas, "wholly human."[22]

These biblical cities, these sanctuaries of life, point not to the past, but to a future where persecution ceases because life is no longer under the threat of death, and where violence is no more. In the Jewish tradition from which Levinas draws, to speak of such places of refuge and sanctuary is to have the fullness of Jerusalem in mind, a "city of the authentic Torah," "a more conscious consciousness, completely brought down to earth," where the other is visible in the fullness of their humanity.[23] The profound religious humanism embedded into the cities of refuge is also echoed in the early Christian tradition of church sanctuary, which, in its own particular context, served to resist cycles of violence and death.

Refuge in the Church

The origins of church sanctuary illustrate that it was understood as a religious and pastoral response to persons in need of protection from violence and death. In this section, I examine some of the earliest Christian references to church sanctuary, mostly from the mid-to-late fourth century. The references illustrate the diverse ways in which this

---

[20] Levinas, 45.
[21] Levinas, 50.
[22] Levinas, 52.
[23] Levinas, 50.

ecclesial tradition was invoked with the participation of ecclesiastical leaders of the time, even before it had been formally codified within the church or the Roman Empire. While the fourth-century bishops could theoretically presume upon ancient Greek and Roman traditions of sacred spaces as places of refuge,[24] their confrontations with imperial authorities illustrate that they protected persecuted persons because it was the church's religious and pastoral duty to advocate and intercede on their behalf, not because it was permitted.[25] Despite the vast differences that exist between the church in the fourth century and the realities of the twenty-first century, the need for protection remains a constant, as do the political and legal tensions to which refuge in the church gives rise.

The earliest reference to what we call church sanctuary comes from the Council of Serdica. Held in 343, it gathered about 170 bishops from the Eastern and Western part of the empire who attempted to reconcile political, ecclesiastical, and theological conflicts.[26] Part of the tension had to do with Athanasius of Alexandria and other bishops who had been deposed in 335 by bishops who sympathized with Arius. The Western bishops who supported the Nicene Creed had reinstated Athanasius and the other deposed bishops, leading to a back-and-forth struggle that the council sought to address. Most of the canons that resulted from the council dealt with disciplinary matters of the episcopate such as excommunication, bishops going to the imperial court, the right of appeal of bishops, and refuge for bishops or clergy who were persecuted for their theological positions. For example, canon twenty-one states:

> If anyone is forcefully and unjustly expelled [from his church] because of [his] doctrine or catholic confession or defense of the truth, fleeing peril, guiltless and devout, comes to another city, whether bishop or presbyter or deacon, he shall not be forbidden to remain there until he can either return [to his church] or has

---

[24] Philip Marfleet, "Understanding 'Sanctuary': Faith and Traditions of Asylum," *Journal of Refugee Studies* 24 (2011), 440–55.

[25] Jan Hallebeek, "Church Asylum in Late Antiquity: Concession by the Emperor or Competence of the Church?" in *Secundum Ius. Opstellen aangeboden aan prof. mr. P.L. Nève* (Nijmegen, NL: Gerard Noodt Instituut, 2005), 164.

[26] Hamilton Hess, *The Early Development of Canon Law and the Council of Serdica* (New York: Oxford University Press, 2002), 95, 101.

received remedy for his injury; for it is hard for him who has suffered persecution not to be received.[27]

Athanasius of Alexandria, whose life was marked by various forced exiles and flights from threats of violence, is an example of the kinds of situations to which these canons referred.[28] Within this broader context of determining ecclesiastical norms for bishops, and for their interactions with each other and with the imperial courts, we also find the earliest references to church sanctuary and the responsibly of bishops to intercede for condemned and persecuted persons. Canon eight states:

> A bishop should make his intercession [for those] who are oppressed by disadvantages in life or the afflicted widow or exploited orphan . . . [and] since it often happens that those who suffer a wrong or who as offenders are condemned to exile or an island or at any rate receive some sentence flee to the mercy of the Church, they are to be given relief, and forgiveness is to be asked for them without hesitation.[29]

To "flee to the mercy of the Church" (*ad misericordiam ecclesiae confugiant*) is arguably the first ecclesiastical reference to church sanctuary within what the late theologian Hamilton Hess calls an "ecclesiastical rule of law"[30] that would eventually become codified into the church's canon law in the following centuries.[31] The text conveys the conviction of these early prelates that the tradition of refuge should encompass a wide scope of who could seek the church's intervention. A bishop's duty to "give relief" concerned persons oppressed by any number of social, economic, or political reasons. Particular attention was given to those

---

[27] Council of Serdica, canon twenty-one, from the Latin version. Hess, 225.

[28] Jennifer Barry, *Bishops in Flight: Exile and Displacement in Late Antiquity* (Berkeley: University of California Press, 2019), 2–5.

[29] Council of Serdica, canon eight, from the Latin version. Hess, *The Early Development of Canon Law,* 217. For the Greek version see canon seven, Hess, 231.

[30] Hess, 203.

[31] Since the Latin version of the canon says "flee to the mercy of the church" and the Greek version says "flee to the church," it is possible to interpret the canon as referring to both the church as an institution and its intercessory role, as well as to the particular role that church buildings have in providing refuge. See Hallebeek, "Church Asylum in Late Antiquity," 165.

who had actually been condemned to exile. In the fourth century, exile could serve as an alternative to the death penalty, especially for the more privileged classes, so a condemnation to exile was a forced displacement to avoid death.[32] In such cases, whether it was because the accused suffered a wrong or because they were in fact offenders, if they fled to the church, the church was tasked with interceding and seeking their forgiveness before the emperor "without hesitation."

The Council of Serdica sought to discipline bishops who frequented imperial court for "ambitious" and "self-serving petitions," or, as canon eleven says, who "wishe[d] to climb with ambition more than to please God."[33] However, if the matter concerned the life of those in need, then the bishop was not only encouraged to go to the imperial court but was obliged to do so. Hess writes, "Although the presentation of frequent and ambitious petitions is condemned, a clear distinction is drawn between the evil of this and the propriety of intercession for the poor and the oppressed and for widows and orphans."[34] That those who were "oppressed by disadvantages in life," who were "afflicted," and who were "exploited," were placed together with the "condemned" in the canon's instructions for bishops points to the variety of persons who found themselves in need of the intercession of bishops before courts and to the way in which such categories are often interrelated in the vicissitudes of life. Canonically speaking, the bishop's personal involvement with persons whose life was threatened was not an optional extra demand added to his responsibilities but a constitutive dimension of his faith and ecclesiastical duty.

The intercession of bishops on behalf of sanctuary seekers was a reflection of the theological affirmation that clerics could and must mediate the mercy and justice of God to those who seek their protection. The ancient biblical duty to intercede for the poor and oppressed as expressed in the biblical law codes of Exodus, Deuteronomy, and Leviticus, which is captured in the traditional formula of the stranger, the orphan, and

---

[32] Barry, *Bishops in Flight,* 6–8.

[33] Hess, *The Early Development of Canon Law,* 202. See also Christopher W. B. Stephens, *Canon Law and Episcopal Authority: The Canons of Antioch and Serdica* (Oxford, UK: Oxford University Press, 2015), 74.

[34] Hess, *The Early Development of Canon Law,* 203.

the widow,[35] was reaffirmed and codified to also include persons who may fall into crimes and who faced the possibility of death.

The Council of Serdica established a framework for how ecclesiastical leaders were to respond to the practice of persons taking refuge in the church. The council did not establish the practice of sanctuary in the church, for it was already happening at the time of the bishops' gathering at Serdica regardless of whether they approved of it or not. The bishops, though, recognized and affirmed the legitimacy of a merciful response to the practice. In addition to the agreement that bishops should intercede on behalf of those who sought the mercy of the church, did the council suggest that bishops should actively prevent, if necessary, the extraction of those who took refuge in the church? This is, in fact, what may be implied by the canons of the council, at least while the intercessory process plays out.

In her detailed analysis of the emergence of sanctuary in the fourth century, Anne Ducloux suggests that if nothing was attempted between the moment when the condemned person fled and took refuge in the church and the moment when the possible imperial favor or indulgence reached the local authorities, it could be too late for the one who had taken refuge.[36] Thus, the intercession of the bishop also meant the active protection of the refugee from being apprehended by local authorities until a solution to the critical, life-altering situation could be found in the court. The phrase from canon eight—"they are to be given relief"—may

---

[35] See Lohfink, SJ, "Poverty in the Laws of the Ancient Near East and of the Bible," 34–50. In speaking of the earliest law code (Covenant code) and the poor, Lohfink writes: "In Exodus 22:21, after the law on the stranger, we have a law on widows and orphans. They are mentioned once again in 23:11, in the law of the fallow year, which precedes the law on the Sabbath where the stranger occurs the last time. In my opinion, we find here the origin of the series of *personae miserae* which will be typical for the rest of the Old Testament. It is not yet the fixed formula 'the stranger, the orphan, the widow,' which does not appear before Deuteronomy. But here, in the framework of the laws on the poor in the Covenant Code, its foundation is laid" (40–41). Additionally, for a brief analysis of "the stranger" in Israelite law codes, see Pietro Bovati, "My Father Was a Stranger: Biblical Teaching on Migrants," *La Civilta Cattolica*, February 15, 2017 (Hong Kong: Union of Catholic Asian News, 2017), 18–32.

[36] Anne Ducloux, *Ad Ecclesiam Confugere: Naissance du droit d'asile dans les églises* (Paris: De Boccard, 1994), 30.

refer to such direct protections, relief that was to accompany and make possible a legitimate process of episcopal intercession. In the 340s, when the canons of Serdica were agreed upon, there were no protections that would theoretically keep the local authorities of the empire from entering a church and extracting whoever had taken refuge, which highlights the pastoral conviction that undergirded the responsibility they placed upon themselves. Ducloux clarifies that retaining refugees who had already been condemned was contrary to secular law and even constituted concealment of wrongdoers.[37] Yet the bishops chose to stand with those who sought refuge and mercy in the church.

It would be too simplistic to say that the Council of Serdica pitted the mercy of the church against civil law, for this fails to account for how bishops were to use the legal systems of the time to find a resolution. Emphasis should be placed on the conviction that mercy was a pillar of the church for those who sought refuge and for the bishops themselves. Furthermore, refugees and church leaders alike recognized the need to live courageously into this mercy regardless of the unexpected effects.

From its beginning, refuge in the church was for both the innocent and the guilty, the just and the unjust, the righteous and the unrighteous. In light of the preceding discussion of innocence and guilt in relation to the cities of refuge, and of what will later become a stricter association of sanctuary with criminality that survives to this day, it is important to note that, in the earliest references, people took refuge in the church and sought the bishop's intercession for a multitude of reasons that had to do with the preservation of their life and dignity before civil authorities, irrespective of whether they were actually guilty or innocent of some crime. Refuge in the church was an act of desperation because, in one way or another, their life was in danger. However, there were no guarantees of life for those who took refuge in the church or for the bishops who interceded.

At the Council of Serdica the bishops made legible a popular practice that had already been taking place but for which an agreed-upon term did not exist. The bishops avoided calling it "asylum," which evoked pagan practices and customs from previous centuries that had some legal recognition.[38] Throughout the fourth century and into the fifth,

---

[37] Ducloux, 30.
[38] Ducloux, 34.

what we now refer to as sanctuary was simply referred to as fleeing to the church, or more specifically at its roots, to the mercy of the church. The reference was not simply that of fleeing to *a* church, as in an individual church building or cathedral, but to *the* church (*ad misericordiam ecclesiae confugiant*), to the whole community of what church points to in both its human and divine aspects. In the latter half of the fourth century this practice would be further established through the preaching and personal involvement of some of the key bishops of the time. Beyond the canons of Serdica, their words and witness would more firmly establish an ecclesial tradition that would bind refuge in the church with the responsibilities of bishops. The Council of Serdica did not provide details laying out the specifics about church sanctuary because its focus was on elaborating a principle of ecclesiastical conduct. Therefore, one must turn to later patristic writings that offer insight into the practice and into the theological understanding of this tradition.

In Gregory of Nazianzus's funeral oration for his friend Basil, the bishop of Caesarea who died in 379, we find the example of Basil protecting a sanctuary seeker who fled to the church altar. The situation concerned a judge who was forcing a woman into marriage after the death of her husband and the woman's "daring" attempt "to escape this oppression."[39] Gregory writes, "She fled to the holy table and made God her protector against outrage." He then rhetorically asks, purposely adopting the language of a courtroom, what any bishop or priest ought to have done in a similar situation: "Was it not his duty to act in her defense, to receive her, to protect her, to raise his hand on behalf of the mercy of God and the law which commands respect for the altar? Was it not his duty to be willing to do and suffer all rather than take against her any inhuman measure, and outrage the holy table and the faith of her supplication?"[40] Gregory's affirmation that to take refuge at "the holy table" was to take refuge in God is at the core of Gregory's dramatic retelling.

Gregory's words point to a sacramental relationship between sanctuary and the mercy of God made manifest in that place through the church and, more particularly, through the bishop who was to serve as God's

---

[39] Gregory of Nazianzus, "On St. Basil the Great," *The Fathers of the Church*, vol. 22 (New York: Catholic University of America Press, 1953). All quotations of this recollection are in sections 56–57.

[40] Gregory of Nazianzus.

instrument for her protection. To hand over the one who took refuge at the altar was to carry out an "inhuman measure" that prioritized the bishop's self-preservation over the needs of the persecuted person. To reject the one seeking relief from oppression was to betray both the sacramental presence of God at the altar of mercy and the faith of the one who sought it, or as Gregory frames the situation, it would make Christians "traitors to their own laws," which is what the judge apparently wanted. What laws did Gregory have in mind? In the 370s there were no civil laws that recognized sanctuary, but the canons of Serdica could have certainly been a point of reference. More profoundly than any one law, though, it appears that Gregory is pointing to the divine law of mercy that exceeds any codification and is most profoundly captured in the reference to the altar. Ducloux argues that Gregory and Basil, through their teaching and preaching, propagate the principle that there is a divine law that commands respect for the altar, and that this principle was already being recognized inasmuch as it was being challenged, as the case with the judge shows.[41] But theologically speaking, a principle of respect for the altar, if it was to be more than a general notion of the holy present there, would have been grounded in the divine mercy that the altar represented in its material reference to the life, passion, and death of Jesus Christ. There is a whole christological context in the background of this confrontation with the judge, which is why Gregory later compares Basil to Jesus.

The peak of the situation takes place when the judge attempts to extract the woman from the church, or more specifically, from the "holy table." Gregory only writes that "the judge sought to seize the suppliant, but Basil protected her with all his power." Does this mean that the judge entered the church to extract the woman or that he merely gave orders? Or did the judge send soldiers into the church to take her away? If either of these two scenarios took place, did Basil physically intervene in locating himself between the judge or soldiers and the "holy table" where the woman was located? These are questions in search of details that the text does not provide, but Gregory is unambiguous that Basil did everything he could to keep the woman from being taken away from the church by force. Gregory adds that the judge sent magistrates to Basil's bedroom, with the implication that Basil was sexually involved with the woman

---

[41] Ducloux, *Ad Ecclesiam Confugere*, 49.

and that this would dishonor the bishop. Finally, in light of Basil's non-cooperation with the judge's orders, the judge began to persecute him and "ordered him to appear in court and justify himself . . . as if he were a man condemned."[42] At this point Gregory compares Basil to Jesus before Pilate, both standing in judgment for their actions. But paradoxically, as Gregory clarifies at the end of this recollection, the judge was on trial before the judgement of God, and Basil would end up protecting the judge from the anger and possible violence of the crowd that gathered in defense of the bishop. If, at the beginning of the situation, the woman who took refuge in the church was described as suppliant, by the end, the judge was described as such. The bishop, as he had interceded for the woman, also interceded with the crowd in defense of the judge's life. The whole recollection ends with Gregory emphasizing that the defense of life is the work of God: "And why should not He who divided the sea, and stayed the river, and subdued the elements, and by the stretching of hands set up a trophy to save a fugitive people, why should not He have also delivered this man from his dangers?"[43]

As Gregory's funeral oration for his friend Basil testifies, getting involved with persecuted or condemned persons in the fourth century could lead to a bishop's own persecution and perhaps condemnation by the judges of the empire. Basil's defense of church sanctuary is one of the earliest Christian references to the specificity of the altar as a site of refuge and protection for the persecuted.[44] Sacramentally, by the 370s, the life of the bishop and the life of those seeking refuge in the church had become interdependent around the "holy table," bound together before the mercy of God. This sacramental relationship would be affirmed by other bishops in the following decades.

Let us consider an account that concerns Ambrose, who, around 396, is reputed to have tried to defend a man named Cresconius at the Cathedral of Milan.[45] The account reaches us through Paulinus's *Life*

---

[42] Gregory of Nazianzus, "On St. Basil the Great."

[43] Gregory of Nazianzus.

[44] Ambrose of Milan, in his treatise *On Virgins* 11.65, also makes reference to a similar situation where a woman took refuge at the altar, though he does not further elaborate on the practice. See Boniface Ramsey, *Ambrose* (London: Routledge, 1997), 91.

[45] Paulinus of Milan, *Life of Saint Ambrose,* in *The Fathers of the Church*, vol. 15 (New York: Catholic University of America Press, 1952), 34. All quotations are

of Saint Ambrose, written about thirty years after the events. The narrative, though brief and hagiographical in nature, offers insights into the ongoing practice of refuge in the church and the religious dimensions associated with sanctuary. The forceful extraction of Cresconius from the church took place while the child emperor Honorius and his guardian, Stilicho, were in an amphitheater in Milan, about to watch a show with live wild animals. Soldiers were sent to the church and entered it, which led Cresconius to take refuge not only in the church itself, where he already was, but more specifically "at the altar of the Lord." Paulinus writes that "the holy bishop with the clerics who were present at the time gathered around to defend him, but the multitude of soldiers . . . prevailed over the few." Up to this point in the narrative it is clear that soldiers and the civil leaders who sent them did not hesitate to confront and oppose one of the most prominent and well-connected bishops of the time. Ambrose and the rest of the clergy, even though they tried physically to intervene, could not keep Cresconius from being taken from the altar. All Ambrose could do at that point was to pray, in lamentation, "prostrate before the altar of the Lord." One could ask whether Ambrose was lamenting the forced apprehension and removal of Cresconius, or the fact that it was done from the altar itself, but to separate the two would fail to acknowledge the growing relationship between the altar and the life of persecuted persons.

The rest of the narrative communicates what could be termed a miraculous divine intercession, or a response to Ambrose's laments. Just as the soldiers returned to the amphitheater with Cresconius, they were attacked by leopards and left wounded. What initially seemed like a "triumph over the church" ends up becoming an opportunity for the civil authorities to be "moved with repentance," to make "amends to the bishop," and to unbind "unharmed the one who had been snatched away." Certainly, all of this was meant to convey the sacredness of the tradition of sanctuary and the sanctity of Ambrose as a defender of those who took refuge in the church.[46] Cresconius, who is described as "guilty of the most serious crimes and [who] could not be corrected otherwise,"

---

in section 34. See also Neil B. McLynn, *Ambrose of Milan: Church and Court in a Christian Capital* (Berkeley: University of California Press, 1994), 164.

[46] Claudia Rapp, *Holy Bishops in Late Antiquity* (Berkeley: University of California Press, 2005), 258.

was initially sent into exile but then granted a pardon. The whole situation echoes canon eight of the Council of Serdica and enfleshes the canon through the actions of Ambrose.

At the end of the fourth century John Chrysostom provides one of the most powerful reflections on taking refuge in the church. Two of his homilies from 399 concern a consul to Emperor Arcadius, Eutropius, who, after his political downfall and condemnation, took refuge in the church of St. Sophia in Constantinople.[47] Chrysostom points out that Eutropius had fought to eliminate the practice of taking refuge in the church, succeeding to some degree with laws he was able to pass against this practice in the 390s, only to then find himself the beneficiary of what he previously persecuted. In the first homily given while Eutropius was in the church, Chrysostom says: "In thy misfortune I do not abandon thee, and now when thou art fallen, I protect and tend thee. And the church which you treated as an enemy has opened her bosom and received thee into it."[48] The bishop uses this homily to try to convince his own congregation in the cathedral to not be angry and indignant that refuge has been extended to one who, as Chrysostom says, "made war upon the church." To a cathedral so full that Chrysostom compares it to the paschal feast celebrations, he asks that they "hasten to produce some fruit of mercy,"[49] imploring the merciful God and interceding before the emperor. Chrysostom extends the responsibilities for bishops set forth in canon eight of the Council of Serdica to the whole church community, for when persons flee to the mercy of the church they flee not only to a building, or to an altar, but to a people whose faith must bind them to the persecuted in their midst. According to Chrysostom, that a person live becomes in and of itself "an offering to the Holy Table," for God, he says, desires mercy and not sacrifice.[50]

In a second, much longer, homily given after Eutropius had left the church, Chrysostom uses highly symbolic language and adds details of

---

[47] For details of Eutropius's political rise and fall, and the emperor's proclamation against him, see Chris Doyle, *Honorius: The Fight for the Roman West, AD 395–423* (New York: Routledge, 2019), 106–7.

[48] John Chrysostom, "Homily One on Eutropius: On Eutropius, the Eunuch, Patrician, and Consul," in *Nicene and Post-Nicene Fathers: First Series,* ed. Philip Schaff, vol. 9 (Grand Rapids, MI: Eerdmans, 1956), 1.

[49] Chrysostom, 4.

[50] Chrysostom, 5.

the firmness with which the church stood when soldiers attempted to forcefully apprehend and extract Eutropius from the altar. The church did not cooperate with the soldiers, but Eutropius surrendered shortly thereafter and was eventually beheaded. Chrysostom writes:

> A few days ago the church was besieged: an army came, and fire issued from their eyes, yet it did not scorch the olive tree; swords were unsheathed, yet no one received a wound; the imperial gates were in distress, but the church was in security. And yet the tide of war flowed hither; for here the refugee was sought, and we withstood them, not fearing their rage. And wherefore prithee? Because we held as a sure pledge the saying "Thou art Peter, and upon this rock I will build my Church: and the gates of hell shall not prevail against it." And when I say the church I mean not only a place but also a plan of life: I mean not the walls of the church but the laws of the church. When thou takest take refuge in a church, do not seek shelter merely in the place but in the spirit of the place. For the church is not wall and roof but faith and life. . . . Ye were present on that day, and ye saw what weapons were set in motion against her, and how the rage of the soldiers burned more fiercely than fire, and I was hurried away to the imperial palace. But what of that? By the grace of God none of those things dismayed me.[51]

Chrysostom's vivid imagery locates the refugee and the practice of taking refuge in the church explicitly within a horizon of life and death that echoes war. As the homily emphasizes, the protection of those who sought the mercy of the church resided not so much in the church walls that could demarcate a place of refuge or sanctuary, but rather in the embodied community of faith who could enflesh it peacefully ("the olive tree"), with a sense of security in God and without being overcome by the fear of armed soldiers. His recalling of Jesus's promise to Peter (Mt 16:18) that death—"the gates of hell"—shall not prevail makes of the defense of those who take refuge in the church an embodied memorial enactment of that salvific promise that ultimately life shall prevail, and that the church has been entrusted with upholding in

---

[51] John Chrysostom, "Homily Two on Eutropius: After Eutropius Having Been Found outside the Church Had Been Taken Captive," in *Nicene and Post-Nicene Fathers: First Series,* vol. 9, 1.

practice this fundamental principle of faith. It is also a promise that the church, if faithful to Christ, will always be marked by a confrontation with whatever seeks to deny life and make of it a living hell. Death and life, condemnation and salvation, the reign of war and the reign of God were all implicated in the struggle to protect persons seeking refuge in Chrysostom's fourth-century context.

The homily, meant not only as a defense of what Chrysostom had done in protecting a once-powerful man despised by the population, was also an opportunity for him to question his own congregation's love of wealth, of security, and their fear of the powerful instead of sin. Making them aware of their precarious position to judge Eutropius and Chrysostom's own actions, he asks them: "Didst thou not yesterday kiss his hands, and call him saviour, and guardian, and benefactor? Didst thou not compose panegyrics without end? Wherefore today dost thou accuse him? Why yesterday a praiser, and today an accuser?"[52] Like Levinas's reflections that all people are already in need of cities of refuge because of humanity's subjective innocence yet objective guilt, Chrysostom aims to dispel from his hearers the notion that they are innocent or somehow pure, unlike the one who has taken refuge at the altar. Echoing the biblical mandate of the centrality of the poor, he tells them, "strip not the widow, plunder not the orphan, seize not his house," and then adds, "I do not address myself to persons but to facts. But if any one's conscience attacks him, he himself is responsible for it, not my words."[53] The members of the congregation are meant to understand that their lives and the life of a condemned man, a fugitive, one who has been made a stranger, may not be that different after all, for both are in need of what the altar provides. Using sacramental language, Chrysostom declares to all, "The Church is thy hope, thy salvation, thy refuge."[54]

This historical review of some key bishops in the fourth century has illustrated two key points about the origins of sanctuary. First, bishops looked at the status of the individuals who took refuge in the church in terms of the oppressions, persecutions, and condemnations that threatened their life and humanity and saw the church's responsibility as one of historically manifesting the mercy of God through their defense.

---

[52] Chrysostom, 4.

[53] Chrysostom, 6.

[54] Chrysostom, 6.

Second, they consistently rejected the view that they could carry out this religious duty of intercession and protection without also risking themselves as ecclesiastical leaders.[55] By the time of Chrysostom, the whole of the church community was being invited to intercede, to risk themselves and face possible consequences before the empire's courts.[56]

The practice of refuge in the church would not be legalized as a positive right within civil codes until decades later. Already in 399 the bishops of Carthage had asked for a law that legalized refuge in churches and that placed sanctions on those who violated this practice, but they would have to wait until 419 in the Western part of the empire, and until 431 in the Eastern part, for a law that made refuge in the church a possibility that was open to all who may have need of it. These laws were essentially the legal codification of a practice, or a custom, that had been taking place in Christian churches for about a century.[57] Although refuge in churches is mentioned in civil law codes as early as 392, the references were to exclude certain categories of persons (e.g. tax evaders), not to institute a positive legal right. The codifications of the practice in the Theodosian and Justinian codes would ensure that refuge in churches would eventually become a tradition of the church in the centuries to come as bishops, kings, and popes negotiated space and cartographies of the sacred. Negotiations were not necessarily carried out as a clash between church and state, for at times they were strategic gifts, such as ecclesiastical exemptions or privileges given to royalty, and royal immunities given to the church, all of which were ways to "construct space, define boundaries, prohibit entry."[58]

---

[55] For details of Chrysostom's legal trial for performing acts of mercy in the church, see Mary Farag, *What Makes a Church Sacred?: Legal and Ritual Perspectives from Late Antiquity* (Berkeley: University of California Press, 2021), 85–93.

[56] Two decades later, in 419, Augustine will preach a sermon after a refugee was extracted from the church in Carthage and Augustine will further emphasize this point, that a person who takes refuge in the church can only be protected with the presence and collaboration of the church community. For this text, which is a fragment of a sermon that has been attached to Augustine's sermon 302 delivered earlier in his career, see Augustine of Hippo, "Sermon 302: On the Birthday of St. Laurence," in *The Works of Saint Augustine*, vol. 8 (Hyde Park, NY: New City Press, 1994), 310–11. See also Ducloux, *Ad Ecclesiam Confugere*, 179–81.

[57] Pierre-Clément Timbal, *Le Droit d'asile* (Paris: Librairie du Recueil Sirey, 1939), 73–89.

[58] Barbara Rosenwein, *Negotiating Space: Power, Restraint, and Privileges of Immunity in Early Medieval Europe* (Ithaca, NY: Cornell University Press, 1999), 18.

There is no linear progression of the legal or canonical "right" of refuge or asylum in churches in the Middle Ages, for it is a tradition that adapted with the restrictions, possibilities, and ecclesiastical and secular leaders of a given time. However, as Pierre Timbal has argued, by the fifteenth and sixteenth century, procedural questions dominated canonical debates about refuge or asylum in churches, dealt with under the broader framework of immunities or privileges of the church,[59] rather than attempts to elaborate or deepen the theoretical or theological foundation for this practice as the bishops had done in the fourth century.[60]

By the late twentieth century, ecclesiastical leaders questioned the necessity and validity of references to refuge in the church, which still existed in the Code of Canon Law, paving the way for the canonical erasure of this tradition in the post–Vatican II church. The many centuries of church sanctuary as a recognized right within kingdoms and empires had led the church to depend on the legal recognition of this tradition for its existence, tragically eroding its early Christian roots as a religious and pastoral duty that transcended any codification in civil law. The rest of this chapter analyzes how the last reference to church asylum disappeared from canon law and argues for an ecclesial reconsideration of the principle and practice of refuge in the church.

Disappearing the Ecclesiastical Right of Asylum

The ecclesiastical recognition of sanctuary or asylum in the church formally existed until the early 1980s. The current Code of Canon Law, established in 1983, does not explicitly prohibit refuge in the church, but it no longer mentions the existence of this tradition. The last official acknowledgment is found in the 1917 Code of Canon Law, which, in canon 1179, states: "Churches enjoy the right of asylum, which implies that criminals seeking refuge therein may, except in case of urgent necessity, not be taken out without the consent of the Ordinary or at least of

---

[59] At the Council of Trent, although the topic of sanctuary or church asylum was not directly addressed, indirectly it is implied in the council's documents dealing with "the immunities, liberty, and other rights of the church" (Session 25, Chapter 20). See John O'Malley, *Trent: What Happened at the Council* (Cambridge, MA: Harvard University Press, 2013), 232, 236, 253.

[60] Timbal, *Le Droit d'asile*, 268.

the rector of the church."[61] Long gone are references to persons "oppressed by disadvantages in life," or to the "afflicted widow or exploited orphan" that were mentioned by the bishops at Serdica. The only reference now is to criminals, a reflection of the ways that the practice had been codified for centuries as it became more standardized and narrower in meaning.

The 1917 Code of Canon Law recognizes that persons in sanctuary may be removed "in case of urgent necessity" without the consent of the ecclesiastical leader. While theoretically this clause is an acknowledgment that the state can forcefully remove persons from the church, as we saw in the example of Ambrose of Milan in 396, the clause can also be interpreted as a further means of protection for the person who takes refuge in the church. For example, one commentary on this canon states: "In cases of urgent necessity no permission is required [to remove someone without the bishop's consent]. Such a case would be that of threatening mob violence, from which officials might save the criminal by quick action."[62] The commentary assumes that the state's motives for forcefully removing someone from the church would be in furtherance of their life, to protect them from the possibility of violence or death rather than to expose them to it.

The process of revising the Code of Canon Law began with Pope John XXIII and then Pope Paul VI. It was concluded under Pope John Paul II, who, as John Coughlin writes, "desired that the church's law reflect the ecclesiology of Vatican II."[63] In 1971, a commission gathered to discuss canon 1179 of the 1917 Code of Canon Law, and the head of the commission advised eliminating the reference to the right of asylum in churches. The reasons given were that civil society no longer recognized the right and that it was no longer invoked by people seeking sanctuary.[64] In agreement, others on the commission added that civil laws increasingly guarantee and defend the rights of

---

[61] Charles Augustine Bachofen, *A Commentary on the New Code of Canon Law* (St. Louis: Herder, 1918), 47.

[62] Bachofen, 48.

[63] John J. Coughlin, *Canon Law: A Comparative Study with Anglo-American Legal Theory* (New York: Oxford University Press, 2011), 37.

[64] For the official Latin record, see Pontificia commissio codici iuris canonici recognoscendo, "Coetus studii 'De Locis et de Temporibus Sacris' (Sessio I)," *Communicationes* 35.1 (2003), 72.

citizens, even those of criminals, because penalties they said, have been "humanized."[65] In contrast, some members of the commission argued that, even if in practice the right of asylum or sanctuary within churches was not recognized by civil society, the affirmation of such a principle before civil society depended on whether the canon was suppressed or retained within canon law.[66] These members of the commission even suggested revising the canon in order to more explicitly transform sanctuary in churches into something similar to the diplomatic immunity of embassies, with clear processes for requesting it. The discussions actually led to new wording for the canon, and, with an eight-to-one vote in favor, reference to sanctuary was kept at this stage of the code's revision. Furthermore, the reference to cases of "urgent necessity" for extracting someone from sanctuary was removed, arguably to strengthen the principle of sanctuary and its possible practice. Thus, the temporary canon in the early 1970s affirmed that whoever flees to a church or sacred place to obtain asylum is not to be removed without the consent of the competent ecclesiastical authority.[67]

The former canon 1179 of the 1917 Code of Canon Law became canon 14 in the working draft that was sent out for consultation to various episcopal conferences, dicasteries, and other church entities in 1977. In 1979, a commission composed of both new and previous members of the 1971 group gathered for a second stage of revisions, and canon 14 was simply eliminated. The primary reasons provided by the commission were that civil law does not recognize the right of asylum in churches and that the church does not have a need of its existence.[68] The previous commission's insights on the importance of affirming the *principle* of sanctuary before civil society, even if civil law did not recognize its practice as a *right*, came to an end.

The final stages of the process that led to the disappearance of sanctuary from canon law were marked more by a reference to legal rights than by an understanding of sanctuary as an ecclesial and pastoral duty with

---

[65] *Communicationes* 35.1, 72.

[66] *Communicationes* 35.1, 72.

[67] *Communicationes* 35.1, 72.

[68] Pontificia commissio codici iuris canonici recognoscendo, "Coetus Studii 'De Locis et de Temporibus Sacris,'" *Communicationes* 35.2 (2003), 289.

deep roots in fourth-century pastors and theologians. To a degree, this is understandable, since episcopal conferences, dicasteries, and other church entities that provided feedback to the commission may not have been familiar with the roots of sanctuary practices or its ongoing tradition in the twentieth century. After all, aside from examples such as the village of Le Chambon-sur Lignon in France or the Assisi Network in Italy during World War II,[69] or the late 1960s and early 1970s declarations of sanctuary in the United States for civilian and military personnel opposed to serving in the Vietnam War,[70] the practice of church sanctuary was largely absent from collective consciousness until the 1980s sanctuary movement for Central Americans. In the perceived absence of a living tradition, and without legal standing in the modern nation-state, maintaining references in canon law to the right of asylum in the church could seem antiquated and irrelevant to the church's existence.

The 1979 commission could have allowed for omitting mention of the *civil legal right* of asylum in churches while still affirming the *principle* of refuge in the church, since one arguably depends more on legal recognition and the other on Christian faith and pastoral duty. In fact, the wording that the 1971 commission approved did away with references to a right of asylum, for it simply said that those who flee to the church to obtain asylum are not to be removed, thus recognizing that a positive legal right for church asylum no longer existed in the modern nation state. On a related point, some of the members of the commissions expressed their positive assessment of civil laws and the belief that penalties had been humanized, even for criminals, as reasons for why church asylum was no longer needed. One must wonder how much interaction commission members had with legal systems and their penalties, for both historically and presently they have served to persecute poor black and brown bodies across the world. *Humanized* is not an

---

[69] The Assisi Network was led by Father Aldo Brunacci and Bishop Giuseppe Nicolini, who coordinated churches, monasteries, and convents to serve as places of refuge. See Nicola Caracciolo, *Uncertain Refuge: Italy and the Jews during the Holocaust* (Urbana: University of Illinois Press, 1995). For the experience at Le Chambon-sur Lignon, see Peter Grose, *A Good Place to Hide* (New York: Pegasus, 2015).

[70] Ignatius Bau, *This Ground Is Holy: Church Sanctuary and Central American Refugees* (Mahwah, NJ: Paulist Press, 1985), 161–71.

adjective that adequately represents the experience of penalties or legal systems endured by communities from the global South.

It is necessary to discern whether in fact church asylum or sanctuary is no longer needed, not as a civil legal right, but as a principle and practice of the church for welcoming and protecting those who flee to the church.[71] Vatican II's ecclesiological vision expressed in *Gaudium et Spes* described the church as the people of God who make "the griefs and anxieties . . . especially [of] those who are poor or in any way afflicted," its own (no. 1). Furthermore, *Lumen Gentium* tells us that in its sacramental nature, the church is a sign and instrument of God's salvific presence throughout history (nos. 1, 48). In light of Vatican II, the church's contemporary need of and for sanctuary becomes a living question that the 1979 commission silenced, ironically, while trying to have canon law reflect the spirit and ecclesiology of Vatican II.

As demonstrated in the previous section, from the earliest references to sanctuary one encounters a practice that was tied to the church's very identity. When persons seeking refuge located themselves by the altar, a sacramental logic was invoked, for God became the ultimate reference in the midst of their threatened existence.[72] It was the duty, first of bishops and then of the whole church community, to embody a Christian response, to intercede even to the point of their own condemnation, for the veracity of the church as a historical mediation—a sacrament—of the mercy of God was at stake.

In the United States, even some of the most pastorally grounded Roman Catholic bishops and clergy are hesitant to associate with the church's tradition of sanctuary, which points to the need to continue grounding this tradition in the church's own lived history and theology. For example, a 2017 letter from Cardinal Cupich says:

> We have not named our churches as "sanctuaries" solely because it would be irresponsible to create false hope that we can protect people from law-enforcement actions, however unjust or inhumane

---

[71] Pope Francis uses four key verbs and categories for outlining the church's shared responsibility toward migrants and refugees: "to welcome, to protect, to promote, and to integrate." See Francis, "Message of His Holiness Pope Francis for the 104th World Day of Migrants and Refugees 2018," Rome, August 15, 2017.

[72] This is made particularly clear in the Spanish phrase for sanctuary—*acogerse a sagrado* or *asilo en sagrado* (embrace of, asylum in, the sacred/holy).

we may view them to be. Moreover, immigration law does impose criminal penalties and fines for anyone who conceals, harbors or shields from detection, in any place, an alien who has come to, entered or remains in the United States in violation of the law.[73]

The statement that sanctuary creates false hope is found in various bishops' statements regarding sanctuary and is not unique to the cardinal's letter. But, as this chapter has shown, church sanctuary has never been a guarantee of protection. It has served as a possible means of refuge from violence and forced exile. Strictly speaking, persons who seek refuge in churches now are attempting to avoid a second exile, a forced return to a place from which they fled, too often by necessity.

The cardinal's letter rightfully invokes immigration law and its penalties and fines for anyone, and more particularly for clergy or bishops who conceal, harbor, or shield a person whose presence in the United States is a violation of this law. The fears are legitimate. However, one must always ask why a law has been violated. It is reasonable to assume that no one wants to bear the burden of illegality or criminality, neither the person who crosses borders seeking protection nor the person who crosses civil law in providing it. Yet, as the cardinal also wrote in a piercing letter against the Trump Administration's Family-Separation Policy in 2018, "Scripture tells us that God requires no one to follow unjust laws," and that, "every so often, history presents circumstances that test the soul of a nation. We are living in one of those moments. Whatever this nation of immigrants does for the least of these brothers and sisters of ours will define us for decades to come, in the world's eyes, and in God's."[74] To his words can be added those of his fellow bishop from the fourth century, John Chrysostom, who, after he was taken away by soldiers for refusing to hand over Eutropius from the cathedral, said:

---

[73] Blase Cupich, February 28, 2017. Bishop Libasci of Manchester, New Hampshire, on April 7, 2017, issued a letter to clergy prohibiting sanctuary in churches when sanctuary is understood as allowing "individuals in fear of deportation to *live* in the church," stating it "creates a false hope" of protection the church cannot deliver. Bishop Jaime Soto provides a more nuanced approach to the tradition of sanctuary, while still echoing the notion of false hope. See Jaime Soto, "Adopt the Religious Meaning of 'Sanctuary,'" *Sacramento Bee* online, January 17, 2017.

[74] Blase Cupich, "Statement of Cardinal Blase J. Cupich, Archbishop of Chicago, on the Administration's Family-Separation Policy," Archdiocese of Chicago online, June 20, 2018.

I was being forcibly dragged away, but I suffered no insult from the act; for there is only one real insult, namely sin: and should the whole world insult thee, yet if thou dost not insult thyself thou art not insulted. The only real betrayal is the betrayal of the conscience: betray not thy own conscience, and no one can betray thee.[75]

In our age, as in Chrysostom's time, the church cannot invoke sanctuary as a civil legal right, but the fundamental principle of sanctuary as a response in faith to those who seek refuge in the church must not be forgotten.

Some Christian denominations have begun to codify anew the principle and practice of sanctuary. The legislative bodies of the United Methodist, Evangelical Lutheran, Presbyterian (USA), and Episcopal churches, among others, have institutionalized the possibility of providing church sanctuary as an expression of their pastoral and religious commitment.[76] At a minimum their bishops or ecclesiastical leaders have left the door open for local congregations to decide where they stand in regard to providing sanctuary if someone seeks refuge in their congregation. The Episcopal Church has even developed sanctuary insurance for parishes (coverage of up to $100,000 at an annual cost of $100) in order to address the costs of legal defense that may arise as the local community of faith intercedes with and on behalf of the sanctuary seeker(s) toward a resolution that protects their life and the integrity of their family.[77] In Germany there are Roman Catholic parishes and religious communities practicing church asylum/sanctuary for persons threatened with deportation to dangerous situations.[78] Mother Mechthild Thürmer, a Benedictine abbess, has faced legal consequences for providing refuge in

---

[75] Chrysostom, "Homily Two on Eutropius," 2.
[76] See Kathy Gilbert," United Methodist Churches Offer Sanctuary," *UM News* online, January 23, 2017; Evangelical Lutheran Church in America website, "Sanctuary Denomination"; Presbyterian Office of the General Assembly website, "Sanctuary"; The Episcopal Diocese of New York website, "Bishop Dietsche Writes on Sanctuary," April 10, 2017.
[77] Church Pension Group, "Sanctuary Church Insurance," online fact sheet 2019.
[78] Dale Gavlak, "German Churches Act as Buffer for Refugees with Sanctuary Program," *America* online, December 20, 2017.

her monastery to asylum seekers with orders of deportation.[79] As in the United States, there are risks for living into this tradition of the church.[80] However, fidelity to God and neighbor, and the sacramental horizon that holds them together, continues to challenge the church to become a living sanctuary, a place of refuge that communicates unequivocally the merciful love of God.

The analysis of cities of refuge using the insights of Emmanuel Levinas, combined with the witness of prominent bishops in the fourth century who protected those who sought refuge in the church, shows that these traditions are as relevant now as they were in their time. These are traditions to be creatively invoked in new contexts of persecution, oppression, and condemnations that erode the fundamental value of all life. To echo Levinas, in a world where the privileges of some mean the death of others, we are all already in need of refuge, in both the cities in which we find ourselves as innocent-yet-guilty and also in the church, for it is in relation to those whose existence is most threatened that the church must continually define itself.

---

[79] Madoc Cairns, "Cardinal Voices Support for Abbess Facing Trial for Sheltering Refugees," *The Tablet* online, July 30, 2020. Cardinal Michael Czerny, prefect of the Dicastery for Promoting Integral Human Development, and the son of refugees himself, has expressed support of Mother Mechthild Thürmer's efforts to prevent the deportation of asylum seekers.

[80] Asyl in der Kirche website, "German Ecumenical Committee on Church Asylum."

4

The Sacramental and Humanizing Vision
of Vatican II

A Firm Foundation for the Reconstruction of Church Sanctuary

The 1980s sanctuary ministry and the potential for church communities to transform society gave rise in Part I to the theological question of what the church is, and more specifically, to the question of the church's proper relationship to historical, social, and political challenges that threaten humanity. Jim Corbett and the Tucson community provided their own response to this question in light of the ecumenical and interreligious particularities of their borderland experience. Although a significant number of church communities who provided sanctuary in the 1980s were Roman Catholic, very few bishops spoke publicly in support of sanctuary because they dismissed it as too political and illegal. In ecclesiastical circles the profound connections between church and sanctuary that once existed had been severed.

In this chapter I engage the ecclesiological vision of the Second Vatican Council as the most authoritative contemporary understanding of what the church is and what it is for. By locating sanctuary in reference to Vatican II, the chapter contextualizes the tradition of ecclesial refuge not simply or primarily as a political action, but as an expression of the church's own nature and mission in history. I begin by highlighting the influence of the incarnational theology of Marie-Dominique Chenu, who, before and during the council, helped establish the practice of reading the signs of the times in light of the challenges brought forth by war and the spirit of modernity. He helped form Vatican II as a council focused on the humanization of the church and the world, a focus that was crystalized with Pope John XXIII at the beginning of the council, and with Paul VI at the end. The core of the chapter provides an analysis of the sacramental and missionary nature of the church, its fundamental existence as a people of God, and its relationship to the sociopolitical challenges of history—key elements of the two ecclesiological constitutions, *Lumen Gentium* and *Gaudium et Spes*. This examination shows that the humanizing vision of Vatican II echoes the ecclesial practice of refuge and protection upheld by bishop theologians in the early church, and that the church's sacramentality as a sign and instrument of salvation is a solid foundation for a contemporary reconstruction of church sanctuary.

Incarnating the Church in History—Chenu and John XXIII

During the Second Vatican Council (1962–65) the Roman Catholic Church entered deeply into a self-analysis of its nature and mission in dialogue with the perennial challenges facing humanity. It affirmed that the church, as a sacrament of salvation, could not think itself apart from the world, but rather, had to be in the heart of human history. To grasp theologically why the church recommitted itself to its mission of accompanying humanity in the joys and sorrows of history, it is first necessary to inquire into the church's understanding of the presence of God manifest in history, or what came to be referred to as the signs of the times. Reading history with the eyes of faith to discern the presence of God active through the Holy Spirit has become an ecclesial means of recommitting to the struggle to work for all that is life-giving and against all that denies life.

One of the theologians who greatly influenced the council's approach to reading the signs of the times was the Dominican friar Marie-Dominique Chenu, whom Gustavo Gutiérrez has called the youngest theologian at the council, not in age but in spirit.[1] His fundamental

---

[1] See Giuseppe Alberigo and Joseph A. Komonchak, *History of Vatican II,* vol. 5 (Maryknoll, NY: Orbis Books, 2006), 579–84. Alberigo and Komonchak argue that Chenu had a clear grasp of John XXIII's understanding of the concept of aggiornamento, which necessitates a reading of the signs of the times, as well as of John XXIII's emphasis on a "pastoral" council, which does not refer to an application of theology but rather to a way of theologizing. On aggiornamento and the signs of the times, Chenu wrote: "The specific way of bringing about the *aggiornamento* of the Church is to watch for the 'signs of the times,' these being so many reminders of the gospel and so many indicators, written in the hearts of human beings, of their capacity for

belief in God's active presence throughout history marked the style of some of the council's key documents (especially *Gaudium et Spes*), and his passion for theological and ecclesial renewal continues to influence generations.[2] Chenu's engagement with contemporary developments as a source for theological reflection was the result of his detailed studies of Thomas Aquinas's own commitment to the world of his time.[3] By returning to one of the great thinkers of Christianity and to the spirituality that undergirded Aquinas's approach to the task of theology, Chenu was able to envision a renewal of theology and of the church that was positively open to the historical events of the world.[4] In the early twentieth century when the Catholic Church had a profound distrust of what it called "modernist" ways of thinking that challenged long-held neo-Scholastic approaches for doing theology,[5] Chenu's commitment to doing theology

---

receiving the grace of Christ." Chenu, "Dans la coulée de *Pacem in Terris:* Idéologies et mouvements de l'histoire," in *Peuple de Dieu dans le monde* (Paris, 1966), 57. Also in Alberigo and Komonchak, 580. On the nature of "pastoral," Chenu wrote: "The pastoral aspect has become the primary criterion used in formulating and proposing the truth and not simply the motive for practical decisions to be adopted. 'Pastoral,' therefore, describes a theology, a way of thinking theology and teaching the faith, or, better, a vision of the economy of salvation." Chenu, "Un concile 'pastoral,'" *La Parole de Dieu*, vol. 2: *L'Évangile dans le temps* (Paris: Cerf, 1964), 655–672. Also, in Alberigo and Komonchak, 581. See also Bernard Lonergan, *Collected Works of Bernard Lonergan: A Third Collection*, vol. 16 (Toronto: University of Toronto Press, 2017), 218ff. As for Gustavo Gutiérrez' comment about Chenu, it was made in a personal conversation about Chenu's influence on Vatican II and on liberation theology.

[2] See Giuseppe Alberigo and Joseph A. Komonchak, *History of Vatican II,* vol. 1 (Maryknoll, NY: Orbis Books, 1995), 461; for Chenu's influence on *Gaudium et Spes*, see Joseph Komonchak, "Augustine, Aquinas, or the Gospel *sine glossa*? Divisions Over *Gaudium et Spes*," in *Unfinished Journey: The Church Forty Years after Vatican II*, ed. Austen Ivereigh (New York: Continuum, 2003), 102–18. See also, Mary Kate Holman, "'Like Yeast in Dough': The Church-World Relationship in the Evolving Thoughts of Marie-Dominique Chenu," *Theological Studies* 81 (2020), 788–809.

[3] Marie-Dominique Chenu, *Une École de Théologie: Le Saulchoir* (Kain-lez-Tournai, Belgique: Le Saulchoir, 1937), 52.

[4] See Marie-Dominique Chenu, *Aquinas and His Role in Theology* (Collegeville, MN: Liturgical Press, 2002).

[5] In 1907, Pope Pius X promulgated the encyclical *Pascendi Dominici Gregis,* in which he sought to protect the deposit of the faith from what he saw as a multitude of threats coming from advances in scholarship in various fields. By 1910, an oath against modernism was required of church leaders and theologians to ensure that their ways of doing theology conformed to established neo-Scholastic philosophical traditions.

with the challenges of history was a courageous and prophetic approach, and one for which he eventually paid a price.[6]

In 1942, the Vatican suppressed Chenu's book *Le Saulchoir: une école de théologie*, published in 1937, and stripped him of his leadership and teaching duties. According to Paul Philibert, "Chenu had formed and directed a school that breathed intellectual freedom and that took pastoral problems seriously, emphasizing participation, communication, and practical engagement with the church. At that time, none of that was desirable in Rome."[7] As a result of his inability to continue teaching at Le Saulchoir, Chenu began a period of more direct engagement with pastoral concerns and social movements in Paris, such as the Young Christian Worker Movement and later the worker-priest movement.

The accompaniment Chenu provided for these groups, as well as the violent experience of the Second World War, became essential elements for discerning the signs of the times and for better understanding the profound pastoral challenges facing the church, especially from marginalized poor sectors of society. During the war, in 1941, reflecting on the form that Christian witness needed to take in his contemporary context, he wrote:

> As a first step, we must absolutely enter, each and every one of us, into the distress of the world, the suffering of souls and bodies, even those of our momentary conquerors, in this darkness, in this social, economic, and political breakdown on a global scale, *massa peccati*. Original sin is reaching maturity. I cannot remove myself from this and live in a pseudo-fervour, in a pseudo-detachment.[8]

---

[6] For more on the renewal of theology and Chenu's influence in the 1930s and beyond, see Joseph Komonchak, "Returning from Exile: Catholic Theology in the 1930s," in *The Twentieth Century: A Theological Overview*, ed. Gregory Baum (Maryknoll, NY: Orbis Books, 1999), 35–48.

[7] Thomas O'Meara and Paul Philibert, *Scanning the Signs of the Times: French Dominicans in the Twentieth Century* (Adelaide, South Australia: ATF Theology, 2013), 24.

[8] Chenu, "Retraite au Saulchoir," 34, Archives of the Order of Preachers in France. Cited in Christophe Potworowski, *Contemplation and Incarnation: The Theology of Marie-Dominique Chenu* (Montréal: McGill-Queen's University Press, 2002), 31. This notion of entering into a sinful reality to witness to the suffering of "souls and bodies" who endure that reality will be echoed by the 1968 Medellín documents in their treatment of poverty and a church of the poor. Medellín will

Instead of retreating from the chaos of violence, war, and the breakdown of the social fabric, Chenu advocated for an embodied presence and witness in its midst, not only to those most vulnerable, but even to those "momentary conquerors" causing the violence. While recognizing the sinfulness of situations that inflict violence and suffering, Chenu did not believe that the Christian response was to flee from them, to become detached for one's own protection or from a false sense of purity. Following the principle of the incarnation of the Word of God in history, the church's response must always be to enter fully into the complexity of the human condition. Reflecting a few years later on the presence the church must have in marginalized sectors of society, Chenu wrote: "For the church to be present to this world of the working poor, the priest also has to be inserted there along with the laity. Priests have to be attentive to the people's problems, their questions, their needs, and observe and listen to make sure that the people hear the response that the church has to offer them."[9] In time, his focus on the church's failure to accompany whole sectors of society in the 1940s and 1950s, especially oppressed communities, would profoundly influence his contributions at Vatican II. Chenu is clear that the church's presence in the midst of the world's distresses is not simply the responsibility of the laity, as though they were the arms and feet of the church for the hierarchy.[10] Instead, the whole church, the ordained ministers (bishops, priests) and the laity, are mutually called to witness and be a presence in the world as one church that continues to become incarnate in history.

According to Chenu, the church's being-in-history, being-in-the-world, is also the church's participation in the ongoing dynamism of creation and redemption that continues in time, in corporality, and in

---

be more direct on the need to eradicate the sinful reality of poverty. See Chapter 5 herein.

[9] Olivier de la Brosse, ed., *Le Père Chenu: La Liberté Dans La Foi* (Paris: Les Éditions du Cerf, 1969), 120. Also in O'Meara and Philibert, *Scanning the Signs of the Times*, 29.

[10] In relation to the 1980s sanctuary movement examined in Chapter 2 and the contemporary challenge of those seeking sanctuary that will be further examined in Chapter 7, Chenu's point that the church as a whole—including the hierarchy— must accompany those in need demands emphasis. In such sociopolitical struggles it is not uncommon for priests and bishops to abandon the laity in their struggle to make the church present in the midst of suffering.

the social structures of human existence.[11] God's incarnation and the eventual recapitulation of all in Christ through the Holy Spirit is the fundamental reality that gives meaning both to the church's being and mission in the world and to the theologian's task to discern the signs of the times therein. Chenu writes:

> The Incarnation of Christ develops and consumes itself in an incorporation in which every reality, every human value becomes part of his Body—his Body in which all creation will be "recapitulated." . . . The incarnate, redeeming Logos accomplishes the work of the creative Logos: personal identity which does not allow the redemptive work to be separated from the creative work, and gives the Incarnation its cosmic dimension, where creation finds its unity.[12]

There is, then, no creation that is separate from the redemptive act of the incarnation. Therefore, there is no dimension of human existence (temporal, material, or social) that is not a locus for the church's presence. If the mystery of the incarnation continues in time, in history, through Christ's incorporation of all that is human, then it can also be said that a new creation is continually coming to be, which must also continually renew the church's self-understanding as a witness to all that is human and divine. This theological perspective radically questions any notion of church as separate from creation, from "the world," from human values and aspirations, or simply from human efforts in the transformation of history and society.

The Chalcedonian affirmation that, through the mystery of the hypostatic union, Christ was truly human and truly divine is the classical formula that frames Chenu's historically attuned theology. The unity of

---

[11] Chenu refers to these three categories that define the contemporary context of human existence and that must mark theology and the church's life as temporality, corporality, and sociality. See Potworowski, *Contemplation and Incarnation*, 96.

[12] Chenu, "Les laïcs et la 'consécration du monde,'" in *Peuple de Dieu dans le monde* (Paris: Les Éditions du Cerf, 1967), 87–88. Also in Potworowski, *Contemplation and Incarnation,* 174; The notion of all reality being incorporated into the body of Christ, and thus of the body of Christ becoming incorporated into all aspects of history will be revisited toward the end of Chapter 7 with Ignacio Ellacuría's understanding of the church as a historical sacrament of salvation that is called to make salvation a reality in history.

creation and redemption through the incarnation lies in this mystery. For the church, as the continuation of Christ's sacramental presence and mission in history, this union also frames its relation to the world and the redemptive value of all that is genuinely human and that serves the further humanization, and thus divinization, of the world.[13] By entering more fully into the human condition and being present to humanity in all its distresses, the church is able to discern the ongoing presence of Christ at work, who is creating and redeeming humanity from within. Reading the signs of the times, those signs of genuine human growth in history and of God's presence therein, as well as the signs of all that dehumanizes, becomes a fundamental ecclesial task. The church has a responsibility to listen attentively to how the Word of God is speaking in the movements of history.

Discerning the signs of the times, understanding the meaning of the unfolding events of history, is not only the task of the formal craft of theology and of theologians. More important, it is the task of the church as a whole, which is baptized into the prophetic Spirit of Christ.[14] Echoing Chenu's insights into the role of the prophetic charism for discerning the signs of the times, Potworowski emphasizes that

> the prophet stays close to the movement of history. In the sometimes dramatic and ambiguous struggles for peace, justice, and liberation, the prophet perceives the exigencies of the future, precisely because he or she is situated in the perspective of a future promise in the process of realization. The prophet identifies with the hopes of the poor and the oppressed, because, paradoxically, it is they who have a sense of history's progress.[15]

---

[13] On the question of the hypostatic union and its relation to the church, Potworowski writes: "The hypostatic union is therefore, at least indirectly, the doctrinal basis for the autonomy of terrestrial values, for the involvement of lay people in the Church, for the presence of the Church in the world. In this context, Chenu warns against a contemporary form of idealistic monophysitism that views the created world only as matter for a possible sacralization." Potworowski, *Contemplation and Incarnation,* 175.

[14] For a more detailed analysis of the role of the Holy Spirit, the prophetic charism, and discerning the signs of the times, see Yves Congar, *I Believe in the Holy Spirit,* vol. 2 (New York: Crossroad, 1997), 29–35.

[15] Potworowski, *Contemplation and Incarnation,* 188.

The Holy Spirit ultimately reveals and leads the church in the interpretation of the signs of the times. The Holy Spirit is the ground for prophetic witness in history. A church that stays close to the movements of history and to the sometimes ambiguous struggles for peace, justice, and liberation; a church that opens itself to the depth of interpretation that the signs of the times may have for it to better understand its nature and mission in the world; a church that begins a transformative process of identifying with the hopes of the poor, oppressed, and persecuted—this is a church that has been grasped by the prophetic Spirit of Christ, and, in many ways, this was the Second Vatican Council.[16]

I have focused on the theological and ecclesial vision of Marie-Dominique Chenu because his understanding of the presence of God in history and his profound openness and optimistic spirit echoed Pope John XXIII's vision for the council. Chenu wrote the first draft of what became the opening 1962 "Message to Humanity" or "Message to the World" at the beginning of Vatican II, which tried to capture the tone of John XXIII's statements leading up to the council. John XXIII convened a council that he tasked with reading and understanding the signs of the times in order for the church to enter into its own fuller incarnation in history.

A year before, in 1961, John XXIII had published a brief apostolic constitution (*Humanae Salutis*) that officially convoked Vatican II and that set the tone and method for the necessary theological work. In that constitution, he wrote that "distrustful souls see only darkness burdening the face of the earth. We, instead, like to reaffirm all our confidence in our Savior, who has not left the world which He redeemed." To this faith-filled perspective he added: "Indeed, we make ours the recommendation of Jesus that one should know how to distinguish the 'signs of the times' (Mt. 16:4), and we seem to see now, in the midst of so much darkness, a few indications which auger well for the fate of the Church

---

[16] Pope John Paul II affirms this prophetic spirit of the Council: "The Second Vatican Ecumenical Council was truly a prophetic message for the Church's life; it will continue to be so for many years in the third millennium which has just begun." John Paul II, "Address of the Holy Father John Paul II to the Conference Studying the Implementation of the Second Vatican Council" (Vatican City: Dicastery for Communications, February 27, 2000).

and of humanity."[17] The horizon for John XXIII's statement was that of radical trust in God's presence throughout history, in a God who does not abandon creation but redeems it through God's own incarnation. Jesus's recommendation to "know how to distinguish the 'signs of the times'" crystalized his hoped-for method or approach for the council, a method whose intelligibility fundamentally relied on having the eyes of faith to see the light of Christ illuminating a way forward for humanity.

John XXIII does not ignore the impact of "bloody wars," "the spiritual ruins caused by many ideologies," or the scientific progress that led to "catastrophic instruments for [humanity's] destruction"—all of these were all too real. However, reading the signs of the times also meant seeing the accelerated "progress of closer collaboration and of mutual integration toward which, even though in the midst of a thousand uncertainties, the human family seem[ed] to be moving."[18] Priority was given not to the apocalyptic readings one could have in the midst of darkness,[19] but to "the light of Christ [that] reveals men to themselves; it leads them, therefore, to discover in themselves their own nature, their own dignity, their own end."[20] These same sentiments and hopes were again echoed in John XXIII's opening speech to the council: "We feel we must disagree with those prophets of gloom, who are always forecasting disaster, as though the end of the world were at hand."[21] Further clarifying the pope's method for the council was his assertion that

> the substance of the ancient doctrine of the deposit of faith is one thing, and the way in which it is presented is another. And it is the latter that must be taken into great consideration with patience if necessary, everything being measured in the forms and proportions of a magisterium which is predominantly pastoral in character.[22]

---

[17] Pope John XXIII, "Humanae Salutis," in *The Documents of Vatican II*, ed. Walter M. Abbott (New York: Herder and Herder, 1966), 704.

[18] *Humanae Salutis,* 704.

[19] For an analysis and critique of the signs of the times from the Reformed tradition, with a particular focus on messianic and apocalyptic distinctions, see Jürgen Moltmann, *Church in the Power of the Spirit* (London: SCM Press, 1977).

[20] *Humanae Salutis,* 707.

[21] John XXIII, "Pope John's Opening Speech to the Council," in Abbott, *The Documents of Vatican II*, 712.

[22] John XXIII, "Pope John's Opening Speech to the Council," 715.

The urgent need to communicate beyond the internal boundaries and structures of the church was at the core of John XXIII's approach. The church is only able to communicate the mysteries of the deposit of faith to the rest of humanity through embodied presence and witness in a pastoral encounter, a conviction that Pope Francis has unequivocally affirmed half a century after the council.[23]

Out of this desire that the council be one of pastoral communication, Chenu drafted an initial message to the world, which the council fathers could publish as they began their theological and ecclesial work.[24] The final result was the "Message to Humanity," addressed to all persons and not just Roman Catholics—a first in the history of ecumenical councils. In it, the council fathers write: "As we undertake our work, therefore, we would emphasize whatever concerns the dignity of man, whatever contributes to a genuine community of peoples. 'Christ's love impels us' [2 Cor 5:14] for 'he who sees his brother in need and closes his heart against him, how does the love of God abide in him?'" [1 Jn 3:17]."[25] Through these very words, the council fathers acknowledged that the church could not close itself off to those who seek the mercy of the church, for the very presence and dwelling of God was encountered in such openness. The council referenced 1 John 3:17, a verse at the heart of Jim Corbett's discernment in the early 1980s, when he wrestled with the implications of collaborating in a transnational sanctuary ministry that would accompany Central Americans as they crossed borders into ecclesial refuge. The council's message, grounded in God's love for the world and the church's love for humanity, especially for the "lowly, poor, and the weak,"[26] emphasized the church's desire for renewal and for peace among persons and nations. This brief message from the council's first days in 1962 also foreshadowed the opening lines of the council's last and

---

[23] See, for example, Pope Francis, *Evangelii Gaudium*, nos. 87–92.

[24] Chenu attended the council as a theological adviser to Bishop Claude Rolland of Antisirabé in Madagascar who had been a seminary student at Le Saulchoir between 1930 and 1938. Because Chenu was there to assist an African bishop, he found himself in the company of other bishops and theologians from the global South. Marie Dominique Chenu, *Vatican II Notebook* (Adelaide, Australia: ATF Press, 2015), 68n22.

[25] Council fathers, "Message to Humanity," in Abbott, *The Documents of Vatican II*, 5.

[26] "Message to Humanity," 5.

most debated document, *Gaudium et Spes* (1965). The council fathers' affirmation that they carried in their hearts "the hardships, the bodily and mental distress, the sorrows, longings, and hopes of all peoples" and the "anxieties by which modern man is afflicted,"[27] was a pastoral guide for the opening days of the council, and it attempted to communicate the very humanity of the church to the rest of humanity.

In the following sections I address more specifically how the nature and mission of the church were renewed at Vatican II. Originally, there was to be one single document on the church, but, in the evolution of the document, the bishops and theologians at the council deemed it necessary to have two documents that addressed the church, one more interiorly focused and the other more outward in its gaze. *Lumen Gentium* focuses more on the church's own reality, and *Gaudium et Spes* places this reality more explicitly in relation to the world—our common home, to use a phrase from Pope Francis—in which the church journeys.

Lumen Gentium contains eight chapters, treating the church's sacramental nature; constitution as a people of God in history; the hierarchical dimensions of the church; the laity, or what could be called the horizontal dimensions of the church; the call to holiness that is for all persons regardless of rank or state in life; the various forms of religious life that are found within the church; the eschatological dimension of the church as a pilgrim people in history; and the role of Mary within the church. I focus on the first two chapters, for they serve as a foundation for analyzing the core reality of the church as both a divine mystery and a human community.

Gaudium et Spes contains two parts, the first of which focuses on the dignity of the human person, the call to community, the meaning of human activity in history, and the relation or dialogue between the church and the world. The second part considers particular challenges facing humanity, which include the role of marriage, culture, socioeconomic and political life, and peace in the global community. The analysis of central themes from *Lumen Gentium* and *Gaudium et Spes* leads to an initial incorporation of church sanctuary within the ecclesial vision of Vatican II at the end of the chapter. This incorporation will continue in the remaining chapters.

---

[27] "Message to Humanity," 5.

The Nature of the Church as Sacrament, as a People of God

Perhaps the most succinct manner of speaking of the nature of the church—of what the church is—is to say that it is a mystery, as the first chapter of *Lumen Gentium* states.[28] To claim that the church is a mystery does not preclude an analysis of this mystery, but rather, it sets the parameters of the question at stake. In other words, whatever is said of the church's nature must always follow the theandric (God-human) mystery to which it belongs and from which it derives—Jesus Christ. To say that the church is a mystery is to evoke the early church's theological understanding of Christ as the sacrament (*sacramentum* in Latin; *mysterion* in Greek) of God through whom God has communicated God's very self to humanity. The church, as the community of persons who, in faith, are the historical continuation of the mystery and sacrament that is Jesus, is also a mystery and sacrament that communicates the communion between God and God's creation. *Lumen Gentium* affirms: "The church, in Christ, is a sacrament—a sign and instrument, that is, of communion with God and of the unity of the entire human race."[29] As a *sign*, the church points beyond itself, to its source, who is Christ. As an *instrument*, the church is a means through which the presence of God can be effectively communicated. As sign *and* instrument, the church makes manifest the invisible presence of God in history but never exhausts the mystery of God and God's plan of salvation. *Lumen Gentium* makes it clear in its first sentence that the church is to reflect the light of Christ, who is the "light of the nations," by communicating the gospel of good news to humanity, but the church itself is not the

---

[28] The focus on the church as mystery was introduced during the second session of the council (1963). The title that appears in the first session is "the nature of the church militant." By locating the nature of the church within the category of mystery, the council unequivocally locates it within a transcendent horizon that is beyond visible structures. Reference to the church as mystery occurs in *Lumen Gentium* (nos. 1, 5, 39, 44, 63). For further references of church as mystery in other Vatican II documents, see Bonaventure Kloppenburg, *Ecclesiology of Vatican II* (Chicago: Franciscan Herald Press, 1974), 14–22.

[29] *Lumen Gentium*, no. 1. All citations are from Austin Flannery, *Vatican Council II: The Basic Sixteen Documents: Constitutions, Decrees, Declarations* (Northport, NY: Costello Publishing, 1996). The documents are also available on the Vatican website.

source of that light. The mystery that the church serves is always greater than the church's comprehension of it.

The sacramental reality of the church's existence must always be at the service of God's universal mission of salvation. One cannot properly speak of the church's nature without also speaking of this mission in which it participates. In commenting on the sacramental reality of the church expressed in *Lumen Gentium*, Gustavo Gutiérrez argues:

> The Church can be understood only in relation to the reality which it announces to humankind. Its existence is not "for itself," but rather "for others." Its center is outside itself, it is in the work of Christ and his Spirit. It is constituted by the Spirit as the "universal sacrament of salvation" (*Lumen Gentium*, no. 48); outside the action of the Spirit which leads the universe and history towards its fullness in Christ, the Church is nothing.[30]

Ultimately, the church's sacramental nature is inseparable from its salvific mission. Because it does not exist for itself but for the work of Christ through the Holy Spirit present in history, the church can only be at the service of proclaiming the reign of God, but it is not identified with the reign of God.[31] This mission will be analyzed in greater depth through *Gaudium et Spes*, but it is important to emphasize that, because of the sacramental nature of the church's existence, the nature and mission of the church are indelibly bound, and one becomes meaningless without the other. The church's *missionary nature*, especially in relation to the poor, is particularly clear toward the end of *Lumen Gentium*'s first chapter:

> The church, although it needs human resources to carry out its mission, is not set up to seek earthly glory, but to proclaim, and this by its own example, humility and self-denial. Christ was sent by the Father "to bring good news to the poor . . . to heal the broken hearted" (Lk 4:18), "to seek and to save what was lost" (Lk 19:10). Similarly, the church encompasses with its love all those who are afflicted by human infirmity and it recognizes in those

---

[30] Gustavo Gutiérrez, *A Theology of Liberation* (Maryknoll, NY: Orbis Books, 1988), 147.

[31] *Lumen Gentium*, no. 5.

who are poor and who suffer, the likeness of its poor and suffering founder. It does all in its power to relieve their need and in them it endeavors to serve Christ.[32]

The Christocentric nature of the church binds it to Christ's own mission to the poor. For the church to partake of Christ's theandric mystery, to be constituted by both human and divine elements, the church must also mirror Christ's life. The church cannot seek earthly glory as though it were simply another human organization. It is called to follow Christ to new historical manifestations of oppressive and suffering contexts and there participate in the healing of the brokenness of humanity, for, in doing so, it enters into its own healing in the salvific depths of the mystery from which it is constituted.

Thus far, I have emphasized the fundamental essence of the church as mystery and sacrament, complementary categories that point to both a visible and an invisible element in its constitution. Furthermore, I have echoed *Lumen Gentium*'s assertion that the nature of this mystery/sacrament is for salvation. I have not yet explored the relationship between the visible elements or concrete form of the church and its invisible nature, which can only be grasped through the eyes of faith. Before touching on other elements of the nature of the church presented in *Lumen Gentium*, let us further engage the fundamental claim that the church is a sacrament of salvation.

To a contemporary reader, the description of the church as a sacrament of salvation may appear as a lofty theological statement from a bygone era. However, the bishops who supported a sacramental view of the church's nature sought to address a prior understanding of church that was considered too clericalist, legalist, and triumphalist.[33] Walter Kasper writes: "The intention in pressing for a sacramental view of the church was anything but a bid for its ideological elevation. On the contrary,

---

[32] *Lumen Gentium*, no. 8.

[33] The first schema of the document on the church did not use a sacramental framework to speak of the church's nature, and instead sought to understand the church more as a perfect society, thus placing greater emphasis on the visible elements or structures rather than on the invisible ground from which it has its being. A sacramental framework was introduced for the second session, but not all of the council fathers supported a description or definition of the church as a sacrament. See Walter Kasper, *Theology and Church* (New York: Crossroad, 1989), 113–116.

The Sacramental and Humanizing Vision of Vatican II   107

the aim was to get away from the encrusted, narrow and one-sided elements of the traditional view held by scholastic theology."[34] If Kasper's description of the church before Vatican II is generally accurate, then the hope of a sacramental approach was to ground the church's nature in a more flexible, broad, and multifaceted understanding of its being. A sacramental approach sought to create greater openness and creative possibilities for understanding the church's nature, rather than close off possibilities for comprehension and communication.[35]

While *Lumen Gentium* emphasizes that the church is a sacrament of salvation, there are other descriptions of the church drawn from scripture that are used to approximate its nature. From the church as a sheepfold or flock with Christ as the good shepherd, to a building, temple, or sanctuary built of living stones where God dwells, to understanding the church as an exile journeying in a foreign land,[36] these and more are images used to communicate that the church is neither the simple aggregate of persons or visible structures nor an other-worldly spiritualized entity. The church is "one complex reality comprising a human and a divine element" that is analogous to "the mystery of the incarnate Word."[37] As previously stated, the church is not the incarnate Word, but it participates in and is called to serve the incarnate Word. In the ways in which it serves, the church's sacramental character can be properly discerned. When the church does not serve God and humanity as it is called to do by its sacramental nature, it risks obscuring the mystery of its foundation and becoming an empty sign or a counter sign to God's dwelling among humanity. However, instead of denying the church's sacramental nature because of human limitations, a sacramental approach aids in understanding the church as a living entity that is always in need of renewal in Christ through the Spirit. As Kasper writes: "To talk about the church as a sacrament is not to deny the scandal of the church as it actually is. On the contrary, the term is intended to make the scandal clear."[38]

---

[34] Kasper, 113.

[35] For a good example of creative possibilities for thinking through various ways of conceiving of the church, see Avery Dulles, *Models of the Church* (New York: Image Books, 1974).

[36] *Lumen Gentium*, no. 6.

[37] *Lumen Gentium*, no. 8.

[38] Kasper, *Theology and Church*, 117.

Lumen Gentium's opening chapter on the mystery of the church and its sacramental nature ends with an honest and humble assessment that it is "at once holy and always in need of purification."[39] The sobering reality that its difficulties in communicating the good news are the result of external opposition and an internal lack of faithfully living its sacramentality are a reminder of the eschatological horizon and hope that ultimately gives meaning to the church's journey through history. As a sacrament that is already in history, attempting to serve and communicate the Word who became flesh, the church will only find the fullness of the primordial sacrament that is Christ at the end of time. In history, the church can only entrust itself to the Spirit of Christ, who both sanctifies it and continuously calls it to renewal in its visible manifestation. By not forgetting the eschatological horizon toward which it moves, the church can hold itself accountable to enfleshing its invisible nature in its own visible structures and, as a sacrament, to serving as a living sign and instrument of God's life-giving grace.

To summarize, by its sacramental nature, the church is tasked with communicating the ultimate depth and meaning of reality, the fullness of life that is called salvation. Such communication, if it is to be genuinely human and free, must be a dialogic encounter among persons in the infinite diversity of creation and varieties of human experience. To echo John XXIII's hopes for what the church of Vatican II could achieve in its self-analysis and renewal, we cannot forget that "the substance of the ancient doctrine of the deposit of faith is one thing, and the way in which it is presented is another."[40] *Lumen Gentium*'s description of the church as a sacrament of salvation sought to present the church in a different light to better help humanity's understanding of what the church is and can be at its core—a loving dialogue between God and humanity. Cardinal Walter Kasper thus calls the church "a dialogistic sacrament," which means that, in its very nature, "the church has itself a dialogistic constitution."[41] The church, then, has the task or mission to communicate the salvific presence of God, and it can only do so if it also listens to the rest of God's creation, which is longing for life, and if it

---

[39] *Lumen Gentium*, no. 8.
[40] John XXIII, "Pope John's Opening Speech to the Council," 715.
[41] Kasper, *Theology and Church*, 143.

communicates in a manner that can be understood. Pope Francis's efforts to reconstitute the church as a synodal church that listens continues this vision of Vatican II. The aim of this dialogue is a communion, as *Lumen Gentium* states, "with God and of the unity of the entire human race."[42] This longing and hope for communion and unity, which is already present and revealed in the church's sacramental nature, is nonetheless an ever-present challenge for the people of God.

Everything said thus far about the church as mystery and sacrament of communion with God and humanity leads to *Lumen Gentium*'s teaching that, at a most fundamental level, the church is the people of God. This simple affirmation that, at first glance, appears unproblematic, generated much discussion in the textual evolution of *Lumen Gentium*. The decision to title the first chapter "The Mystery of the Church" and the second chapter "The People of God" communicates a movement from an exploration of the church's invisible nature, which ultimately can only be grasped in faith, to the church's more visible aspects—the people—who, through history, have borne and continue to bear witness to the mystery of God and God's manifestation through Jesus Christ.

The first draft of the schema discussed during the first session of the council in December 1962 did not have a chapter devoted to the category of the people of God. Instead, the original draft had a chapter on the laity. The phrase "people of God" was initially introduced into the draft in reference to the laity. However, during the second session in 1963, the biblical and theological breadth of this category of the people of God found its proper context as a category that holds the diversity and peoples who constitute the church's visible nature in creative tension. In other words, before the chapters that more fully introduce distinctions within the church's constitution as a visible organization, the church is first and foremost the ongoing event of the people of God without whom no institution can exist. Yves Congar believed that the decision to describe the church as the people of God and to place this after "the mystery of the church" and before the chapter on the hierarchy had "the greatest promise for the theological, pastoral,

---

[42] *Lumen Gentium*, no. 1.

and ecumenical future of ecclesiology."[43] After centuries of a church that was too closely defined by its juridical elements and structures, and by a hierarchical primacy that made the rest of the faithful into appendages of the church, the category of the people of God became a means to recover the communal dynamism of the church's human foundation in history.

The opening paragraphs of the chapter in *Lumen Gentium* provide a moving narrative of God's initiative in history to reveal God's self for the sake of entering into a lasting relationship. We read that God has willed "to make women and men holy and to save them, not as individuals without any bond between them, but rather to make them into a people who might acknowledge him and serve him in holiness."[44] In the long history of God's self-revelation, the people of Israel first became the people of God through whom God's vision for humanity was established. A holy covenant marked their relationship, a covenant that would serve—and which continues to serve—not only the community's constitution as a people, but God's salvific intentions for all of humanity.[45] In time, these intentions would be extended through and beyond the people of Israel in the person of Jesus, a Galilean Jew from the margins of the society of his time. For Christians, this Galilean Jew is the fullness of the revelation of God's very self in human history, the primal sacrament that communicates the mystery of God and through whom his followers are also constituted as a people of God. Of these followers *Lumen Gentium* states, "He called a people together made up of Jews and Gentiles which would be one, not according to the flesh,

---

[43] Yves Congar, "The People of God," in *Vatican II: An Interfaith Appraisal*, ed. John H. Miller (Notre Dame, IN: University of Notre Dame Press, 1966), 197.

[44] *Lumen Gentium*, no. 9. In Pope Francis's encyclical *Fratelli Tutti*, no. 32, we hear echoes of this when he says that we are not saved alone, but together.

[45] The reintroduction of the category of the people of God in Vatican II raises crucial questions about supersessionism and Jewish-Christian relations. Although *Lumen Gentium* uses the term "new people of God" to refer to Christians (no. 9), it also clearly affirms that "God never regrets his gifts or his call" when referring to the call and covenant with Israel (no. 16). For more on the Catholic Church's position on these complex set of questions since Vatican II, see the Vatican's recent document "The Gifts and the Calling of God Are Irrevocable (Rom 11:29): A Reflection on the Theological Questions Pertaining to Catholic-Jewish Relations on the Occasion of the 50th Anniversary of 'Nostra Aetate' (no. 4)," (Vatican City: Dicastery for Promoting Christian Unity, 2015).

but in the Spirit."[46] These followers, who, through their lives and witness, acknowledge Jesus's message and uphold the commandment to love God and neighbor, are the people of God entrusted to the guidance of the Holy Spirit. The gathering of individuals into a people and the creation of bonds through a communal and diverse faith is always to serve God's plan. On this point, Congar insists: "The People of God is consecrated to know God, and to praise him, but also to be his witness. It is not set apart in order to remain separated, but rather to serve God in the fulfillment of his universal plan of salvation. It is dedicated to an action, to serve the dynamism of a mission."[47] There is an inseparable bond between the gathering of a people as a community of faith in history and the transhistorical task for which they have been gathered.

The brief and broad historical sketch of God's revelation in history presented in *Lumen Gentium*'s chapter on the people of God profoundly enriches the question of who constitutes the church. In reflecting on this point, Congar writes that "this People of God is *de iure* coextensive with humanity,"[48] for, ultimately, all of humanity and all of creation are ordained for relationship with God. However, even if eschatologically speaking the people of God is coextensive with all persons, there are certain elements that demarcate a people and that give meaning to the category by virtue of their particular relationship and covenant with God. Thus, Congar argues, "The People of God, in its historical, public and concrete form, is identified with the Church."[49] Clearly there is a dialectical tension present in these affirmations that the people of God includes all of humanity and that the people of God is visibly identified with the church. This last point, however, is crucial for understanding the basic question of what the church is, for it retrieves the essential notion that the church is a people, and more particularly, a people of peoples historically situated and bound by their gifts and limitations. Because the church is composed of human persons who make up a people of peoples, and because of the dialectical tension that the people of God is also coextensive with all of humanity, the church is marked by a universality or catholicity.

---

[46] *Lumen Gentium*, no. 9.

[47] Congar, "The People of God," 200.

[48] Congar, "The People of God," 199.

[49] Congar, "The People of God," 202.

In presenting the people of God as church, *Lumen Gentium* does not speak of membership in the church, but rather of the notion of incorporation and varying degrees of communion. Within the broader affirmation of the church as the people of God, the more particular distinctions are explicitly made between incorporation in the Catholic Church, communion among the diversity of Christian churches, and the bond with non-Christians made possible by the Holy Spirit, whose active presence and grace overflows the visible boundaries of the church. This last point is succinctly captured in the following statement: "The effect of [the Holy Spirit's] activity is that whatever good is found sown in people's hearts and minds, or in the rites and customs of peoples, is not only saved from destruction, but is purified, raised up, and perfected for the glory of God . . . and the happiness of humanity."[50]

The decision to include a chapter on the people of God allowed Roman Catholicism to open the door to an ongoing reassessment of its constitution not so much as a juridical institution, but as a living and diverse people of peoples, called to serve God and one another and to work with all persons for unity and peace. The document states: "All are called to this catholic unity of the people of God which prefigures and promotes universal peace. And to it belong, or are related in different ways: the Catholic faithful, others who believe in Christ, and finally all of humankind, called by God's grace to salvation."[51] The vision of unity and peace that is embedded into this statement echoes the already examined conviction that the church is, and is always called in its human limitations, to be a genuine sacrament of salvation, a sign and instrument of "communion with God and of the unity of the entire human race."[52] Salvation consists of such sublime and concrete realities as unity and peace. However, to echo a piercing question left by Yves Congar at the end of his assessment of *Lumen Gentium*'s chapter on the people of God, "Is the Church—and with it other Christians who belong basically to the People of God—effectively a source of peace and unity for the world, the hope of a better order?"[53] This is a question that requires radically honest discernment. I now turn to *Gaudium et Spes*, the last and most

---

[50] *Lumen Gentium*, no. 17.

[51] *Lumen Gentium*, no. 13.

[52] *Lumen Gentium*, no. 1.

[53] Congar, "The People of God," 206.

debated document of Vatican II, in order to analyze more explicitly not only what the church is, but what it is for.

The Mission of the People of God

The opening words of *Gaudium et Spes* are arguably the most recognized words of any document from Vatican II: "The joys and hopes, the grief and anguish of the people of our time, especially of those who are poor or afflicted, are the joys and hopes, the grief and anguish of the followers of Christ as well."[54] The capacious vision of humanity's joys and hopes, and also the tender awareness of the suffering realities that mark so much of humanity, imbues the document with a theological horizon that echoes Marie-Dominique Chenu's and John XXIII's conviction of a church that must be present in the vicissitudes of history. The iconic words, the fruit of Chenu's efforts within the commission tasked with drafting what eventually became *Gaudium et Spes*,[55] allude to the same pastoral sensitivity expressed at the council's opening three years prior. In this final document the hopes and wishes of John XXIII to have a pastoral council concerned with the world's pressing concerns was most fully realized. The man who envisioned and opened the pastoral council did not live long enough to see the final fruit of his efforts, but *Gaudium et Spes* continues to be a source of inspiration for understanding the church's nature and mission in history.

The textual evolution of the document was marked by an initial marginalization that paradoxically brought the document to the center of the council's activities at its closing in December 1965. Rev. Mark McGrath, who was part of the drafting commission, wrote that "almost down to the last few days of harried labor many doubted that the document would ever see the Conciliar light of day."[56] This was the result of a complex process made more difficult by some council fathers who questioned the document's inherent value. Since *Gaudium et Spes* was not originally envisioned during the opening of the council, the first draft of

---

[54] *Gaudium et Spes*, no. 1.

[55] O'Meara and Philibert, *Scanning the Signs of the Times*, 38.

[56] Mark McGrath, "The Constitution on the Church in the Modern World," in Miller, *Vatican II*, 398.

the document, known then as schema 17 and later as schema 13, arose after the end of the first session in 1962.

In addition to the document not having the priority of other schemas, there was much disagreement about the proper approach or method for a document that was to speak of the church *in* the world. Some of the drafters desired a more deductive approach that emphasized a traditional theological method; others advocated for a more inductive approach that began with the contemporary experience of humanity and its questions. The latter approach appeared too sociological or temporally focused for those who hoped for a timeless ecclesial document. McGrath summarized these conflicts:

> Some of the members of the Doctrinal Commission, most of whom were former professors of Scripture or theology, as well as some of their theologians, could only come with difficulty to accept this "social" document as truly Conciliar. For a few of them, of course, its new approach to today's problems and its effort to illuminate these problems precisely, rather than repeat older expositions of theology on the various areas treated, went against the grain.[57]

Time, however, served as an unstoppable pressure that forced decisions upon the various commissions involved in its drafting. In early 1965, a new draft was created (referred to as the Ariccia document) with the help of professional lay experts whose insights enriched the timely topics the document sought to address. Through their inclusion the document began to model the dialogic approach for which it advocated.

Gaudium et Spes's final form took shape during the last session of Vatican II, between September and December 1965, in a series of public readings and votes. The initial marginal existence of the document had shifted, and it was now on the center stage of the council. Additionally, it had become the longest text of any church council in history. The more inductive method was ultimately adopted, which resulted in a document that attempted to understand the human situation in the fullness of its social and historical context before responding theologically to those realities.[58]

---

[57] McGrath, 403.

[58] Intense theological discussions took place in 1964 and 1965 to decide schema 13's method. At issue was the desire by some theologians, such as Joseph

I now turn to some of the key contributions of *Gaudium et Spes* and to the ways in which it attempted to clarify questions about the church's presence and mission in the world. These contributions are useful for continuing to lay a theological foundation for a reconstruction of church sanctuary.

Gaudium et Spes seeks to both uphold the distinction between the world and the church while simultaneously integrating the church and the world by affirming the integral vocation of humanity. If the church is a sacrament constituted by divine (mystery of God) and human elements (people of God), serving as both a sign (points to divine presence) and instrument (can effectively communicate divine presence) of God's communion with humanity, the "world" in which all of this happens is, according to *Lumen Gentium*, the "total environment" in which humanity lives, "the theatre of human history, bearing the marks of its travail, its triumphs and failures."[59] The world is not so much a spatial category demarcating the church's boundaries or the limits of its presence as a visible institution. It does not, primarily, refer quantitatively or juridically to where the church is or is not. Rather, "world" is the very reality of creation that is in the historical process of living out its God-given freedom and its ultimate longing for the divine.

Karl Rahner argued that the world with which the church began to dialogue during Vatican II was "the world of the modern mind, that is,

---

Ratzinger, to start with a strong Christological presence at the beginning of the document and from there derive a properly Christian anthropology. Other theologians, such as Marie-Dominique Chenu, strongly advocated for an inductive approach that worked its way up to the theological anthropology that culminated in Christ. Karl Rahner was somewhat of a mediating figure inasmuch as he advocated for an inductive approach that started with the human condition, but he was critical of a certain lack of success in the execution of the method. Other critiques by theologians who worried about an inductive approach included an insufficient focus on the reality of sin, a too-optimistic outlook of human progress, and not enough focus on the cross as a complement to the strong incarnational focus of the document. See Brandon Peterson, "Critical Voices: The Reactions of Rahner and Ratzinger to 'Schema XIII' *Gaudium et Spes*," *Modern Theology* 31, no. 1 (2015): 1–26; Also, Joseph Komonchak, "Augustine, Aquinas, or the Gospel *sine glossa*? Divisions over *Gaudium et Spes*," in Ivereigh, *Unfinished Journey*, 102–18.

[59] *Gaudium et Spes*, no. 2; *Gaudium et Spes* also uses the word *world* in a negative sense in other sections. For example, in *Gaudium et Spes* no. 37 *world* refers to "a spirit of vanity and malice whereby human activity from being ordered to the service of God and humanity is reduced to being an instrument of sin."

the world of a pluralistic, scientific, technically oriented society of vast scope and multiplicity of insights and tendencies, a world of a contrasted and divided Christianity, one of world religions, a world with an immense future waiting to be planned."[60] *Gaudium et Spes* wanted to distinguish this world and the church in order to safeguard the autonomy of society and the human person as a genuine subject in and of history.[61] This distinction was particularly important both in a world of rising secularization and in light of periods in church history marked by the collapse of distinctions that led to a confusion of the church's mission. One only needs to consider how church and state were collapsed into each other in Christendom or the ways in which religion became the justification for colonial conquests and the subjugation and enslavement of whole peoples. While *Gaudium et Spes* distinguishes between the world and the church, it does not separate the world from the church or the church from the world. Rather, following an incarnational and eschatological framework that recognizes the profound and ultimate unity of the human and divine, *Gaudium et Spes* speaks of an integral vocation toward greater humanization, acknowledging that what is truly human is also the very soil of the divine.[62]

The document's introduction attempts to read the signs of the times in which modern humanity lives.[63] In a few short paragraphs the mystery of the human person and the paradoxical effects of human creativity and freedom are addressed and summarized:

> In the light of the foregoing factors there appears the dichotomy of a world that is at once powerful and weak, capable of doing what is noble and what is base, disposed to freedom and slavery, progress and decline, amity and hatred. People are becoming conscious that the forces they have unleashed are in their own hands and that it is up to themselves to control them or be enslaved by them. Here lies the modern dilemma.[64]

---

[60] Karl Rahner, "The Task of Theology after the Council," in Miller, *Vatican II*, 590.

[61] See, for example, *Gaudium et Spes*, no. 36.

[62] See *Gaudium et Spes*, nos. 57, 10, 11.

[63] See *Gaudium et Spes*, nos. 4, 11.

[64] *Gaudium et Spes*, no. 9.

The Sacramental and Humanizing Vision of Vatican II   117

To complement these deepest longings and anxieties of the human person, a theological anthropology is developed that illustrates an organic unity that is both anthropocentric and theocentric. *Gaudium et Spes* speaks of the dignity of conscience which is "people's most secret core, and their sanctuary";[65] of genuine freedom which is "an exceptional sign of the image of God in humanity";[66] and of the conviction that it is "only in the mystery of the Word made flesh that the mystery of humanity truly becomes clear."[67] In other words, through the incarnation Christ becomes present in all persons, and, as *Gaudium et Spes* writes, "all this holds true not only for Christians but also for all people of good will in whose hearts grace is active invisibly."[68] These theological statements recognize the integral unity of the mystery of the human person and the mystery of God in the drama of history—a history forged by both human activity and the presence of God. If the church is a pilgrim people of God who also journeys and shares in the joys and hopes, griefs and anxieties of humanity as a whole, the question arises about the relationship between human activity "in the world" and the ultimate horizon of salvation; more particularly, about the church's mission and relationship to social and political challenges, among which we can certainly include the urgent and ongoing challenge of forced human displacement.

Gaudium et Spes is clear that the mission of the church is a religious mission, and thus, that it is also "supremely human."[69] This approach in regards to the church's mission is a reflection of the document's desire both to clarify the church's work in the world and to remain open to the reality of the diversity of situations and cultures that constitute what is human.[70] However, there are various key passages that succinctly attempt to define its mission in this world of worlds. For example, the church's mission is defined as carrying on the work of Christ: "The church is not motivated by earthly ambition but is interested in one thing only—to carry on the work of Christ under the guidance of the Holy Spirit, who came into the world to bear witness to the truth, to save and not to judge,

---

[65] *Gaudium et Spes*, no. 16.
[66] *Gaudium et Spes*, no. 17.
[67] *Gaudium et Spes*, no. 22.
[68] *Gaudium et Spes*, no. 22.
[69] *Gaudium et Spes*, no. 11.
[70] *Gaudium et Spes*, no. 91.

to serve and not to be served."[71] In this description the document builds upon the very etymology of the word *mission*—"to be sent"—for the follower or disciple of Christ is one who continues Christ's own mission in the world of witnessing, saving, and serving. Pope Francis's insistence on using the term *missionary disciples* in his encyclicals builds upon this basic point from Vatican II.[72] Whatever will be the specific content of collaborating with Christ's witnessing, saving, and serving, it must ultimately find coherence with Christ's own vision for the world, a vision that is particularly manifest in his encounters with the poor of his time. In recalling Christ's words, "As you did it to one of the least of these my brothers and sisters, you did it to me" (Mt 25:40), *Gaudium et Spes* emphasizes that, "today, there is an inescapable duty to make ourselves the neighbor of every individual, without exception," regardless of whether this neighbor is an elderly person, a foreign worker who is despised, or a refugee.[73] The church's mission is to make neighbors of the very persons whom dominant society relegates beyond the margins of desirability, to recognize that, according to the scriptures, there is an indelible unity—a communion—between the "least of these" and the salvific presence of Christ. This point will be analyzed at greater length in the next chapter.

The church's mission to carry on the work of Christ can also be summarized in a desire echoed in the prayer Jesus taught his followers: "Your kingdom come, your will be done, on earth as it is in heaven." These words, binding an eschatological time with the present time, touch the core of *Gaudium et Spes*'s response to the relationship between human activity now and its meaning for the ultimate horizon of salvation. The call to transform the world through love, to work for peace and justice, to "make life more humane,"[74] all of this work is intimately related to the reign of God. The crux of the question is how such earthly work is related, and *Gaudium et Spes* responds in the following manner: "Although we must be careful to distinguish earthly progress clearly from the increase of the kingdom of Christ, such progress is of vital concern to the kingdom of God, insofar as it can contribute to the better ordering of human society. . . . Here on earth the kingdom is mysteriously

---

[71] *Gaudium et Spes*, no. 3.

[72] See Francis, *Evangelii Gaudium*, nos. 119–21.

[73] *Gaudium et Spes*, no. 27.

[74] *Gaudium et Spes*, no. 38.

present; when the Lord comes it will enter into its perfection."[75] The document seeks to distinguish between these two realities so as not to collapse the kingdom into human progress or human progress into the kingdom. A positive description of the relationship is only captured in the words "of vital concern" and in the affirmation that the kingdom is already—though not fully—mysteriously present on earth. At another point *Gaudium et Spes* restates this mission:

> The church has but one sole purpose—that the kingdom of God may come and the salvation of the human race may be accomplished. Every benefit the people of God can confer on humanity during its earthly pilgrimage is rooted in the church's being "the universal sacrament of salvation," at once manifesting and actualizing the mystery of God's love for humanity.[76]

In this latter description of the church's mission, it becomes clear that the church is to serve the reign of God, but the church is not the reign of God. Because of the church's sacramental nature, it is called to manifest and live out God's life-giving love in service to humanity, in actions that are "rooted" in its work of salvation and that make it a "leaven" in humanity's ongoing transformation.[77]

Although *Gaudium et Spes* clearly states that the church's mission is not properly in the political, economic, or social order, because of its religious mission the church must be present to and witness in the political, economic, and social order. *Gaudium et Spes* strongly critiques the separation between faith and sociopolitical action and how this is connected to the church's ultimate mission, writing: "Let there, then, be no such pernicious opposition between professional and social activity on the one hand and religious life on the other. Christians who shirk their temporal duties shirk their duties towards his neighbor, neglect God himself, and endanger their eternal salvation."[78] Using the word *pernicious* unequivocally communicates that such a separation is destructive and, in the full sense of the etymology of the word, deadly—deadly toward the neighbor whose very life may depend on the social, economic, or

---

[75] *Gaudium et Spes*, no. 39.
[76] *Gaudium et Spes*, no. 45.
[77] *Gaudium et Spes*, no. 40.
[78] *Gaudium et Spes*, no. 43.

political activity of those who profess themselves followers of Christ, and deadly toward the Christian community whose credible existence is also at stake. There is no opposition between the pursuit of one's religious activity and one's involvement in the historical transformation of the world toward a more humane and humanizing society, and the love of God and the love of neighbor are inseparable, placing upon the church an obligation "to initiate action for the benefit of everyone, especially of those in need."[79]

Gaudium et Spes assumes all that was affirmed about the church's nature in *Lumen Gentium*,[80] so the word *church* refers to the whole people of God, laity and ordained ministers, as well as to its concrete structures by virtue of its sacramentality. However, there are instances where *Gaudium et Spes* explicitly makes a distinction in its use of the word. For example, in clarifying the church's relationship to the political community, *Gaudium et Spes* insists on the importance of distinguishing clearly "between the activities of Christians, acting individually or collectively in their own name as citizens guided by the dictates of a Christian conscience, and what they do together with their pastors in the name of the church."[81] While a distinction is important, it cannot be a separation if in fact the people of God fundamentally constitute the church. Furthermore, if it is not a separation, then the church as a whole, because of its sacramentality, is called to live the salvific message that it preaches in its very institutional and concrete structures. To summarize with the words with which *Gaudium et Spes* began: "The joys and hopes, the grief and anguish of the people of our time, especially of those who are poor or afflicted, are the joys and hopes, the grief and anguish of the followers of Christ"—*the church*. If they are not, then one can legitimately question whether the church is in fact carrying on the salvific work of Christ, whether it is church at all.

A Human and Humanizing Church

The ecclesiological frameworks expressed in *Lumen Gentium* and *Gaudium et Spes* invite their concretization in dialogue with particular contexts

---

[79] *Gaudium et Spes*, no. 42.
[80] *Gaudium et Spes*, nos. 2, 40.
[81] *Gaudium et Spes*, no. 76.

and historical challenges. The concept and practice of church sanctuary examined in Chapter 3 serve as a dialogue partner for understanding what the church is and what it is for in an age of forced displacement. In attempting to read ancient traditions along with contemporary ecclesial and theological developments there is always the risk of imposing one reality upon another. However, by turning to ancient sources and dialoging with their historical reality, new insights for our times can emerge, which is a practice that guided many of the theologians who were present at Vatican II.

During the first session of Vatican II, Cardinal Leo Joseph Suenens presented a distinction between the church ad intra and the church ad extra, which, although analytically beneficial, also introduced the possibility of too strong a distinction between what the church is called to be and what it is called to do.[82] The distinction allowed for a document on the church (*Lumen Gentium*) to emerge that focused more on the church itself and its internal structure, as well as a document that focused more explicitly on the church's external presence or mission in the world (*Gaudium et Spes*). Given this distinction, it is imperative to understand both documents as part of an integral reality.[83] To avoid too strong a distinction or dualism between an ad intra and ad extra understanding of church, I must emphasize that both *Lumen Gentium* and *Gaudium et Spes* are constitutions—they both speak of the church's very being and reason for being, and, as previously shown, these two aspects cannot be separated without making the church unintelligible.

---

[82] Cardinal Suenens (Belgium) had already proposed this distinction in the spring of 1962 as a response to the preliminary drafts of documents circulated before the council began. He felt that by making the distinction, there was a greater possibility of actually addressing questions of the church in light of contemporary challenges. Pope John XXIII, in agreement with the benefits of making such a distinction, incorporated the idea into a radio speech he gave one month before the beginning of the council (September 11, 1962) that began to set the tone for his hopes of what the council could accomplish. See Alberigo and Komonchak, *History of Vatican II*, vol. 1, 343, 437.

[83] Richard McBrien famously spoke of the "twin pillars" of Vatican II's ecclesiology. See Richard McBrien, *The Church* (New York: Harper One, 2008), 182. Arguably, to these two pillars one could add the first document agreed upon by the bishops at the council, *Sacrosanctum Concilium*, which lays the groundwork for rethinking the church in sacramental terms and as a worshipping community. See Massimo Faggioli, *True Reform: Liturgy and Ecclesiology in Sacrosanctum Concilium* (Collegeville, MN: Liturgical Press, 2012).

The church's mission is its reason for being. Its task is fundamentally *constitutive* of all that it is, and is called to be.

These theological claims lead to a key point: to speak of the church's involvement and protection of poor, oppressed, and persecuted persons and communities is both to engage with social ethics *and* to deal with constitutive elements of what it means to be church. In Chapter 3's analysis of church sanctuary in the fourth century, I highlighted that this ecclesial tradition was not only for persons who had committed a crime, but that it was also a form of refuge and protection for the oppressed and all whose life was persecuted. This essential relationship was evident in the Council of Serdica's canons that affirmed a bishop's religious duty to intercede for those "who are oppressed by disadvantages in life or the afflicted widow or exploited orphan" who along with "offenders" tended to "flee to the mercy of the church."[84] The practice of church sanctuary differs from what is a more typical spatial imaginary associated with mission that envisions the church as going out to assist persons. Sanctuary and notions of refuge challenge the church to wrestle with the dynamic not necessarily of going out, but of the oppressed and persecuted coming into the church. If *Gaudium et Spes* talked about the church in the world, here the emphasis falls on the complementary movement of the world—the grieved and anguished people of our time, whether Christian or not—in the church. The challenge is not only that of the poor, oppressed, and persecuted coming into the church building and community for refuge and protection (which must remain a real possibility), but also of them participating, belonging, and transforming all that the church is, has, and does. The concept and practice of sanctuary is about more than the church's mission ad extra, for it has much to do with the church ad intra—it questions the church's own self-understanding as a community and institution of merciful refuge.

The degree to which the church had to undergo a transformation toward the poor and oppressed was a point of discussion at Vatican II, but this did not ultimately become a central focus of the council. It is well known that, in a radio speech one month before the start of the council, Pope John XXIII spoke of the church in the following words:

---

[84] Council of Serdica, canon 8; Hamilton Hess, *The Early Development of Canon Law and the Council of Serdica* (New York: Oxford University Press, 2002), 217.

The Sacramental and Humanizing Vision of Vatican II 123

"Confronted with the underdeveloped countries, the Church presents herself as what she is, and wants to be, as the Church of all, and particularly, the Church of the poor."[85] Cardinal Lercaro, the archbishop of Bologna, took up this theme of the church of the poor at the end of the first session with a passionate attempt to make this the central focus of the council, but without much success.[86] The vision of a church of all, and particularly, a church of the poor, is essentially a way of affirming that the church is and must be a universal sacrament of salvation.[87] This fundamental ecclesial principle demands that Christians of every generation ask the following questions in their local context: Is the church a sacrament of salvation for the poor, oppressed, or persecuted who flee to the mercy of the church? Is the church their sanctuary? Is their life constitutive of the church's being and mission? If the church is not a sacrament of salvation for them, if it does not actually defend and promote their humanity, then it is difficult to say that the church is in fact a *universal* sacrament of salvation, assuming that, at the very least, salvation has to do with life itself.

A second theme that emerges in the dialogue between the ecclesial tradition of sanctuary and the ecclesiological frameworks of Vatican II is the question of violence. Cities of refuge and church sanctuary served as concepts and practices to interrupt and resist cycles of violence and death. In light of its sacramental nature, the church is called to reconstitute itself as a sign against violence and an instrument of peace. In Chapter 3, I presented the ambiguity surrounding who could qualify for protection in cities of refuge based on the difficult task of ascertaining intentionality and argued that focusing only on the juridical aspects of this tradition risked losing sight of the purpose of these cities—to protect the life "of anyone who kills a person without intent" (Num 24:15). A narrow reading of these cities makes them applicable only to persons who have committed a crime by taking the life of another. However, Emmanuel Levinas's insights opened up a more capacious horizon for understanding that, in a world marked by profound inequality, the advantages available to some at the expense of others, especially the poor, can certainly serve as

---

[85] John XXIII, "Radio Message of September 11, 1962," in *Council Daybook, Vatican II, sessions 1 and 2*, ed. Floyd Anderson (Washington, DC: National Catholic Welfare Conference, 1965), 18–21.

[86] Komonchak, "Augustine, Aquinas, or the Gospel *sine glossa*?" 111–12.

[87] *Lumen Gentium*, no. 48.

the cause of another's agony and death. Understanding the act of killing as more than an individual matter between two persons that are in direct contact allows those who previously considered themselves innocent to reflect on their possible "subjective innocence" and "objective guilt" in the taking of another's life.[88] Collectively, it allows for whole communities or societies, including the church, to ask both about their participation in the act of killing without intent and for their own possible need for refuge from those seeking justice through violence. These Levinasian insights on intentionality and culpability in an interrelated and globalized world question the people of God and their participation in the multiple forms of violence that ultimately lead to the killing of others.[89]

Gaudium et Spes, in fact, recognizes the close relationship that exists between profound inequality and the taking of life. In a section devoted to the topic of socioeconomic life, the text reads: "Faced with a world today where so many people are suffering from want, the council asks individuals and governments to remember the saying of the Fathers: 'Feed the people dying of hunger, because if you do not feed them you are killing them.'"[90] It is not sufficient to avoid direct killing because avoidance alone does not free a person or community from participation in death-dealing violence. In fact, according to the statement in *Gaudium et Spes*, it is avoidance of such issues—that is, not becoming involved to address them—that implicates one in the killing of others. While these statements are directed to individuals and governments, they must also apply to the church itself, since its sacramentality calls it to be a real sign and instrument, in other words, to live out the message it proclaims. Unlike *Gaudium et Spes*, *Lumen Gentium* does not mention the category of violence or the possibility of its relation to the church, but, as I have already pointed out, it does affirm that the church is "at once holy and always in need of purification,"[91] an affirmation that is made in the same context in which it speaks of the poor and the church's duty to do "all

---

[88] Emmanuel Levinas, *Beyond the Verse: Talmudic Readings and Lectures* (Bloomington: Indiana University Press, 1994), 39–40.

[89] This notion of the church's participation in the act of killing and the moral ambiguity between subjective innocence and objective guilt will be revisited in Chapter 7.

[90] *Gaudium et Spes*, no. 69.

[91] *Lumen Gentium*, no. 8.

in its power to relieve their need."[92] Decades later a key aspect of the church's need for purification lies in witnessing against the violence that persecutes the poor and displaces them across the globe.

In addition to the quoted axiom from the early church that connects poverty and killing, *Gaudium et Spes* at various times uses the term *violence* to speak of injustice and its effects, and calls for the rejection of such violence: "We cannot fail to praise those who renounce the use of violence in the vindication of their rights";[93] "insofar as men vanquish sin by a union of love, they will vanquish violence as well";[94] "we can and we should work together without violence and deceit in order to build up the world in genuine peace."[95] *Gaudium et Spes* does not make an unequivocal condemnation of violence, for it recognizes the complex history of this topic within a just-war tradition, but, ecclesiologically speaking, the church has the responsibility to communicate, through its being-in-the-world, a nonviolent way of life that contributes to the building of peace ad extra and ad intra. Perhaps it is such theological aspirations to nonviolence that one glimpses in the early church's tradition of church sanctuary, where not only sanctuary seekers were prohibited from carrying weapons into the church, but even the emperor had to divest himself of such instruments when he entered a church building. Church sanctuary, as a means to resist deadly violence that persecutes humanity, is a manifestation of a church becoming an instrument of peace.

The practices of refuge and sanctuary of the early church and now, and the ecclesial vision expressed during Vatican II, both seek the greater humanization of society. As analyzed in Chapter 3, in Gregory of Nazianzus's homily about his friend Basil's defense of a woman seeking sanctuary, he asked the following rhetorical question: "Was it not his duty to be willing to do and suffer all rather than take against her any inhuman measure, and outrage the holy table and the faith of her supplication?"[96] For Basil not to receive and protect her through church sanctuary would have been a violation of his duty to practice God's mercy as the head

---

[92] *Lumen Gentium*, no. 8.

[93] *Gaudium et Spes*, no. 78.

[94] *Gaudium et Spes*, no. 78.

[95] *Gaudium et Spes*, no. 92.

[96] Gregory of Nazianzus, "On St. Basil the Great," Oration 43, *The Fathers of the Church*, vol. 22 (New York: The Fathers of the Church, 1953), 55–57.

pastor of the local church and a violation of his own humanity.[97] In the process of interrupting and resisting the violence pursuing the woman, Basil was upholding both of their humanity, and, as a servant of Christ, he had to take upon himself any consequences for doing so. Violence, in its multiple manifestations, dehumanizes, and working toward the greater humanization of society entails working against all that wounds and destroys what it means to be fully human.

Gaudium et Spes is the most human conciliar document, for it envisions a church fully immersed—incarnated—in all that is genuinely human. It is no surprise then, that the word that appears most often in the English translation of *Gaudium et Spes* is the word *human*. After *human,* the top three terms in descending order are *man, life,* and *God*."[98] These details do not on their own provide theological insights, but, in light of the council's hope of dialoging with humanity and of renewing the church's presence in the real world of history, they demonstrate that the point of reference is, in fact, humanity.

In the shadow of the atrocities of the Second World War and in the midst of the terror of the Cold War, the church cast its gaze upon the hopes of a more human, humane, and humanizing world. In presenting a church that serves the indivisible unity of God and neighbor,[99] Vatican II opened the doors for the church to enter into the brokenness and beauty of humanity, and for greater humanity to enter more fully into the nature and mission of the church. Faithful to the mission of Christ, the church—the people of God—is called to serve as the sanctuary of God and of the human person. This is not simply a duty of the church. It is a way for the church to live and become incarnate and present to the griefs, anguishes, and joys of a persecuted and displaced humanity, for, in them, it encounters Christ.

---

[97] Pope Francis continually invites the church to welcome, protect, promote, and integrate migrants and refugees. See Francis, *Message of His Holiness Pope Francis for the 104th Day of Migrants and Refugees 2018* (Vatican City: Dicastery for Communications, January 14, 2018).

[98] The word *human* appears 229 times; *man* 197 times; *life* 154 times; *God* 145 times; *church* 118 times. By comparison, in *Lumen Gentium, human* appears 27 times; *church* 276 times; and *God* 246 times.

[99] *Gaudium et Spes*, no. 3; *Lumen Gentium*, no. 8.

5

The Church of the Poor

A Sacrament of and for Christ

Vatican II articulated a new understanding of the nature and mission of the church, but it did not sufficiently clarify the relationship between the poor and the church. Some of the most luminous and piercing insights into the indelible unity between the poor and the church arose in Latin America, where inequality and the legacies of colonialism continued to generate a separation between the world of the poor and the world of the church. Continuing to lay a firm theological foundation for a reconstruction of ecclesial sanctuary for displaced and persecuted persons requires the sacramental understanding of the church examined in the previous chapter, and, more particularly, a sacramental understanding of the poor as a manifestation of the church itself—as a living sanctuary of the true and real presence of Christ.

In 2021, in his message for the fifth World Day of the Poor, Pope Francis spoke of the poor as a sacrament of Christ,[1] words that echo Pope Paul VI's 1968 homily right before the Latin American bishops gathered in Medellín, Colombia, for a historic meeting that would alter the direction of the church in that continent. In that homily Paul VI spoke of a mystical correspondence among the poor, the Eucharist, and Christ, adding specificity to the sacramental relationship by placing the poor in reference to the sacrament that is traditionally at the heart of the Roman Catholic Church—the Eucharist. But, if the affirmation that the poor are a sacrament is not to remain a vague and romanticized notion that ends up spiritualizing the poor and sanctifying poverty as though

---

[1] Pope Francis, *Message of His Holiness Pope Francis for the Fifth World Day of the Poor* (Vatican City: Dicastery for Communications, November 14, 2021).

it were a good, then it is essential first to clarify the theological status of poverty and of the poor, clarifications that are needed for every generation, especially in the global North.

To this end, after contextualizing Paul VI's statement on the Eucharist, the poor, and Christ, and the vision of the Medellín conference, I enter into the inner logic of the most influential documents of the 1968 conference—the documents on justice, peace, and poverty. Because of their particularity, these documents are arguably still the clearest articulation for becoming a church of and for the poor, not only in Latin America but wherever persons are made to be insignificant and, thus, expendable. With the clarifications of a church of the poor in place, the chapter returns to the core question of how the poor are a sacrament, and more particularly, how the sacrament of the poor, the sacrament of the Eucharist, and the sacrament of the church can be grasped in a life-giving relationship to one another. Henri de Lubac's classic study of the mystical body of Christ provides a framework for holding in creative tension this sacramental unity that serves as a cornerstone for the reconstruction of the ecclesial tradition of sanctuary.

Learning to Listen to the Poor

Pope Paul VI's encouragement at the end of Vatican II for the renewal and growth of the Latin American church opened the doors to a profound ecclesial transformation. In late November 1965, Bishop Manuel Larraín of Chile, who was then president of the Latin American Bishops Conference (CELAM), arranged for Paul VI to meet with the Latin American bishops to commemorate the tenth anniversary of CELAM. This gathering became a bridge between the spirit of Vatican II and a future regional gathering in the Americas that would seek to make the Catholic Church in Latin America "more substantial in doctrinal principles and more solid in practice" in order to meet the challenges of the continent.[2] The Latin American bishops participating in Vatican II committed themselves to finding a way to reflect on the Latin American reality in light of the spirit of renewal that had been present at the council. Three years later, in 1968, Pope Paul VI became the first pope to visit Latin America, and in so doing, inaugurated one of the most

---

[2] Pope Paul VI, "Discorso di Paolo VI nel X anniversario del CELAM" (Vatican City: Dicastery for Communications, November 23, 1965).

significant ecclesial events of the Latin American church to this day—the bishops' conference in Medellín, Colombia. What Vatican II was for the universal church, the conference in Medellín became for a continent marked by vast poverty and institutionalized violence. As will be shown, the vision of Medellín is an ongoing challenge for Latin America and for the global church. Paul VI's visit to Colombia also coincided with the 39th International Eucharistic Congress in Bogotá. This was the first such congress after Vatican II, and it took place immediately before the Medellín conference.[3] The two events bind together reflections on the sacrament of the Eucharist and on the sacrament of the church.

At the Eucharistic Congress, Paul VI provided insights that reflected a renewed sense of the unity of Christ in both the Eucharist and the poor. These insights were particularly pronounced in his homily, delivered on August 23, 1968, to about 200,000 campesinos who had gathered in San Jose de Mosquera, outside of Bogotá.[4] Paul VI opened his homily by stating that he had traveled to Colombia to render homage to the presence of Jesus in the Eucharistic mystery, a presence, he told them, that is also "in your persons." He added: "You are a sign, an image, a mystery of the presence of Christ. The sacrament of the Eucharist offers us his hidden presence, living and real; you are also a sacrament, that is to say, a sacred image of the Lord in the world, a reflection that represents and does not hide his human and divine face."[5] In the latter part of this chapter, I analyze more closely the sacramental theology embedded in such a statement, but, for now, I simply wish to highlight the indelible

---

[3] The 39th International Eucharist Congress took place August 18–25, 1968, and the second Latin American Bishops Conference in Medellín took place August 26–September 8, 1968.

[4] Bernhard Bleyer, "Los pobres como sacramento de Jesucristo: la homilía de Pablo VI en San José de Mosquera (1968)," *Revista latinoamericana de teología* 75 (2008): 265–78.

[5] Pope Paul VI, "A los Campesinos," August 23, 1968, Conferencia General del Episcopado Latinoamericano (CELAM), La Iglesia en la actual transformación de América Latina a la luz del Concilio, vol. 2, 12th ed. (Bogotá, Colombia: Secretariado General del CELAM, 1981), 247–53. All translations of this discourse are my own from the Spanish original. For a full English translation, see CELAM, "Address to the Peasants," The Church in the Present-Day Transformation of Latin America in the Light of the Council, vol. 2 (Washington, DC: USCC, 1970), 254–59. The original Spanish text reads: "Sois vosotros un signo, una imagen, un misterio de la presencia de Cristo. El sacramento de la Eucaristía nos ofrece su escondida presencia, viva y real; vosotros sois también un sacramento, es decir, una imagen sagrada del Señor en el mundo, un reflejo que representa y no esconde su rostro humano y divino."

link that the pope established between the mystery of Christ's presence in the Eucharist and the mystery of Christ's presence in the poor.[6] The poor reveal the presence of Christ in history; they are the image of the image of God. Paul VI's proclamation echoed *Lumen Gentium*'s affirmation that "the church encompasses with its love all those who are afflicted by human infirmity and it recognizes in those who are poor and who suffer, the likeness of its poor and suffering founder."[7] The scriptural text of Matthew 25:31–46, to which Paul VI also referred, is at the root of these affirmations that indelibly bind Christ and the poor, for, there, Christ promises communion with suffering humanity. This scriptural foundation allowed the pope to go on to say that "the whole tradition of the church recognizes in the poor the sacrament of Christ, not in an identical manner to the reality in the Eucharist, but certainly in perfect analogical and mystical correspondence with it."[8] The presence of Christ

---

[6] The question of the presence of Christ in the poor and in the Eucharist was a question raised by Giacomo Cardinal Lercaro, the archbishop of Bologna, on December 6, 1962. In the previous chapter this point was briefly discussed. In 1968 Lercaro traveled to Colombia and was present for the International Eucharistic Congress. Here I quote part of Lercaro's intercession at the end of the first session of the council because in the homily at San Jose de Mosquera Pope Paul VI echoes, and in some ways validates, Lercaro's insights and concerns: "The Mystery of Christ in the Church is always, but particularly today, the Mystery of Christ in the poor, since the Church, as our Holy Father Pope John XXIII has said, is truly the Church of all, but is particularly 'the Church of the Poor.' . . . We shall not be doing our task sufficiently well, and our spirit will not be sufficiently responsive to God's design and man's expectation unless, we place the Mystery of Christ in the poor and the preaching of the Gospel to the poor at the heart and centre of our doctrinal and legislative work at this council." "In all the subjects the Council will deal with, may the ontological connection between the presence of Christ in the poor, and the two other profound realities of the Mystery of Christ in the Church, namely the presence of Christ in the Eucharistic action by means of which the Church is made one and is constituted, and the presence of Christ in the sacred hierarchy which instructs and governs the Church, be brought out and clarified." Paul Gauthier, *Christ, the Church, and the Poor*, trans. Edward Fitzgerald (Westminster, MD: The Newman Press, 1965), 153–55; Rohan Michael Currow, *The Preferential Option for the Poor* (Milwaukee, WI: Marquette University Press, 2012), 26–27.

[7] *Lumen Gentium*, no. 8.

[8] Pope Paul VI, "A los Campesinos." Translation my own. The original Spanish text reads: "Y toda la tradición de la Iglesia reconoce en los Pobres el Sacramento de Cristo, no ciertamente idéntico a la realidad de la Eucaristía, pero sí en perfecta correspondencia analógica y mística con ella."

in the Eucharist and in the poor, while distinct, cannot be separated, for a sacramental unity binds these two realities.

Paul VI communicated to the poor community gathered before him that he loved them with an affection and a "predilection" because he was aware of the conditions of their existence, "conditions of misery" that were "inferior to the normal exigencies of a human life.[9] He assured them that he and the church heard the cries that arose from their suffering and from the vast majority of humanity, and that the church desired to be in solidarity with their cause. In his homily Paul VI went on to critique the international structures that were the cause of so much poverty and the reforms that were needed to address such inequality and injustice. He also spoke of the spirit of poverty that was necessary if the church was to be faithful to Christ's preaching and witness.[10] The sacramental insights delivered by the pope immediately before the Medellín conference provided a rich context and point of reference for reflecting on the church's task—a task that the Latin American bishops would begin to examine in the days to come that August 1968. If, as Paul VI told the poor campesinos, "you are Christ for us,"[11] then it required that the church follow its reason for being, that it enter the world of the poor where Christ was already present, and that the poor have a preferential place within the church.

The conference at Medellín became a means for the Latin American church to begin incarnating John XXIII's vision of a church of all, but especially a church of the poor. This entailed becoming a community of faith that, following the love of Christ and the logic of the incarnation, entered the world of the poor to take up their struggle for life, sharing in their joys and their hopes, their griefs and anguishes. Such a radical process, which would go to the roots of the church's identity and reality of poverty in Latin America, required an honest self-analysis and a willingness to suffer and even die with the poor. As Bishop Pironio said at the bishops' conference, "Medellín hurts because it demands radi-

---

[9] Pope Paul VI.

[10] See *Gaudium et Spes*, no. 88, and *Lumen Gentium*, no. 8, for more on the church's call to a spirit of poverty and witness.

[11] Pope Paul VI, "A los Campesinos." The original Spanish text reads: "Amadísimos hijos, vosotros sois Cristo para Nos."

cal changes and an abandoning of certain privileged positions."[12] The Medellín conference was a key part of the process by which the church, especially in its institutional dimension in Latin America, was coming to know itself and was entering into its own maturity on the continent, forging a new path distinct from its colonial history.[13]

At the opening of the conference Cardinal Juan Landázuri Ricketts, co-president of CELAM, gave the inaugural address and asked the simple yet piercing question, "Who are we?"[14] The question went to the core of the church's identity, and it continues to challenge the church on the continent today. Landázuri gave his own response: "this is the hour of love, so that for a questioning world we have only one answer: we are witnesses to love."[15] This is a love that finds its expression in the indivisible commandment to love God and neighbor, and God through neighbor, or, as Landázuri stated, "our supreme law is the welfare of the flock which has been entrusted to us, not as masters, but as pastors."[16]

---

[12] Latin American Episcopal Council (CELAM), *The Church in the Present-Day Transformation of Latin America in the Light of the Council*, vol. 1 (Washington, DC: United States Catholic Conference, 1970), 9: Pironio and Óscar Romero were friends and supporters of each other's commitment to a church of the poor. Romero writes the following in his diary on June 26, 1978, when he visited Cardinal Pironio in Rome: "I told Cardinal Pironio that I was being accused of serving as an instrument of communism in Latin America, and he told me, 'It doesn't surprise me since they have even published a book about me titled, "Pironio, Pyromaniac." This is the inheritance of all who desire to preach social justice and the promotion of Latin America.'" Óscar Romero, *Su Diario* (San Salvador: UCA editores, 2006), 47.

[13] In November 1965, when Paul VI met with the CELAM bishops in Rome, he spoke of an "organic weakness" that required a revitalization and reanimation of Catholic life in order to meet the demands of the continent. It is in this regard that he said that the faith of the Latin American people had not yet reached its full maturity in development. Pope Paul VI, "Discorso di Paolo VI nel X anniversario del CELAM," November 23, 1965. Also see Gustavo Gutiérrez, "Significado y alcance de Medellín," in *Irrupcion y Caminar de la Iglesia de los Pobres* (Lima, Peru: Instituto Bartolomé de las Casas, 1989), 39.

[14] Juan Landázuri Ricketts, "Inaugural Address," in CELAM, *The Church in the Present-Day Transformation of Latin America in the Light of the Council*, 1:50. In his home diocese of Lima, Peru the bishop and then cardinal was commonly referred to simply as Landázuri, which I will follow.

[15] Landázuri, "Inaugural Address," 51.

[16] Landázuri, "Inaugural Address," 50.

Those gathered at Medellín were gathered to rekindle their love, presence, and commitment to the mystery of the body of Christ in history, whom they were called to serve and to whom they were responsible. This purpose is further expressed in Landázuri's response to his own question of "Why have we come together?," to which he answered, "Brethren, we are urged on by the same Lord who is present in the people whom we lead, waiting to be recognized."[17] The presence of Christ in history, in the church, and preferentially in the poor of the continent was leading those gathered at Medellín to listen to the signs of the times so that they would know how to be. Landázuri argued that knowing how to *listen* and knowing how to *be* were the two core tasks for Medellín.[18] Landázuri used the verb *estar* rather than *ser* for "to be," thus emphasizing that the church's constitution is fundamentally relational, and more particularly, that its existence is tied to its capacity to listen to others.[19]

The Latin American church was being called to listen to God and to neighbor, for the incarnation bound the two together. Echoing the humanizing and missionary spirit of *Gaudium et Spes,* Landázuri proclaimed in his opening talk: "The Word of God was made man and lives among us, giving meaning to all that is human. Thus, when we listen to man we listen to Christ; whenever we worry about man, we worry about Christ. And, to the degree that we are with man, learning and knowing how to approach him, we are encountering our Lord Himself."[20] The presence of Christ in the human person prevents an unchristian division between listening to the Word of God on the one hand, and the voice of humanity on the other, for the Word of God dwells in the world, where we encounter the one history of humanity and of salvation. Christ's presence in history through the incarnation allows for the world, for humanity as it is, to be the bearer of the presence and the possibility of communion with God. The church was being tasked with learning the

---

[17] Landázuri, "Inaugural Address," 52; *Gaudium et Spes*, no. 39.

[18] Landázuri's pithy response to the question "why have we come together?" was: "I would summarize it briefly: knowing how to listen, knowing how to be." Landázuri, "Inaugual Address," 1:52.

[19] Juan Landázuri Ricketts, "Discurso Inagural," *La Iglesia en la Actual Transformación de América Latina a la Luz del Concilio*, Segunda Conferencia General del Episcopado Latinoamericano, vol. 1, 48.

[20] Landázuri, "Inaugural Address," 1:53; *Gaudium et Spes,* nos. 22, 32.

depths of human persons situated in their concrete history so that it could hear what humanity was saying in all its joys and sorrows, for there it would also have to hear and discern what God was communicating.

The mystery of God's presence in the human person was such that, referencing Paul VI's closing speech at Vatican II, Landázuri said, "To know God we must first know man."[21] He argued that the church had to learn to approach—to go near—the human person, and, in the context of Latin America, that meant learning how to grow near to the poor, for they were and are the vast majority of human persons and communities who inhabit the continent. To learn how to approach the poor, in whom God dwells, was to become a church that, like John the Baptist, prepares the way for the Lord and for the coming of the reign of God. Landázuri wanted to make this reference to one who was also persecuted and killed for his witness to Jesus Christ when he said: "In the world and in its history we find the only Shepherd who expects from us the attitudes and the cry of the precursor: It is the Lord."[22]

In learning to *listen* to the Word present in the world, especially the world of the poor, the church in Latin America could also learn how to *be* (*estar*)—how to live simultaneously out its nature and mission. The radical challenge that faced the Latin American church was captured in the following words: "To know how to be means to carry out, in a spirit of faith and hope, the prophetic function of love: to denounce all that which oppresses man; to live that charity which demands a positive stand."[23] The church's capacity to be was singularly marked by a call to be an active presence of love in history that could communicate communion between God and humanity. To communicate God's love was not only to denounce oppression. As Landázuri affirmed, it was to take a definitive stand with the poor and oppressed, to accompany and journey with them, for, in doing so, the church as a whole would accompany its reason for being: God incarnate who seeks that all may have life and have it to the fullest (Jn 10:10).

---

[21] Landázuri, "Inaugural Address," 1:54; Pope Paul VI, "Address of Pope Paul VI during the Last General Meeting of the Second Vatican Council," December 7, 1965.

[22] Landázuri, "Inaugural Address," 1:53.

[23] Landázuri, 1:54–55.

A Church of Love
Witnesses against Injustice

The final documents of the Medellín conference reflect a church that was indelibly marked by listening to the cries of the poor—the cries of Christ—that defined for the church how to be present, how to be a sign and sacrament of salvation in the history of Latin America. The church that was envisioned at Medellín was fundamentally a church whose reason for being was love. The documents that dealt most explicitly with the historical challenges facing Latin America—*Justice, Peace,* and *Poverty of the Church*—locate the dynamism of love as the central force for the church's renewal and transformation. At the heart of these documents is not a theory of justice, of peace, or of poverty, but the urgent need and call to incarnate the love of God in history, a dynamic that is a response to God's own gratuitous self-giving in Christ. In the document on justice we read that God "sends his Son in the flesh, so that He might come to liberate all men from the slavery to which sin has subjected them: hunger, misery, oppression and ignorance, in a word, that injustice and hatred which have their origin in human selfishness."[24] God's incarnation in history for the sake of humanity's liberation from all forms of injustice and hatred makes categories such as hunger, misery, oppression, and ignorance theological concerns and ecclesial challenges, not simply social questions. The reality of sin as a rejection of love of neighbor and of God is at their root.

Love is the force that overcomes the sin that gives rise to structures of injustice. As Medellín proclaims: "Love, 'the fundamental law of human perfection, and therefore of the transformation of the world,' is not only the greatest commandment of the Lord; it is also the dynamism which ought to motivate Christians to realize justice in the world, having truth

---

[24] *Justice*, no. 3; Citations of the Medellín final documents on justice, peace, and the poverty of the church are taken from CELAM, *The Church in the Present-Day Transformation of Latin America in the Light of the Council,* vol. 2, and also from the original Spanish text, Conferencia General del Episcopado Latinoamericano, *La Iglesia en la actual transformación de América Latina a la luz del Concilio,* vol. 2, 12th ed. (Bogotá, Colombia: Secretariado General del CELAM, 1981). I refer to each Medellín text by name and paragraph.

as a foundation and liberty as their sign."[25] If sin generates the social and historical forces that make misery the daily bread of the poor, then love is what can redeem and give new life to a history of suffering and death. The love made present in the struggle for liberation from the chains of injustice is the same love with which God transformed human history by taking flesh and dwelling among humanity. Medellín's call for the institutional church and for all Christians to embody the transforming love of God was neither simply nor primarily a moral exhortation. It was a proclamation of the fundamental framework of salvation in history. The call to justice, a call to individuals, to society, and to the church, was a call to holiness or, as the document says, to "human perfection" that ultimately transforms the world.[26] Love, in its social dimension, generates justice, and freedom from subjugation is love's own verification as a fundamental truth of what it means to be human.

In the interplay between the personal and social transformation of which love is the root, Medellín emphasizes that, while structural changes are necessary, they are not sustainable without personal conversion. Justice, then, is an interdependent dynamic between the personal and the social: "We will not have a new continent without new and reformed structures, but, above all, there will be no new continent without new men, who know how to be truly free and responsible according to the light of the gospel."[27] The liberation of a people, and, more particularly, the liberation of the church from all that keeps it from understanding its reason for being as indelibly bound with the life or death of the least in society, cannot take place only through an external reform of structures. Ultimately, it depends on a maturation of faith that is made manifest in the church's historical commitment to follow Jesus to the margins with the marginalized. From there, the church must commit to live into a new and liberated creation in the radical freedom of God. As the bishops said, "In the economy of salvation the divine work is

---

[25] *Justice*, no. 4. There is a parallel in this Medellín statement to Gandhi's emphasis on ahimsa as a positive force of love expressed through the search for truth, the practice of nonviolence, and the willingness for self-suffering. See Chapter 2 herein.

[26] This call to perfection echoes the universal call to holiness expressed in *Lumen Gentium*, no. 40.

[27] *Justice*, no. 3.

an action of integral human development and liberation."[28] The work of justice, founded on love, is already divine work that sanctifies and heals humanity, and it begins to bring about salvation in a history that is marked, but not overcome, by sin.[29]

A Church of Peace Witnesses against Violence

Medellín's document on justice was initially one with the document on peace, for they are two dimensions of the same reality. A church that works for justice, that embodies justice, and that ushers in a more human world with and for the victims of injustice, is also a church of peace. In the bishops' conception of peace, the absence of violence does not guarantee peace. The process by which persons become subjects of their own lives and not objects of structures of violence guarantees peace. The bishops wrote that this requires a social order where "men can fulfill themselves as men, where their dignity is respected, their legitimate aspirations satisfied, their access to truth recognized, their personal freedom guaranteed; an order where man is not an object, but an agent of his own history."[30] Certainly the greatest challenge to the fulfillment of these principles came from the historical experience of the poor and marginalized in Latin America, for whom these principles were not a reality. The poor of history, above all, have their dignity violated, aspirations destroyed, are systematically lied to by those in privilege and power, have no guarantees to personal freedom, and are essentially reduced to byproducts of so-called progress. The church was coming to see that the poor were the forced servants of another's history, but not agents of their own humanity. For the church to be complicit in the objectification of the poor was also for it to be complicit in the objectification of the presence of Christ.

The struggle for peace and against injustice and violence is always in direct relation to God. For the bishops at Medellín, "peace with God is the basic foundation of internal and social peace. Therefore, where this social peace does not exist, there will we find social, political, economic

---

[28] *Justice*, no. 4.
[29] *Justice*, no. 5.
[30] *Peace*, no. 14.

and cultural inequalities, there will we find the rejection of the peace of the Lord, and a rejection of the Lord Himself."[31] In establishing a direct relationship between God and internal and external peace, the bishops affirmed the unity between social relations and humanity's relationship with God. Because work that promotes peace is a manifestation of God's will for humanity, and thus a historical actualization of God's presence,[32] whatever does not promote genuine and peaceful relations is contrary to God. Conversely, any person or community who works for peace is already grounded, by the grace of the Holy Spirit, in the peace of God and the love of God.[33] The bishops leave no ambiguity that social, political, economic, and cultural inequalities are against peace and against God. Another way of saying this is that structures that maintain and promote such inequalities—at times by suppressing and not dealing with the root conflict—are structures of sin contrary to the reign of God. Eradicating these sinful realities entails their transformation into humanizing structures, which is work that is never finished. The bishops point to this ongoing process of humanization when they write: "Peace is a permanent task. A community becomes a reality in time and is subject to a movement that implies constant change in structures, transformation of attitudes, and conversion of hearts."[34] As expressed previously, changing structures without changing hearts is unsustainable in the long term, for, without addressing the violence of sin that is the root of selfishness, structures will continue to conform to the will and desire of the few rather than serving the majority who are the poor and oppressed of history. External structures of sin are a manifestation of internal sin, which promotes dehumanizing violence rather than humanizing peace. A church of the poor is founded on, constructed with, and becomes a communal artisan of peace in the midst of violence.[35]

The Medellín document on peace locates the overwhelming reality of violence in Latin America within the structural mechanisms that promote

---

[31] *Peace*, no. 14; Matthew 25:31–46.

[32] There is a correlation between the doing of the will of God and God's dwelling/presence. This is fundamentally expressed in the Lord's prayer, for the coming of God's kingdom is the coming of God's very self: " . . . Your Kingdom come, your will be done . . . "

[33] *Peace*, no. 14; *Gaudium et Spes,* no. 78.

[34] *Peace*, no. 14.

[35] *Peace*, no. 14.

that violence. Thus, the primary focus is not on overt and direct violence, such as armed violence, for, although that was and is a reality, such violence is more a symptom of a deeper unexamined injustice. Medellín called this less visible but equally deadly state of injustice institutionalized violence.[36] Such violence is manifest in economic, cultural, and political structures that keep a people deprived of the basic goods for daily living, and deprived of genuine participation in the economic, cultural, and political spheres of society, where they would be able to exercise their rights and responsibilities as agents of their own future. Institutionalized violence is a structural means of keeping whole sectors of society subservient to those with access to dominant power, wealth, and culture, and using direct violence to ensure that this imbalance continues for the benefit of the elite minority.[37] Institutionalized violence engenders further violence, creating a cycle that intensifies into ever more deadly means of control. The slow killing that is characteristic of institutional violence gives rise to the overt violence of repression and persecution at the hands of the state or powerful sectors of society whenever a people struggle for social transformation. While Medellín's document on peace recognizes that direct violence also arises from those who endure institutionalized violence, echoing a homily from Paul VI given a few days prior, the bishops call this violence "explosive revolutions of despair,"[38] which are provoked by those who oppose necessary systemic transformation.[39]

The document's position on the contentious question of violence conveys a careful and honest response about what is possible and what is preferred. For example, the bishops write: "The Christian man is peaceful and not ashamed of it. He is not simply a pacifist, for he can fight, but he prefers peace to war."[40] The bishops do not fundamentally prohibit the possibility of a people fighting back against the violence

---

[36] *Peace*, no. 16. To my knowledge this is the first time the term *institutionalized violence* appears in ecclesial documents. The following year, 1969, Johan Galtung coined the term *structural violence*. See Johan Galtung, "Violence, Peace, and Peace Research," *Journal of Peace Research* 6, no. 3 (1969): 167–91.

[37] *Peace*, no. 17.

[38] *Peace*, no. 17.

[39] In his third pastoral letter, Romero addresses and distinguishes the different types and sources of violence in El Salvador.

[40] *Peace*, no. 15. For *Gaudium et Spes'* position on conscientious objectors, see no. 79.

that is indirectly or directly taking their life. However, this possibility is not preferred, as they quote Paul VI, "violence is neither Christian nor evangelical."[41] Herein lies the tension on the question of violence, for, although theologically it could not be clearly justified, the bishops acknowledged the reasons why oppressed persons and communities were tempted to respond to violence with violence. In response to both institutionalized violence and overt armed violence, the document centers the productiveness of peace and the fruitfulness of nonviolence.

Peace and nonviolent actions were bound together with a creative process of conscientization on an individual and collective level. The document says that "justice, and therefore peace, conquer by means of a dynamic action of awakening (*conscientización*) and organization of the popular sectors, which are capable of pressing public officials who are often impotent in their social projects without popular support."[42] For sectors that do not have access to wealth or political power as a means for transforming oppressive institutions, the alternative to giving in to the temptation of violence is to cultivate the resource that they do have—vast numbers of people who are capable of entering into solidarity with one another and using their collective agency as a form of power and influence. The awakening of conscience that is necessary requires the ability to imagine what is possible and the practice of creativity to see possibilities into reality without resorting to overt violence as a means for social transformation. In contradistinction to an anemic notion of peace or nonviolence as passivity, the document advocates for peace as a "dynamic action," as a force capable of conquering violence through an internal awakening of self and through the external organization of selves into communities. Citing one of Pope Paul VI's talks in Colombia, the bishops at Medellín understood the challenge as that of transforming the afflictions and suffering of a people not into hatred and violence, but into "the strong and peaceful energy of constructive works."[43] Like Mahatma Gandhi, who, in a different context had awakened a people

---

[41] *Peace*, no. 15. Also see Paul VI, "Homily of the Mass on Development Day," Bogotá, Colombia, August 23, 1968, in *The Church in the Present-Day Transformation of Latin America in the Light of the Council*, 2:265.

[42] *Peace*, no. 18.

[43] *Peace*, no. 19. For an analysis of Gandhi's "constructive program," which he understood as the real basis of political power, see Chapter 2 herein.

to their own power and possibilities through nonviolent alternatives that began to construct in history a new and more just society, the bishops at Medellín also promoted a productive and constructive force that could break cycles of violence. The bishops summarized in the following words the profound cost of violence and the power and potential present in a people's awakening to their own agency as creators of their future:

> If we consider then, the totality of the circumstances of our countries, and if we take into account the Christian preference for peace, the enormous difficulty of a civil war, the logic of violence, the atrocities it engenders, the risk of provoking foreign intervention, illegitimate as it may be, the difficulty of building a regime of justice and freedom while participating in a process of violence, we earnestly desire that the dynamism of the awakened and organized community be put to the service of justice and peace.[44]

In the midst of what they called the "dramatic dilemma"[45] of violence, the bishops gathered at the Medellín conference advocated for and opened a new way of being church that could resist and transform dehumanizing violence. This new way entailed a people of peoples awakening and organizing themselves into a peaceful and "constructive force"[46] that could be infinitely more creative than violence.

A Church of the Poor Witnesses against Poverty

If the documents on justice and peace were responses to institutionalized and overt armed violence, the document on the poverty of the church presented a way for the church to incarnate itself into the suffering and violent reality of Latin America and, from there, to speak and carry out God's liberating message of love. Arguably, the document on poverty contains the richest theological insights that have marked the Latin American church and its theology, which have also come to enrich the

---

[44] *Peace*, no. 19.

[45] *Peace*, no. 15.

[46] Paul VI, "Homily of the Mass on Development Day," 2:267.

universal church's understanding of poverty as a theological challenge that demands a response that is nothing short of the transformation of history.

The document's opening analysis of the situation of poverty in Latin America is explicit in its claim that one cannot remain indifferent to a situation that, at its core, is one of inhumanity. The bishops wrote, "A deafening cry pours from the throats of millions of men, asking their pastors for a liberation that reaches them from nowhere else."[47] The poor turn to their pastors because they do not know to whom else to turn. Governments have failed them, social structures have failed them, history has failed them, and the church, too, has failed them. Yet, the poor intuitively know that they have the potential to evangelize and convert the church to their situation.

The deafening cry of the poor points to a wounded reality. It is a cry that arises from the entrails of the longing for humanity. These communities long for liberation because they are enslaved, trapped, caged, unable to exercise their natural freedom as humans. In contrast to this inhuman reality, the document acknowledges that, to those in misery, the hierarchical church appears to be a church of wealth in support of the rich. Even if the wealth were to be mostly an appearance and not the reality of the Latin American church, it is difficult to overlook the "great buildings, the rectories and religious houses that are better than those of the neighbors, the often luxurious vehicles, the attire, inherited from other eras."[48] These trappings in some ways define the identity of the institutional church, for, in relation to the wealthy of society, the institutional church may not be rich, but, in relation to poor neighbors, the institutional church is certainly not poor. One may ask what is or ought to be the reference point for the church's way of being in the world. The question of perspective or point of reference is essential, for it determines what the church sees and how it sees it. To see from the perspective of the poor neighbor makes a real difference for how the hierarchy and the institutional church understand themselves in relation to the rest of the church and society, which is longing for structural conversion.

To the appearance of the institutional church's wealth, the document adds the reality of the many parishes and dioceses that exist in extreme

---

[47] *Poverty of the Church*, no. 2.
[48] *Poverty of the Church*, no. 2.

poverty. It argues that there are an "exceeding number of bishops, priests, and religious who live in complete deprivation and give themselves with great abnegation to the service of the poor."[49] What does it mean that some parts of the institutional church live in wealth in comparison to other parts of the church? What ought to guide the church's assessment in light of this complex reality of poverty? Instead of focusing on a quasi-universal and superficial assessment of wealth and poverty that stays simply at the level of the amount of goods one ought to have or not have, the document enters deeply into the reality of poverty and its effects in the particularity of Latin America. The church in Latin America must assess itself in light of its own local context, and, as the document says, it is a context of "wretchedness in which the great majority of the Latin American people live."[50] In relation to this particular context of misery and wretchedness, the document argues that those within the institutional church, such as bishops, clergy, and religious, generally have their basic necessities for life met, enjoying a certain security that the poor in their midst lack. In contrast to them, the poor live their everyday life between "anguish and uncertainty."[51] "Anguish" speaks of a threshold close to death, for, without the security of life, the poor merely survive. "Uncertainty" points to a daily living that is always in flux, without the ability to truly settle down, to be still, to give root, or to plan ahead for the long term. For the poor, the reference point is often short-term planning, for there is no reasonable guarantee of life or long-term survival.

Through the contrast between the relative security of bishops, priests, and religious, and the anguish and uncertainty of the poor in their midst, Medellín invites the church as a whole to consider what living under such anguish and uncertainty does to the body, the soul, and to the hopes and dreams of persons and communities. In other words, it invites the church to begin to see the effects of poverty from the perspective of the poor. The document's sensitivity to the perspective of the poor is captured in a statement about how the poor feel about the church. It says: "And incidents are not lacking in which the poor feel that their bishops, or pastors and religious, do not really identify themselves with them, with their problems and afflictions, that they do not always support those

---

[49] *Poverty of the Church*, no. 3.
[50] *Poverty of the Church*, no. 3.
[51] *Poverty of the Church*, no. 3.

that work with them or plead their cause."[52] A plethora of simple yet profound questions arise from this statement: How important are the feelings, thoughts, or perspectives of the poor? How crucial is it that the poor feel that the institutional church stands in solidarity with them? Do their feelings have a say in what the church does? Does the church need to be evaluated by the poor? Are the poor the judges of the church's fidelity and credibility? What does it mean for the church to feel with the poor, to have the problems of the poor, the afflictions of the poor? And why must the church bear such problems or afflictions? Ultimately, it leads to the question of the theological status of poverty and of the poor, and a clarification of what is meant by poverty and by the call to be a church of and for the poor.

The greatest theological contribution of the document on the poverty of the church was to clarify the different meanings of poverty that exist in relation to one another but are fundamentally opposed in the struggle between life and death. Thus, it was necessary to distinguish the terms and the realities to which they point. The document distinguished poverty on three levels. First, poverty is an evil, for it kills. The document says, "Poverty, as a lack of the goods of this world necessary to live worthily as men, is in itself evil."[53] Forced poverty is never good, for it is against the will of God who wills life. Essentially, the poor are trapped, held hostage to an evil that ultimately kills them. In contrast to the theological tradition of understanding poverty as the result of one's personal sin or the sins of one's ancestors (think, for example, of the Pharisees' questioning of the man born blind in John 9:1–41, or in our own day of the prosperity gospel that equates riches with God's blessing and poverty with lack of God's blessing), Medellín locates poverty as the result of injustice, whose root ultimately lies in the sin of selfishness, of being caught up in one's self.[54] The source of the injustice and violence of poverty is fundamentally located in structures, institutions, and the

---

[52] *Poverty of the Church*, no. 3.

[53] *Poverty of the Church*, no. 4.; The original Spanish text does not explicitly include the phrase "necessary to live worthily as men," but this meaning is implied. The Spanish is more succinct and direct inasmuch as it does not raise the question of what constitutes living "worthily." Instead, lacking basic goods to live is itself evil.

[54] See *Justice*, no. 3

overall reality of Latin America, which, although it is ultimately connected to the sin of persons, also overflows the sin of persons and takes root in systems that promote death and not life. This is a radical shift from an individual to a systemic framework for understanding poverty in relation to evil and sin. Poverty, as a lack of goods for life, brings death to God's good creation.

The second distinction of the term centers on spiritual poverty as a category that refers not to the real and historical poverty of lack of goods for life and of what is necessary to live worthily as persons, but to an attitude of openness to God and God's will. The document describes it as a "disposition of one who hopes for everything from the Lord."[55] Spiritual poverty is choosing to make God the point of reference for one's life, and all goods of this world have their ultimate value in reference to God. The reign of God relativizes all worldly goods and power and redirects the life of all who choose to follow Christ. Without spiritual poverty the church cannot be the church of Christ, for, in order to follow Christ, it must be open to what the Holy Spirit is doing with it in history as a pilgrim church that is always in the process of becoming.[56]

The third distinction of the term, which the document calls "poverty as commitment," arises from and is the result of spiritual poverty. In other words, spiritual poverty—here, openness to God's will—leads persons to embrace a life of voluntary poverty as a commitment against the evil of real and forced poverty. The text reads: "We must distinguish poverty as a commitment, through which one assumes voluntarily and lovingly the conditions of the needy of this world in order to bear witness to the evil which it represents and to spiritual liberty in the face of material goods."[57] Poverty as commitment is not the result of coercion but of freedom, which means that persons and communities have come to understand the evil of real poverty, the holiness of spiritual poverty, and the difference between the two. Furthermore, poverty as commitment is carried out "voluntarily and because of love,"[58] the love of the poor in whom Christ dwells. Love guides the church to take upon itself

---

[55] *Poverty of the Church*, no. 4

[56] For more on the church as pilgrim, see *Lumen Gentium,* nos. 48–51.

[57] *Poverty of the Church*, no. 4.

[58] *Poverty of the Church*, no. 4, translation my own. Whereas the English version uses the words "voluntarily and lovingly," I have chosen a more literal translation of

the conditions of those in poverty. In doing so, the church witnesses against the evil of poverty and witnesses to the spiritual freedom that comes when life is not defined and controlled by the world's goods but is lived in reference to the reign of God that gives meaning and definition to existence. In the commitment to the poor, one conforms to the life of Jesus, who accompanied and who continues to accompany the poor in order to witness in love against all that kills them before their time. In resisting the evil of poverty and all that makes people insignificant in their respective societies, the church participates in the ongoing salvific work of Christ.

Clarifying these three interrelated yet distinct meanings of poverty was a crucial contribution of the Medellín conference, especially for further developing the theological implications of Pope John XXIII's desire for a church of all, but especially of the poor. In light of the various meanings of *poverty* and the evil or good to which the term can refer, even half a century later, to speak of a church of the poor can easily lead to a confusion and, ultimately, to a justification of the evil of poverty as good, and more particularly and perniciously, to an uncritical assessment that it is good or holy to be poor. Both to correct such confused understandings of poverty and to avoid future legitimation of poverty, the document defines boldly what constitutes a poor church in the context of the poverty and violence of Latin America.

In relation to the first meaning of poverty, it states that a poor church "denounces the unjust lack of the goods of this world and the sin that begets it."[59] Another way of saying this is that a poor church denounces injustice, the institutionalized violence that keeps people in need and in a state of subserviency. To denounce this injustice is also to denounce the root sin of which poverty is the fruit.

In relation to the second meaning of poverty, the bishops wrote that a poor church "preaches and lives spiritual poverty, as an attitude of spiritual childhood and openness to the Lord."[60] To bind oneself to God, to trust unconditionally in the gratuitous love and mercy that is the church's reason for being, is not a matter of the church's preaching

---

the Spanish text to emphasize that love is the reason for poverty as commitment: "voluntarily and *because* of love" from the Spanish "voluntariamente y por amor."

[59] *Poverty of the Church*, no. 5, translation my own.

[60] *Poverty of the Church*, no. 5.

to others; it is an openess that the church itself, as institution and as a people, embodies through its particular ways of being in the world.

Lastly, in relation to the third meaning of poverty, the document writes that a poor church is "herself bound to material poverty."[61] A poor church commits itself to material poverty as the fruit of spiritual poverty and as a means of struggling against the evil of material poverty. The church becomes poor and, from that reality, works for the liberation of all. The church enters into the hellish reality of anguish, uncertainty, problems, and death that marks the life of the poor in order to participate in the work of salvation from within that reality. This is a dynamic that follows the logic of the incarnation, passion, and resurrection of Jesus. This is why the document says that "the poverty of the church is, in effect, a constant factor in the history of salvation."[62] The church effectively participates in the unfolding of salvation in history through its witnessing with those who struggle for life. A privileged locus of salvation is the reality of the poor, not because that reality is good, but because that is where the struggle for life and against death, the struggle for good and against evil, is being waged and lived by the majority of Latin America's and the world's inhabitants.

Having established and clarified the three distinctions of poverty, the Medellín document begins to use the category of evangelical poverty to refer to the church's fundamental call. Evangelical poverty is effectively the unity of spiritual poverty as openness to God, with poverty as commitment, which together enflesh that openness by following the gospel witness of Jesus who entered the world of the poor to liberate. Evangelical, or gospel poverty, binds together all three distinct meanings without confusing their differences. To speak of evangelical poverty is to speak of a voluntary poverty that is taken up in order to follow the Word made flesh in the struggle against the forces of death. The unequivocal universal call of the church to live evangelical poverty must be contextualized to each circumstance and people, and thus Medellín affirms that "there are diverse vocations to this poverty, that tolerate diverse styles of life and various modes of acting."[63] This openness to the unique ways in

---

[61] *Poverty of the Church*, no. 5.
[62] *Poverty of the Church*, no. 5.
[63] *Poverty of the Church*, no. 6.

which the Spirit of God calls each person and community is necessary if evangelical poverty is to be taken up in freedom and because of love for God and neighbor. Without love as the ground for commitment, evangelical poverty may cease to be a following of Jesus and can become a distorted imitation of the poor that does not work for anyone's liberation. The necessary differences in the ways of living evangelical poverty do not imply that the church can opt out of this witness to the gospel. The bishops write that it is "a challenge and a mission that [the church] cannot sidestep and to which she must respond with a diligence and audacity adequate to the urgency of the times."[64] To sidestep evangelical poverty would also be to sidestep following Jesus, thus rendering the church unintelligible and certainly not an effective sign and sacrament of the mystery of God, who is its source and reason. Active discernment is necessary if the church is to meet the challenge and mission of living genuinely diverse forms of evangelical poverty. However, the "anguished condition of millions of poor people in Latin America,"[65] as the document says, demands that such discernment be accountable to both the poor and to Christ. Evangelical or gospel poverty is a nonnegotiable option for authentic Christian living.

A church of the poor loves the poor as Christ loved. Like Christ, the church must communicate liberation effectively. Effective communication must happen in the entirety of its life, not simply in words, but this is impossible without entering the reality of the poor and understanding that reality from within. This was the mission of Christ, and this is the mission that Christ entrusted to the church, whose vocation is to be the continuation of Christ's presence in history, led by the Spirit. In becoming a church of the poor, the church becomes a "more lucid and authentic sign of its Lord" and more effectively fulfills its redemptive mission.[66] The evangelical poverty of the church becomes "a sign of the inestimable value of the poor in the eyes of God," and thus, "an obligation of solidarity with those who suffer."[67] Perhaps the inestimable value of the poor can

---

[64] *Poverty of the Church*, no. 7. The English translation uses "speed and boldness" instead of "diligence and audacity." I have chosen the latter as a more literal translation from the Spanish text that uses "diligencia y audacia."

[65] *Poverty of the Church*, no. 7.

[66] *Poverty of the Church*, no. 7.

[67] *Poverty of the Church*, no. 7.

only be fully understood from the perspective of God—from the "eyes of God"—through which the church must learn to see.

Spiritual poverty is the means for seeing as God sees, for recognizing God and neighbor properly. Learning to sense as God senses transforms the church and provides it with the foundational point of reference, with the fundamental epistemological ground from which it can come to understand and know as God knows. To be open to God's will is to engage in a process of active contemplation in the world that brings a unity with God akin to that of the prophets and mystics of ages past. When the church learns to hear, touch, and see from the mystery of God's loving gaze, the poor have inestimable value in a way that ordinary ways of thinking, and modernity's rationality, cannot understand. Spiritual poverty teaches the church a divine epistemology, and the church's poverty as commitment and solidarity is the effective sign and instrument that validates the truth of God's inestimable love for suffering and oppressed humanity. The poverty of the church as presented in the Medellín documents is a radically gospel-centric way of knowing, thinking, feeling, and being church in the world, which means that it is at once "paupercentric" and theocentric—its center resides simultaneously in God and the poor. The following of Jesus—salvation made flesh—becomes the means and end horizon of a poor church.

A church of the poor is one incarnated among the poor, living an effective preference for the poor that communicates the gospel. To grow closer to the poor, to enter into solidarity, is, as the bishops said, to "make ours their problems and their struggles."[68] To be a poor church is to continue to fulfill the vocation to enflesh the body of Christ in history and to serve as a sacrament of life in the midst of death.

Having analyzed the contributions of the Medellín documents on the interrelated questions of justice, peace, and poverty, and clarified the theological status of material poverty as an evil and a challenge to the Christian faith, I now turn to the affirmation stated at the beginning of the chapter: the poor are a sacrament of Christ. More particularly, the rest of the chapter enters into the relationship between the presence of Christ in the sacrament of the Eucharist and the presence of Christ in the sacrament of the poor.

---

[68] *Poverty of the Church*, no. 10.

A True and Mystical Sacrament of Life

In his interventions at the end of the first session of Vatican II, Cardinal Lercaro explicitly raised the question of the need to clarify further the connection between the presence of Christ in the Eucharist and the presence of Christ in the poor:

> In all the subjects the Council will deal with, may the ontological connection between the presence of Christ in the poor, and the two other profound realities of the Mystery of Christ in the church, namely the presence of Christ in the Eucharistic action by means of which the church is made one and is constituted, and the presence of Christ in the sacred hierarchy which instructs and governs the Church, be brought out and clarified.[69]

A different way of stating this is to ask about the relationship among the various manifestations of the body of Christ. More explicitly, we can ask about what Pope Paul VI meant when he stated: "The whole tradition of the church recognizes in the poor the sacrament of Christ, not in an identical manner to the reality in the Eucharist, but certainly in perfect analogical and mystical correspondence with it."[70] If poverty is an evil that dehumanizes, humiliates, and kills persons before their time, how is it that the poor are a sacrament, a sign, a mystery of Christ? How do we properly speak of the poor as sacrament of Christ without romanticizing the wretchedness of their poverty, which, at its root, is against the gospel, against any good news? While the close analysis of the Medellín documents on justice, peace, and poverty provides a response, entering more directly into the sacramental frameworks that undergird any conception of a church of the poor will further clarify this ecclesial challenge.

An analysis of the mystical correspondence (to use Paul VI's term) among the body of Christ in the Eucharist, in the church, and particularly in the poor, benefits from the insights of Henri de Lubac's classic study of the term *corpus mysticum* (mystical body) and his clarifica-

---

[69] Cardinal Lercaro, "Extracts from Cardinal Lercaro's Declaration at the First Session of the Vatican Council," in Gauthier, *Christ, the Church, and the Poor*, 155.

[70] Pope Paul VI, "A los Campesinos."

tion of what is meant by reference to the body of Christ. The task of both distinguishing and uniting the various references of the body of Christ—the historical body, the Eucharistic body, the ecclesial body—in a convoluted history that has, at various times and with different understandings, used *corpus mysticum* to refer to Christ's sacramental presence in the Eucharist and, at other times, to refer to Christ's sacramental presence in the church, was at the heart of de Lubac's study. This history created a certain opposition between the "mystical body" and the "true" or "real" body of Christ, an opposition that continues in our day when speaking of the mystical, true, or real presence of Christ in the poor.

In referring to the fundamental relationship between the Eucharist and the church, Henri de Lubac emphasizes the early church understanding that what is received in the Eucharist is a sign and promise of what the followers of Christ are called to form in history. What is received is a mystery of unity and communion, that all may be one in Christ. As he says, "The word communion has, fundamentally, only one sense. For, in the same way that sacramental communion (communion in the body and the blood) is always at the same time an ecclesial communion (communion within the church, of the church, for the church . . .), so also ecclesial communion always includes, in its fulfillment, sacramental communion."[71] This unity between the Eucharist and the church points to the ultimate reality of the one body of Christ, which, despite a history of distinctions, can never be separated. De Lubac clarifies that, in attempting to make sense of distinctions when referring to the mystery of the presence of Christ, the same word, *corpus*, was used to refer to the personal body of Christ born of Mary, to the body of Christ in the Eucharist, and to the body of Christ in the church. In the midst of a history of attempting to distinguish the various manifestations of the body of Christ, the phrase *corpus mysticum* or *mystical body* came into use around the ninth century to specify the sacramental body of the Eucharist.[72] Given the importance of the word *mystical* to refer to the Eucharist during the Patristic and Carolingian era, and not primarily

---

[71] Henri de Lubac, *Corpus Mysticum* (Notre Dame, IN: University of Notre Dame Press, 2007), 21.

[72] De Lubac, 29.

to refer to the body of the church as is mostly understood today, the adjective merits further analysis.

The association of *mystical* with the sacrament of the Eucharist has been a central part of Christianity and its liturgical and theological language from the beginning of the tradition.[73] How then, asks de Lubac, "among so many other analogous expressions, so commonly used . . . could this particular one [*corpus mysticum*] not come one day to fall from the pen of some ecclesiastical writer?"[74] Etymologically speaking, the adjective *mystical* derives from the noun *mystery,* and because of its correspondence to the more or less equivalent Latin terms of *sacramentum* and *mysterium* (at least as they were used in the early church),[75] the term *mystery* is always associated with something sacred that is both "sign" and "secret,"[76] or alternatively stated, something sacred that is visible and yet hidden. De Lubac explains the dynamic relationship between a visible sign that points to a hidden mystery by saying that "the *sacramentum* would therefore play the role of container, or envelope, with regard to the *mysterium* hidden within it."[77] But the mysterium that was hidden within the sacramentum was not primarily a static reality as would be an object, but rather the mysterium—that to which the sacramentum referred—was understood to be an action.

Furthermore, it was not only the content of the mystery that was an action, but also the relationship between the sacrament and mystery itself. The action or reality of the mystery, one can say, overflowed unto the sacrament. In other words, the container or envelope, to use de Lubac's analogy, was permeated by the mysterium hidden within it. To express more intensely the relational action between the sacramentum (sign) and the mysterium (mystery), de Lubac speaks of the "hidden presence of the second term within the first, already at work secretly but effectively."[78]

---

[73] For at least fifty diverse examples of the term *mystical* to refer to the Eucharist and more broadly to all that is entailed in living into the mystery that is at the root of Christianity, see de Lubac, 37–41.

[74] De Lubac, 41.

[75] De Lubac, 45.

[76] De Lubac, 47.

[77] De Lubac, 47. The notion of sacramentum as container will be constructively employed in Chapter 7 when referring to a sanctuary community as an ecclesial container with the potential for healing.

[78] De Lubac, 52.

Understanding that the visible sign points to an invisible action and that the invisible action already permeates the visible sign radically enlivens the relationship between sacrament and mystery. Succinctly stated, to speak of a sacrament is to speak of the mystery to which it points, but also, and primarily, of the action of the mystery that is already present in the sacrament itself.

If these distinctions and clarifications of terms are brought to bear on the phrase *mystical body*, it is understood that the *body* is the sacramentum, the sign, which points to the mystery, to the action that already permeates the body. Thus, the mystical body effectively communicates and makes present, though never fully, the hidden reality that it signifies.[79] So far I have focused on the Eucharist as the mystical body of Christ, but the question arises about the relationship of this mystical body with the other understandings of the body of Christ, particularly Christ's historical body and the ecclesial body of the church.

An understanding of the Eucharist as the mystical body of Christ always exists in relation to the memory or memorial of the life, passion, and resurrection of Jesus and in hope or anticipation of the coming-into-being of the community of justice, peace, and love that the church must be—a people tasked with incarnating the good news of Jesus Christ in history. The sacrament of the Eucharist opens a horizon to a past action made present, pointing to and effecting a future action in the now. The action of the historical body and the action of the ecclesial body are inseparable from the action taking place in the Eucharistic sacrament that gathers together memory and hope, the past and the future, in a present that always overflows its boundaries in our limited conceptions of time and linear history. De Lubac writes: "In its very reality, although through the mediation of the external rite, the Eucharist therefore signifies a thing, or rather an action, which is past. It is a mystery of commemoration. It commemorates and reproduces, that is to say renders once again present . . . this same and unique historical Sacrifice."[80] The

---

[79] De Lubac clarifies that a mystery is revealed, but never fully, lest it cease to be mystery. He writes that it is "precisely the nature of a sacred object not to be open to being fully revealed: it always remains partly secret, always 'mysterious' in itself. A mystery that was not revealed or open to revelation would be totally unknowable, but on the other hand a mystery that was fully unveiled would no longer be worthy of the name." De Lubac, 54n138.

[80] De Lubac, 59.

mystery of the Eucharistic action is therefore the mystery of Jesus's life, death, and resurrection, the mystery of God's historical and ongoing action of redemption and liberation from all that is sin and its consequences. The mystical body of Christ communicated in the Eucharist is, as de Lubac says, "the body engaged in a mystical action, a ritual echo, endlessly reverberating in time and space, of the unique action from which it takes its sense."[81] In terms of the sacrament's relation to the church, de Lubac writes that the Eucharist is "a pledge and image of the reality to come. It does not only reproduce, it also anticipates: pre-signs, pre-figures, pre-demonstrates. . . . It is the effective sign of the fraternal charity which binds its members. . . . It is the effective sign of the peace and unity for which Christ died and toward which we are reaching, moved by his Spirit."[82] Effectively, the mystery of the Eucharist, the mystical body of Christ present in the action of the sacrament, must always exist in relation to the historical and the ecclesial body of Christ, for they are inseparable lest the fullness of the mystery risk becoming unintelligible or incommunicable.

One of de Lubac's key contributions was showing how the term *corpus mysticum* that arose as a common phrase in the ninth century united in the Eucharist the various meanings of the body of the Christ. By the twelfth century, however, the unity of the various meanings of the body of Christ began to erode as the adjective *mystical* underwent a transition from its association with the sacrament of the Eucharist to its association with the church. He explains that, little by little, *body* in reference to the Eucharist came to impose itself without any further qualifications such as "sacrament of . . . " or "mystery of . . . ," and the Eucharist came to be referred to simply as the body of Christ.[83] At the same time, the term *body* in its Eucharistic sense increasingly came to be associated with the historical body of Christ and in contradistinction to the ecclesial body of Christ.[84] By the eleventh century "the first two 'bodies' were moulded into one."[85] By the middle of the twelfth century, expressions and adjectives such as *spiritual flesh* began to appear to distinguish the body of

---

[81] De Lubac, 62.
[82] De Lubac, 66.
[83] De Lubac, 80.
[84] De Lubac, 92.
[85] De Lubac, 95.

Christ in the church,[86] and by the end of the twelfth century, the adjective *spiritual* gave way to *mystical.* Thus, as de Lubac argues, the ecclesial body "would come to have attributed to it more and more the adjective 'mystical,' which fell into disuse to the extent that the sacramental body shed it; so much so that the day would come when 'mystical' would be definitively joined to 'body' as a designation for the Church."[87] In light of the twelfth century's growing identification between the Eucharist and the historical or corporeal body of Christ, and an increasing distinction of the presence of Christ in the church as *mystical,* it can be said that the ecclesial body was being spiritualized while, at the same time, spiritualizing terms were falling away from references to the Eucharist in an attempt to stress the real presence of Christ in the Eucharistic sacrament.

The opposition that arose between terms and their significations around the twelfth century is lamentable. De Lubac summarizes the change: "Sacramental and mystical, which until recently had still been considered synonymous, and are basically the same word, were now separated and placed in opposition to one another."[88] With this opposition, there arose the related opposition of the sacrament of the Eucharist as the true or real body and the church as the mystical body.[89] Once mystical was severed from sacramental, to speak of the church as a mystical body was more akin to using the term as an analogy that referred to a social or juridical body without the sacramental richness the term had previously contained when it was still used in reference to the Eucharist.[90] The eventual result—and this is key—was that speaking of the church as the mystical body did not imply a reference either to the Eucharist or to the sacramental frameworks that had historically undergirded the unity of the various distinctions of the body of Christ.[91] This understanding of the church as the mystical body, severed from the rich sacramentality that had accompanied the term in the first millennium, is what was passed down to the modern era and what Vatican II tried to address.

In the process of this displacement of terms and their significations, part of what was lost was the early church's conception of the ecclesial

---

[86] De Lubac, 99.
[87] De Lubac, 100.
[88] De Lubac, 103.
[89] De Lubac, 111.
[90] De Lubac, 115.
[91] De Lubac, 114.

body as the truth (*veritas*) or true body of Christ inasmuch as this was the body that the Eucharist was effectively bringing about in history.[92] As was said earlier, the sacrament of the Eucharist was integrally related to both the historical body of Jesus, on the one hand, and to the ecclesial body that was coming-into-being, on the other. Since, in the early church, the terms *mystical* and *true* were distinctions rather than oppositions, to speak of the ecclesial body as the true body did not negate the true presence of Christ in the mystical body that was the sacrament of the Eucharist. In other words, the sacrament of the Eucharist was not understood to be less true by being mystical, and the ecclesial body was not understood to be less mystical by being true. That which was true was fundamentally connected with that which was being continually effected, verified—made to be true—by the mystery of the sacrament. De Lubac explains it this way:

> Earlier on, what was "a type" or "a mystery" was the Eucharist itself—*we are celebrating mystically, the mystical body*—while the "truth" revealed within the rite to our spiritual understanding was its effect, its ultimate "thing," that is to say in particular the ecclesial body, still to come to fulfillment. In the final analysis the truth was to be found beyond the sacrament. Now the sacrament itself has become the "thing" and the "truth" of the ancient rites.[93]

In her analysis of de Lubac's ecclesiology, Susan Wood describes the shift by saying that "veritas eventually became identified with the reality of the body and blood whose substance was on the altar under the appearance of bread and wine rather than the completion of the Eucharist in the Church."[94] As was implied earlier, the loss of the association of veritas or true/truth with the church meant that the Eucharistic body and the ecclesial body were understood less and less in terms of their intrinsic connection, and the sacramental dimension of the church

---

[92] For an analysis of these sacramental logics in relation to the truth of a borderlands church, see Roberto Goizueta, "Corpus Verum: Toward a borderland ecclesiology," in *Building Bridges, Doing Justice*, ed. Orlando Espín (Maryknoll, NY: Orbis 2009), 143–66.

[93] De Lubac, 204.

[94] Susan Wood, *Spiritual Exegesis and the Church in the Theology of Henri de Lubac* (Grand Rapids, MI: Eerdmans, 1998), 67.

as a sign that points to a reality beyond itself and to a future fulfillment—the reign of God—which begins in history was also obscured.
By the end of the twelfth century, the unity of the distinctions of the
body of Christ—the ecclesial body, the Eucharistic body, and the historical body—was severed. This unity was made possible through the
ontological symbolism that had undergirded the sacramental system
of the early church,[95] which understood the ecclesial body as the reality, truth, or verification of the Eucharistic sacrament, and which also
understood the ecclesial body as a sacrament always in relation to the
historical body of Christ.[96]

The Second Vatican Council formally addressed some of the sacramental concerns already expressed, but have these theological shifts
transformed the people that is the church? The concluding words of
de Lubac's historical study still serve as a challenge for us decades after
Vatican II: "It seems that it would therefore be of great interest, we might
even say of pressing urgency, given the present state of what remains of
'Christendom,' to return to the sacramental origins of the 'mystical body'
in order to steep ourselves in it. . . . The Church and the Eucharist are
formed by one another day by day."[97]

A Sanctuary for the Body of Christ

This chapter began with the question of the relationship among the
presence of Christ in the church, the poor, and the Eucharist. The
response has entailed acknowledging a perichoretic dimension among
these realities, for, as I have tried to emphasize in turning to de Lubac,
there is a fundamental unity and interpenetration of the distinctions of
the body of Christ at the root of the Christian tradition. To speak of
Eucharist is to speak of the historical body of Jesus and also to speak of
the ecclesial body. Conversely, to speak of the ecclesial body is to also
speak of the Eucharistic body and of the historical body. And to speak
of the historical body is to speak of the life, death, and resurrection of
Jesus, whose action is the foundation for Christ's sacramental presence in

---

[95] De Lubac, *Corpus Mysticum,* 226.
[96] De Lubac, 245–46.
[97] De Lubac, 260.

the ecclesial body and the Eucharistic body. In light of this sacramental matrix, returning to the historically grounded reality of the world of the poor that Medellín addressed is imperative, for this context initially gave rise to these questions of the poor as a sacrament of Christ and of the church of the poor as a concrete manifestation of an ecclesial body that accompanies and responds to the anguish of the mystery of Christ in those who live under constant threat of death.

The true or real presence of the body of Christ, as was understood in the early church, is particularly manifest wherever violence, whose root is sin, threatens to cut short the grace that is life given by the God of life who wills that all may live. The manifestation of the true body of Christ in all who struggle for life is a locus for encountering the real presence of the God who accompanies all who seek liberation and salvation from the evil that destroys their life. As was expressed in Medellín's document on poverty, the church must follow the logic of the incarnation and incarnate itself in the wounded and sinful realities that destroy life in order to eradicate that evil and participate in the healing of that reality. In doing so, the church continues to fulfill its vocation as a sacrament of salvation in history, coming face to face with the sacrament that is also the poor, who, in a preferential manner, constitute the church of Christ. It is one sacramental reality encountering another, distinguished but never separated in the one body of Christ whose mystery is a presence that overflows the visible church and that always calls the church into becoming a sign of God's redemptive act of liberation.

Reading Paul VI's 1968 statements at San Jose de la Mosquera in light of de Lubac's sacramental insights brings forth the depth of his words. In saying to the poor that they are "a sign, an image, a mystery of the presence of Christ"[98] Paul VI was making a profound theological statement about the presence of Christ in a history of suffering and violence. His words bound the suffering reality of the poor to Jesus's own historical journey, especially through the passion and crucifixion, but also through the resurrection. In this manner, the poor reveal the true and real body of Christ in history. In the likeness of the poor, there is the likeness of Jesus, for they are the image of the image of God.

Paul VI goes on to make a further connection by binding the poor with the historical body of Jesus and with the sacramental body of Christ on

---

[98] Pope Paul VI, "A los Campesinos."

the altar. If, as he said, the Eucharist "offers us his hidden presence, living and real," then the poor whom he proclaimed as a sacrament are a source of revelation inasmuch as they disclose "his human and divine face."[99] Reading the connection between the poor and the Eucharist in light of the sacramental matrix analyzed previously leads to the affirmation that, in the poor, the church encounters the presence of the historical body of Christ, the Eucharistic body of Christ, and itself, the ecclesial body that is always coming into being through the Spirit, following Christ, who continues to become incarnate in history.

Paul VI added that the sacrament of Christ in the poor was in "perfect analogical and mystical correspondence"[100] with the Eucharist, though it was not identical with it. In light of the clarifications of the term *mystical*, his use of "mystical correspondence" cannot be spiritualized and rendered in opposition to true or real.[101] Rather, the mystical correspondence between the sacrament of Christ in the Eucharist and in the poor is a piercing reminder that the truth of the sacrament, its historical verification, is to be found in the fruit that it bears in the transformation of history ever more into the reign of God that Jesus preached to all, and especially as a promise to the poor. The life and liberation of the church itself is in the life and liberation of the poor.

The oppressed, the persecuted, the displaced, and all those whose lives are threatened reveal and are a site of holy encounter with the various manifestations of the body of Christ in history, not because the reality in which they are forced to live is holy, but because it is anti-evangelical— anti-gospel. The reality of poverty in its multiple dimensions is against the good news of God's love for all. As such, it is against the "inestimable value of the poor in the eyes of God."[102] To recall Landázuri's words at the beginning of the Medellín conference: "This is the hour of love, so that for a questioning world we have only one answer: we are witnesses to love."[103] Love can allow the church to recognize Christ in the poor and makes the poor constitutive of the church. Love can transform the

---

[99] Pope Paul VI, "A los Campesinos."

[100] Pope Paul VI, "A los Campesinos.".

[101] Paul VI's use of the term *analogical* in this context is an echo to how *Lumen Gentium* uses *analogy* to explain the relationship between the church and Christ (no. 8).

[102] *Poverty of the Church*, no. 7.

[103] Landázuri, "Inaugural Address," 1:51.

church into a church of the poor. Love can lead a poor church to become a sanctuary of and for God's displaced people, where both God and God's threatened creation can dwell in each other's true and real presence. Like Christ, the church will continue to face persecution and death when it witnesses to love, but, by the grace of the Spirit (Rom 8:11), it will also encounter its resurrection.

Part III

6

Archbishop Óscar Romero

A Living Sanctuary for the Persecuted

When the sanctuary ministry began in the US-Mexico borderlands in the early 1980s, Óscar Romero essentially served as the patron saint of the growing movement. On March 24, 1982, and on his anniversary in the following years, churches and cathedrals across North America publicly declared themselves a sanctuary of God for the displaced of Central America. Romero's unequivocal protection of displaced and persecuted Salvadorans made of him an internationally recognized icon of a church that was willing to confront the legalized violence of governments. Romero modeled a bishop's pastoral duty to intercede, echoing the great pastors and theologians of the fourth century who prophetically upheld the tradition of the church serving as a site of refuge. Romero's sacramental vision—and more particularly a Eucharistic vision—of a church of and for the poor in the midst of state violence provided clarity on how to live and die faithfully. Entering into his theological understanding of how to be church in the midst of persecution shows us how to be a community of sanctuary with and for Christ. By serving as a sanctuary for humanity, the church of Romero also served as a sanctuary for God.

By the time Óscar Romero became archbishop of El Salvador in 1977, he could draw nourishment and insights from the documents of Vatican II and from the documents of the Latin American Bishop's conference in Medellín (1968) that sought to concretize and respond to the spirit of Vatican II from the pressing reality of Latin America. In fact, Romero advocated for the Christian liberation expressed in Medellín by referring to those texts as "luminous documents."[1] He said that they were "authentic doctrine of the church and that they must not be feared but rather understood, lived, [and] translated into practice, for they provide the light that will lead the people of Latin America to salvation."[2] These documents guided Romero in defining what the church could be and do for El Salvador. Ultimately, his encounter with the suffering of a whole people clarified for Romero how the church could be present with the poorest and most insignificant of his time.

This chapter historically concretizes the theological foundations for rethinking church as sanctuary that were analyzed in Part II of this book. More specifically, it illustrates how the poor and persecuted became for Archbishop Óscar Romero and for the Latin American church a sacramental encounter with the body of Christ in history and how this encounter transformed Romero and his church into a sanctuary of life in the midst of death. In encountering Christ in the poor, the church entered a process of incarnating itself in the sinful reality of institutionalized violence, persecution, and death in order to struggle against these evils. The poor revealed the church of El Salvador to itself, and, in joining their struggle for life and liberation, the church of this little Central American country has left a lasting impact on the universal church.

I begin with the dehumanizing institutionalized violence of El Salvador in the decades prior to the country's descent into the 1980s civil war. In the closing years of the 1970s, as the church increasingly found itself in the crossfire that was engulfing the country, the poor and those who accompanied the poor became targets of persecution. During this time the persecuted parishes in the northern region of Aguilares left an indelible mark on Romero's first year as archbishop,

---

[1] Romero's reference to the Medellín documents as "luminous documents" echoes John XXIII's use of the phrase "luminous point," which Gustavo Gutiérrez says was used by the pope whenever he wanted to highlight the importance of a point or idea. See Gustavo Gutiérrez, "Significado y alcance de Medellín," in *Irrupcion y Caminar de la Iglesia de los Pobres* (Lima, Peru: Instituto Bartolomé de las Casas, 1989), 33. In English, see Gustavo Gutiérrez, *The Truth Shall Make You Free: Confrontations* (Maryknoll, NY: Orbis Books, 1990), 199n162.

[2] Óscar Romero, *Homilías*, vol. 1 (San Salvador: UCA Editores, 2005), June 19, 1977, 154. Unless specified otherwise, references to Óscar Romero's homilies will be drawn from the original Spanish text and translations are my own.

which became pivotal for Romero's assumption of his role as protector of those whom the government failed to protect and actively persecuted. Using Romero's homilies and actions surrounding the feast of Corpus Christi in 1977 and a historic homily he gave in Aguilares in June 1977, I show how, for Romero, the body of Christ in the Eucharist and the body of Christ in the poor converged into one, so that the protection of one necessarily entailed the protection of the other, for, in their convergence, the depths of communion with God and neighbor were made manifest. In Aguilares, Romero became a living sanctuary for the persecuted, taking upon himself an ecclesial mark that would come to be recognized across the country and the world as a sign of the presence of the Holy.

Living in the Company of the Poor

In the first half of 1977 the persecution of the community of Aguilares and of its surrounding village of El Paisnal left an indelible mark on Óscar Romero's new ministry as archbishop of El Salvador.[3] These months were like a crucible in which Romero was forced to contemplate the nature and mission of the church through the corpus of the magisterium's writings and in the threatened, tortured, and disfigured bodies of his priests and of the parish communities where they ministered. The growing encounter with the violence of poverty and with atrocities that violated any notion of the sacredness and dignity of the human person helped Romero to clarify his role as pastor and refuge of the oppressed and persecuted. To understand these first few months of Romero's ministry, one must also come to know the community of Aguilares.

Since 1972, the parish of El Señor de las Misericordias (the Lord of Mercies) in Aguilares, as well as the rural parishes in the surrounding villages, had been under the leadership of Fr. Rutilio Grande, SJ, and of a mission team associated with Jesuit institutions in San Salvador.[4] Since their arrival, the team had worked to promote religious forma-

---

[3] Aguilares is a town about an hour's drive north of the capital of San Salvador. The village of El Paisnal, where Rutilio Grande, SJ, was killed on March 12, 1977, is located just three miles from Aguilares.

[4] Rutilio Grande had grown up in the neighboring town of El Paisnal, whose parish was part of the larger church of Aguilares.

tion, inspired by the documents of Vatican II and Medellín, along with a social consciousness that addressed the variety of issues affecting the growing community. The people of Aguilares and the surrounding communities depended heavily on work in the sugar cane plantations that provided the raw material for the three major sugar mills in the area. Because of the nature of this work, formation on labor rights became important for the mission team.[5] Additionally, the increasing displacement of families from land they had previously worked, along with a growing lack of employment—and thus a lack of the means for survival—made the campesino community of Aguilares receptive to an ecclesial vision that affirmed their dignity, their right to work, and ultimately, their right to live.

There had never been a strike in the sugar plantations around Aguilares, but within six months of the mission team's arrival, the first one took place in May 1973, spurred by plantation leaders' attempts to pay workers less than what had been previously agreed. Members of the mission team were surprised and concerned by the strike,[6] for they had not foreseen how quickly some of their parishioners would become involved in more direct political action that technically exceeded the church's formation program. The mission team certainly understood that the processes of conscientization and the development of organizational skills in the community for the sake of building small Christian communities that were focused on evangelization could eventually lead to these lay community leaders being involved in the transformation of social structures; they simply had not expected this to happen so soon.[7] The involvement of lay church leaders in the strike, and the rapid escalation of tensions with

---

[5] Rodolfo Cardenal, *Vida, Pasión y Muerte del Jesuita Rutilio Grande* (San Salvador: UCA Editores, 2017), 195.

[6] Cardenal, 231.

[7] Lay leaders involved in the Christian communities established by the mission team soon became leaders within the Christian Federation of Salvadoran Peasants (FECCAS) groups in Aguilares. By 1976, tensions arose between the more political aims of FECCAS and the more explicitly religious aims of the parish. While both institutions sought to address unjust structures affecting the poor and oppressed, the means for doing so necessitated that each have a certain autonomy from the other while still being interrelated. See Cardenal, 366–74. The 1976 tensions with FECCAS deeply affected Fr. Rutilio, who sought advice from Fr. Ignacio Ellacuría on how to navigate the necessary accompaniment of such faith-inspired but politically-directed groups. For Fr. Ellacuria's advice to Fr. Rutilio, see Cardenal, 461–66.

landowners, the sugar mills, and the National Guard, which protected business interests in the region, put Fr. Rutilio and the parish team in a position of having to discern carefully their evangelizing mission.

Fr. Rutilio emphasized the church's religious mission, fully aware that this mission could neither be confused with direct political activity nor separated from the oppressive historical reality of Aguilares. A month later, in June 1973, when El Salvador's president visited Aguilares—a president whom many considered the result of fraudulent elections—local officials expected that Fr. Rutilio would accompany him on his visit to the town's churches. Aware that, in the country's polarized environment, some would interpret such an appearance with the president as a political endorsement of him and others as a betrayal of their struggles for justice, Fr. Rutilio decided not to participate in the official ceremonies and simply left the churches open for the president to visit on his own.[8] Rutilio wrote a letter to the president, explaining the reasons for his decision, affirming his religious role as pastor, and communicating the misery of poverty in which the campesinos of Aguilares lived, but his action effectively placed him in opposition to the government and its local supporters. Within the parish leadership team the question of the church's religious mission and the degree to which it could or could not become directly involved in the political sphere remained an ongoing conversation with both the lay leaders and the fellow priests who desired greater direct action by the church.[9] Throughout the 1970s, paramilitary groups and the military labeled the mission team as communist and violently persecuted the parish,[10] but the work of evangelization and of raising social consciousness continued among the twenty- to twenty-five- thousand persons who lived within the parish boundaries.[11]

---

[8] Cardenal, 243–44.

[9] Both Fr. Boulang, a priest who worked mostly in neighboring Chalatenango, and Fr. Bengoechea, who was part of the mission team in Aguilares, sought greater direct political involvement by the church hierarchy in the activities of its lay members. See Cardenal, 248–49. The participation of laity in the discernment of how the church can engage politics is an essential dimension of discerning the work of the Holy Spirit. In the United States many parishes still do not have participatory structures for the laity to express their voice.

[10] Cardenal, 374, 389.

[11] Cardenal, 291.

By the time Óscar Romero became archbishop and took responsibility for the archdiocese on February 22, 1977, the Catholic Church in El Salvador was enduring an unprecedented and targeted persecution of priests that began with the arrests, torture, and expulsion of missionaries from other countries and quickly expanded to Salvadoran-born priests.[12] On the same day that Romero took office as archbishop, he and the other Salvadoran bishops met with the country's president as a formality, and the president presented the archbishop with a list of priests whom the government considered subversives.[13] Among the foreign priests for whom it was no longer safe to stay were those who worked as part of the mission team in Aguilares. Rutilio, as a native Salvadoran, stayed despite warnings that it was not safe for him. Although priests were increasingly targeted for working closely with poor campesino communities that were becoming organized against institutionalized violence, Romero nonetheless affirmed the committed pastoral work of clergy at his first clergy meeting on March 10, 1977. He especially highlighted the work of Fr. Rutilio and the mission team in Aguilares.[14]

Tragically, two days later, on March 12, Rutilio was murdered.[15] It is well known that government forces assassinated him along with two campesinos who were accompanying him to the neighboring town of El Paisnal for a novena mass to St. Joseph. His companions were seventy-two-year-old Manuel Solorzano and fifteen-year-old Nelson Lemus.[16] Romero, who had spoken with Rutilio just two days before that, arrived in the church of Aguilares that night to witness the cost of living in the company of the poor. The three bloodied bodies were placed in front of the altar for a late-night mass with the campesino community Rutilio had accompanied since 1972. On March 14, a solemn mass was held

---

[12] The first to be deported was Fr. Mario Bernal on January 29, 1977. He was Colombian and pastor of a parish in Apopa on the outskirts of San Salvador. His torture and deportation spurred a public protest—"una manifestación de fe" (manifestation of faith)— on February 13 that ended with a mass preached by Fr. Rutilio Grande.

[13] Cardenal, 497.

[14] Cardenal, 501.

[15] Fr. Rutilio, Manuel Solorzano, and Nelson Lemus are buried in the church of El Paisnal.

[16] For details of the assassination, see Cardenal, *Vida, Pasión y Muerte del Jesuita Rutilio Grande*, 509–15.

in the Cathedral of San Salvador with the three bodies present and a crowd that overflowed the building's capacity. Thus began Romero's public preaching and ministry as archbishop.

The Violation of Sanctuary

Romero's homily at the funeral mass on March 14, 1977, marks the beginning of three years of public reflections that became a dialogue with God and with the concrete reality of El Salvador. That historic homily serves as one bookend of Romero's textual corpus, the other being his last homily before his own assassination three years later, on March 24, 1980. In that first recorded homily Romero made the profound ecclesiological statement that the universal church was also present in the particularity of what the local church in El Salvador was living. The events of the church in El Salvador were—and continue to be—relevant for being church beyond El Salvador. Romero proclaimed in his opening words:

> It seems to me that on some occasions, like this morning, the cathedral becomes the sign of the universal church. It is here that the whole rich pastoral ministry of a local church is gathered together and joined to the pastoral ministry of all the dioceses of our country and the whole world. We feel that the presence not only of the living but of these three deceased persons gives this image of the church a dimension of openness to the Absolute, to the Infinite, to the One Beyond: the universal church, the church beyond history, the church beyond human life.[17]

In his homily Romero brought together the living and the dead, the local church with the universal church, the historical persecution of the church with the eschatological horizon toward which the church journeys, all united in a simple cathedral that would play a significant

---

[17] Óscar Romero, homily, March 14, 1977, *A Prophetic Bishop Speaks to His People: The Complete Homilies of Archbishop Óscar Arnulfo Romero*, vol. 1, trans. Joseph Owens (Miami, FL: Convivium Press, 2015), 59. For the original Spanish, see Romero, *Homilías*, 31.

role as a site of refuge for persecuted Salvadorans in the years to come. The communion present in his words points to the mystery that what particular parishes and communities were suffering in the most isolated corners of the country affected the church in the rest of the country, and, in a particular way, it affected Romero as the pastor of the whole church of El Salvador. Furthermore, because of the church's fundamental unity and communion, the violent and suffering reality of El Salvador affected the church in all of its existence, visible and invisible, in and beyond history.

The assassination of Fr. Rutilio in the company of two peasants was not simply the killing of three individual persons but signified an attempt against a church that was in the process of rekindling the same love with which Jesus carried out his ministry. It was the violent response to a growing unity between the church as institution and the poor and persecuted people of God. Romero conveys this unity when he says that "true love is what brings Rutilio Grande to his death, hand in hand with two peasants. That is how the church loves. She dies with them."[18] For Romero, this message of accompaniment, even unto death, was the message that he said had to be "gathered from that corpse, a message for all of us who continue on pilgrimage."[19] In his homily, on behalf of the whole archdiocese, he thanked Fr. Rutilio and his two companions who were manifesting the true dimension of the church's mission.[20] Let us not forget, he added, that "we are a pilgrim church, exposed to incomprehension, to persecution; but a church that walks serenely because it carries that force of love."[21] The revelatory and unifying force of the three corpses from Aguilares gathered together before the local and universal church in San Salvador continued to shape the contours of Romero's duties as archbishop and the mission of the Salvadoran church in the years to come. The military occupation of Aguilares two months later merits particular attention for understanding how the experience of the desecration and violation of the church and community of Aguilares concretized for Romero his public role as pastor and protector of the poor and persecuted.

---

[18] Romero, *Homilías*, March 14, 1977, 34.

[19] Romero, 31.

[20] Romero, 35.

[21] Romero, 35.

In the early morning of May 19, 1977, the military began Operation Rutilio, a month-long occupation of the city of Aguilares and of the local church community. Three Jesuit priests who had continued the mission work were captured and deported, leaving the community without clergy.[22] One of those deported, Fr. Ortega, later recounted that soldiers and a tank arrived in El Paisnal and Aguilares, killed and disappeared campesinos, and made their way to the church building.[23] The priests and the sacristan slept in the sacristy for protection, since it was considered the safest place.[24] When they sensed the soldiers arriving, they ran up to the bell tower to ring the bells and alert the community, but at that point the city was already heavily guarded. The soldiers forced their way into the sanctuary and began to shoot toward the priests and the sacristan, killing him while he rang the bells. The church was vandalized, the tabernacle was shot multiple times and destroyed, and the Eucharistic hosts were thrown on the floor, stepped on, and desecrated. Soldiers occupied the sanctuary for the rest of the month and made it their barracks.

For Romero, the military occupation of Aguilares and neighboring villages, particularly the direct attack on the sacrament of the Eucharist, became a painful experience of what he understood as violence carried out against the most sacred sign of the presence of God in the world. In a homily delivered a few days after the occupation began, Romero explains that he sent Fr. Vides, the chaplain, to the National Guard to "gather the blessed sacrament from the church in Aguilares, but he was not, and neither was the archbishop himself, allowed to go and fulfill this duty of bringing back the blessed sacrament to prevent its profanation."[25] Romero's sense of duty to protect the blessed sacrament was certainly not

---

[22] Romero issued a bulletin on the situation in Aguilares that was to be read in all masses across the country. In the bulletin he accuses the government of engaging in a campaign whose goal was to remove all priests who were committed to the service of the people. See Óscar Romero, "Boletin informativo del arzobispado No. 16," *Estudios CentroAmericanos* 342/343, 1977, 339–40.

[23] Jose Luis Ortega's recollection of the events is recorded in Maria Lopez Vigil, ed., *Monseñor Romero: Piezas para un Retrato* (San Salvador: UCA Editores, 2011), 157–59.

[24] Cardenal, *Vida, Pasión y Muerte del Jesuita Rutilio Grande,* 550.

[25] Romero, *Homilías,* May 22, 1977, 97.

exclusive or in contradiction to his concern for the people in Aguilares who, as he says, were suffering torture and mistreatments against which the church could not remain silent. In that May 22 homily Romero condemns a false sense of tradition that seeks a "merely spiritualized church, a church of sacraments, of prayers, but without social commitments, without a commitment to history."[26] He adds in that homily: "We would betray our mission as pastors if we sought to reduce evangelization to mere practices of individual piety and to a disincarnate sacramentalism."[27] He strengthened the passion of these words through references to the necessary interplay that must exist between the gospel and concrete life and the need to overcome the "divorce between faith and practical life which is one of the great errors of our times."[28] However, these strong critiques of tendencies in the church that risk making the faith ahistorical or leading it toward a "disincarnate sacramentalism" were in creative tension with Romero's own religious piety.

Romero was certainly leading the church of El Salvador toward a greater incarnation in the historical realities of the country and the suffering of its persecuted people. Yet, during the month of Aguilares's occupation, whenever Romero refers to Aguilares it is almost exclusively in reference to the desecration of the sacrament of the Eucharist. For example, the following Sunday, May 29, he preached a homily on the feast of Pentecost that dealt with the identity of the church—with what the church is. In speaking of the human need to communicate with the transcendent, to dialogue with God, he refers to the church's signs that point to that transcendence and of the "grand and terrible duty" that the church has to defend those signs. In this context, he alludes to the occupation of Aguilares and says:

> How can it not pain the church that the most beautiful sign of the
> presence of God on earth, the Eucharist, was trampled upon in

---

[26] Romero, 97.

[27] Romero, 97. This statement was part of a statement that the bishops' conference of El Salvador published on May 22, 1977, in response to the growing violence. The full statement is titled "Mensaje de la Conferencia Episcopal de El Salvador al pueblo salvadoreño, ante la ola de violencia que enluta el pais" and can be found in *Orientacion*, the archdiocesan newsletter.

[28] Romero, 101.

Aguilares? How can it not pain the church that they used an axe and broke the tabernacle? . . . It was not necessary to strike in that manner the holy relic of our faith: the Eucharist.[29]

Romero's own pain surrounding these events is palpable. Not only were he and his priests prevented from fulfilling what he called their duty to protect the blessed sacrament by removing it from the desecrated church, but the violent manner with which it was attacked—with bullets and an axe—adds a further layer of sorrow to Romero's response to these events. In speaking of the Eucharist as violently struck or hit, Romero communicates the sense that it was Jesus Christ himself who was beaten. He further emphasizes this sense of a violent attack on Christ in that same homily when he refers joyfully to the upcoming celebration of the feast of Corpus Christi that will bring "homage to the consecrated host," and that he proclaims will serve as a "feast of reparations to the blessed sacrament that was vilely profaned."[30] Reparations to Christ become the explicit focus of his homily the following Sunday.

The *Corpus Christi* of Aguilares

Romero's homily for the feast of Corpus Christi presents a penitential church that is in need of making amends for what has been done to Christ through various affronts against the Eucharist. He begins with a vivid image of the universal church concretized in the church of El Salvador, "reverently kneeling to gather with tenderness, with tears, the hosts stomped upon in Aguilares, stolen in Ciudad Delgado, and mistreated by many ill-made communions."[31] In traditional language of Eucharistic devotion, he refers to the church as the spouse of Christ, who received the Eucharist as a living portrait of her husband so that all the children that would be born throughout the ages would remember him. Romero again describes the church kneeling before Christ saying, "Forgive us, beloved! How we treat you! But receive the love of these your children who cry

---

[29] Romero, *Homilías*, May 29, 1977, 115.
[30] Romero, 116.
[31] Romero, *Homilías,* June 12, 1977, 133.

over these shameful abuses."[32] After this striking description, Romero shifts to a reflection on the real presence of Christ in the Eucharist and on the Eucharist as a means of reparation and reconciliation with God. He adds: "In the symbol of the host trampled upon in Aguilares let us see the face of Christ on the cross."[33] In the hosts trampled underfoot, Romero sees both the sinfulness of humanity and the forgiveness and love that Christ offers in the Eucharist, a forgiveness that all Christians are called to practice. Toward the end of the homily, he asks, "What is the greatest need of our mother church?" And he answers: "Reparation. Reparation because she has been spat upon; we must clean her face, make her more beautiful; we must collaborate so that she may be a more beautiful spouse of our Lord Jesus Christ."[34]

Romero's gendered theo-aesthetic insights expand throughout the homily, for, if at the beginning the focus was narrowly on Christ's presence in the Eucharist and on the church's needs to make amends for the sacrilegious insults, by the end it is the beauty of the church that concerns him, a beauty that always exists in relation to fidelity to Christ her spouse.[35] In other words, according to Romero, the church becomes more beautiful the more it faithfully follows Jesus. Although Romero does not expound much on the category of beauty, his references to the

---

[32] Romero, 133.

[33] Romero, 135.

[34] Romero, 136.

[35] For a fascinating study on the convergence of visual adoration and the eating of the Eucharist, see Ann Astell, *Eating Beauty: The Eucharist and the Spiritual Arts of the Middle Ages* (Ithaca, NY: Cornell University Press, 2006). Some of Romero's concerns in his homily for Corpus Christi, including his statement of the Eucharist as a "living portrait" of Christ, are reflected in Astell's reflections: "Because the whole Christ (*totus Christus*) was understood by orthodox medieval Christians to be present in the Host, the questions concerning Eucharistic beauty are inevitably Christological and ecclesial. They address the beauty of Christ in His divinity as the Son of the Father and the preexistent Logos, through whom 'all things were made' (John 1:3) and are refashioned. They meditate on Christ's beauty in His humanity—born of Mary, morally just, cruelly crucified, and radiantly risen. They consider the beauty of the Lord in His salvific, spousal relationship to the church and to the individual soul. Finally they regard the beauty of the sacrament itself as an artwork instituted by Christ and enacted by the church through consecration, adoration, Communion, and charitable service." Astell adds that reflections on Eucharistic beauty reached their climax in the thirteenth century with the institution of the feast of Corpus Christi (19).

church being "spat upon" and thus on the need to "clean her face" evoke elements traditionally associated with Jesus's own passion and suffering on the way to his crucifixion and point to the beauty that is constitutive of a church that imitates Jesus Christ.[36] As Romero says at the very end of the homily, "There is no more beautiful life than the one that embraces the cross of Christ and, from the cross, asks forgiveness for one's self and for others."[37] Those persons listening to his homily who, like Romero, were steeped in Catholic devotional practices would have recognized that the reference to cleaning the face of the church was also a reference to the sixth station of the cross, where tradition has a woman by the name of Veronica cleaning the face of Jesus. Furthermore, the themes of cleaning the face of Jesus and that of the church through reparations for sins are a central theme of devotions to Our Lady of Fatima, whom Romero had evoked in his preparations for the Corpus Christi feast just two weeks before. In that May 29, 1977, homily he had said: "Let us make of our *corpus* an expiation, as the angel taught the children of Fatima: I want to do reparations for those that offend you, I want to love for those that do not love, I want to have faith in you for those who have already lost their faith, and may the blessed sacrament become again the visible soul of our church, of our faith."[38] That Romero would have a devotion to our Lady of Fatima is fitting, since he was born in 1917, the same year that it is believed that Mary appeared at Fatima.

Romero's reflections on the feast of Corpus Christi are an expression of his profound devotion to the sacrament of the Eucharist and a response to its profanation and violation, especially in the church of Aguilares. The homily provides a glimpse into the piety that sustained Romero in prayer as he continued to respond in his new role as archbishop in the midst of an increasingly persecuted church. On Sunday, June 19, 1977, Romero was able to return to Aguilares after the occupation had ended, and the homily and events of that day communicate Romero's widening sacramental horizons and the depth of his own commitment to serve as

---

[36] For example, references to Jesus being spat upon are found in Matthew 27:30, where the Roman soldiers put a crown upon him, spit upon him, and then hit him. Also, according to Matthew 26:67, the Sanhedrin accuse Jesus of blasphemy and spit upon and hit him.

[37] Romero, *Homilías*, June 1, 1977, 137.

[38] Romero, *Homilías*, May 29, 1977, 116.

pastor and protector of the poor and persecuted, even unto death. In some respects his reflections and actions that day became the enfleshment of his devotional insights during the previous month.

"You Are the Image of the Divine One Who Has Been Pierced"

In the homilies that Romero delivered during the month of Aguilares's occupation, he communicated the profound impact that the violation of the sanctuary and the tabernacle had on him, but, in returning to Aguilares, he gazed upon the desecration that had been carried out upon that other constitutive element of the church—the people, particularly the poor and persecuted in whom dwelled the presence of God. The tender tone of his homily is evident from its very beginning, for, instead of using his customary "dear brothers and sisters," he greeted the community as "beloved sons and daughters of Aguilares,"[39] a greeting he did not use in any other homily that year. Then, in one of his most moving statements, he said: "It is left for me to go about picking up the assaults, corpses and all that is left behind by the persecution of the church. Today I have come here to pick up, in this church, in this profaned convent, a destroyed tabernacle but above all a humiliated people, sacrificed indignantly."[40] The rich imagery of Romero's words depicted a pastor whose mission was to go out and gather the wounded and dead in the dangerous wilderness of persecution. Like the Good Samaritan in Luke's parable (Lk 10:25–37), Romero had to risk his own life in order to go near to those whom others had attacked or avoided.[41] However, for the community of Aguilares, El Paisnal, and the surrounding villages who had endured so much, Romero was not only a good Samaritan but a

---

[39] Romero, *Homilías*, June 19, 1977, 149.

[40] Romero, 149. The original Spanish reads: "A mí me toca ir recogiendo atropellos, cadáveres y todo eso que va dejando la persecución de la iglesia. Hoy me toca venir a recoger, en esta iglesia, en este convento profanado, un sagrario destruido y sobre todo un pueblo humillado, sacrificado indignamente."

[41] The scripture readings for that Sunday, June 19, 1977, were Zechariah 12:10–11, Galatians 3:26–29, and Luke 9:18–24. The first reading concerns a prophecy of the pierced one, the second reading addresses the unity of all in Christ, and the gospel reading speaks of discipleship as following Jesus even to the cross.

father and mother seeking out the beloved daughters and sons who had been taken captive and whom he had been prevented from visiting. As he said in his greeting, "I wanted to be with you from the beginning, but I was not allowed."[42] In Romero's brief opening words he referred to the tabernacle and hosts that had concerned him during the previous month and, unexpectedly, he stated that he had come to Aguilares *above all* to pick up "a humiliated people, sacrificed indignantly." In previous homilies, Romero had referred to the human person as the image of God, but in Aguilares he referred to the people as sacrificed, radically uniting their suffering with that of Christ's own suffering. If, on the feast of Corpus Christi, Romero asked his listeners to see in the trampled sacrament of the Eucharist the face of Christ on the cross, now Romero saw in the reality of the community's suffering the sign of the crucifixion. Both the sacrament of the Eucharist and the humiliation and persecution of a people pointed to, revealed, and communicated a God who is preferentially present wherever life is threatened. Although in his opening words Romero referred to Aguilares as sacrificed rather than crucified, the rest of the homily clarified that indeed the sacrifice to which he referred was the event of Christ's own passion.

The persecuted people of Aguilares became for Romero the living image of the suffering and crucified *corpus Christi*—body of Christ. In that day's scripture readings the prophet Zechariah proclaims an oracle of the people of Jerusalem mourning over one who has been pierced,[43] a prophecy that, for John the Evangelist, was fulfilled in Jesus's passion (Jn 19:33–37). In Aguilares those readings take on flesh. Romero proclaims to the community: "You are the image of the Divine One who has been pierced, of which the first reading speaks to us in prophetic and mysterious language, but which represents Jesus nailed on the cross and pierced by a spear; it is the image of all peoples, who like Aguilares, will be pierced, will be violated."[44] In reading scripture through the

---

[42] Romero, *Homilías*, June 19, 1977, 149.

[43] This pierced one of Zechariah 12:10 also finds echo in the suffering servant of Isaiah (52:13—53:12).

[44] Romero, *Homilías*, June 19, 1977, 150. Romero uses the word *ultrajados*, which I have translated as "violated," but one could also translate it as "defiled." Also, the English translation of the homilies has Romero using the past tense: "like Aguilares, have been pierced and violated." I believe the use of the past tense is

wounded reality of Aguilares, Romero gave theological meaning to what had already happened, and the people of Aguilares became part of the signs of the times of what was still to come for El Salvador.[45] Not unlike the event of Jesus's crucifixion, Romero sensed something salvific in the midst of death that led him to say that, in Aguilares, "a holy liberation" had begun, a liberation in which also participated "the many beloved dead—assassinated."[46]

Throughout the homily Romero united the suffering of Aguilares with the suffering of Christ and the church. Among the categories of suffering peoples that he mentioned were the disappeared and those who had fled from the region and did not know what was happening with their family. Of the disappeared he said, "Know my dear brothers and sisters, that before the eyes of God, they are not disappeared, they are very close to the heart of God. . . . For God there are no disappeared."[47] In the only direct reference he makes to the military responsible for the assassinations, rapes, and disappearances, he says, "Violence, wherever it comes from, but above all when it comes from the Armed Forces, who instead of defending the people becomes their violator, is condemned by God and cannot be blessed."[48] With this condemnation, Romero also invited his hearers to find the courage to forgive and free themselves of resentment, hatred, and violence, because, like Christ, all persons have to pick up their cross and entrust their life to the mystery of God, even unto death. Romero crystalized

---

less accurate and is in contrast to the original Spanish that reads: "como Aguilares, serán atravesados, serán ultrajados." For the English, see Romero, *A Prophetic Bishop Speaks to His People*, 162.

[45] On October 30, 1977, Romero preached a homily on the signs of the times. In the introduction to that homily he wrote: "In addition to the readings of scripture, which are the word of God, a Christian who is faithful to that word must also read the signs of the times—contemporary events—to illuminate them with that word." Romero, *Homilías*, October 30, 1977, 421.

[46] Romero, *Homilías*, June 19, 1977, 150.

[47] Romero, 150. In this homily Romero is not yet using the more technical word *desaparecidos* (disappeared) and is still using *perdidos* (lost). However, he is in fact speaking about those disappeared by the repression. A few months later, in his homily for September 11, 1977, he says: "It is a new class of death that has appeared in our Salvadoran society: the disappeared." Romero, *Homilías*, September 11, 1977, 306.

[48] Romero, *Homilías*, June 19, 1977, 151.

this most difficult aspect of discipleship by critiquing a comfortable appropriation of the gospel message:

> Brothers and sisters, I believe that we have mutilated greatly the gospel. We have attempted to live a gospel that is very comfortable, without offering our life, only piety; it has been a gospel that only cheers us up. But here in Aguilares begins a bold movement of a committed gospel. . . . It may lead us to death, but it will surely also lead us to resurrection.[49]

Toward the end of his homily, he asked for the conversion of those who had had the "sacrilegious audacity to touch the blessed sacrament," and who "converted a town into a prison and a place of torture."[50] He prayed for their repentance, that they would have the satisfaction of seeing the one whom they had pierced who could bestow mercy. True to his earlier proclamation that the community of Aguilares had become the image of the Divine One who had been pierced, in Romero's homily, it is difficult to distinguish of whom he is speaking at the end, for the one who bestows mercy appears to be both the crucified One and the crucified ones.[51] Christ and a suffering people become one in sacramental unity.

A Living Sanctuary for the *Corpus Christi*

The liturgy in Aguilares concluded with a Eucharistic procession in the town that enfleshed Romero's call to live an uncomfortable gospel where piety becomes one with the offering of one's life in the following of Jesus. The procession was an opportunity to proclaim visually the consecration of the blessed sacrament in the church and to reconstitute the church as a people who would continue to gather in worship and solidarity, even in the midst of repression. Part of reconstituting the church after the

---

[49] Romero, 152.

[50] Romero, 155.

[51] In Romero's homily it is difficult to ascertain whether in his last reference to the pierced one he is referring only to Christ or to all those who were killed, tortured, violated, and disappeared in Aguilares. See Romero, *A Prophetic Bishop Speaks to His People,* 166.

month of military occupation was the appointment of a new leadership team to accompany the local community.

The team included three Oblate Sisters of the Sacred Heart of Jesus and two Jesuit priests. In attendance that day were many faithful who had traveled from parishes in San Salvador to show their solidarity with the church in Aguilares. Among them was Fr. Jon Sobrino, SJ, who remembers the direct threat that fell upon the community and Romero while carrying the sacrament of the Eucharist in the procession:

> The church filled up completely, but there weren't many from the community itself, a sign of the terror of that month. We never did find out, but people speak of about two hundred who were assassinated, of people tortured, of rapes, and of persons who were disappeared. . . .
>
> At the end of mass Romero invited us to process with the blessed sacrament through the streets, as a reparation for the profanation carried out by the guards. We exited the church singing. There was tremendous heat that day and Monseñor Romero was drenched in sweat under his red pluvial cope. He was carrying the monstrance on high. In front of him, there were hundreds of people. We went around the plaza, singing, praying. The municipal office located in front of the church was filled with guards who were watching us. When we came near, some of them positioned themselves in the middle of the street with their rifles pointed at us. Then more came out. They spread their legs defiantly, with their large boots, and formed a blockade so that we would not pass. Those who were leading the procession did not move, and then those behind them stopped as well. The procession came to a stop. Face to face, us and their rifles. When everyone was completely still, we turned our gaze to Monseñor who was last. He raised the monstrance higher and said in a loud voice so that all would hear: Adelante!—Onward!
>
> So we advanced toward the soldiers, little by little, and they began to retreat, also little by little. We toward them, and they moving back. Then toward their barracks. Ultimately, they lowered their rifles and let us pass.

From that day, and like that day, in any important event that took place in El Salvador, either to follow him or to persecute him, it was always necessary to cast one's gaze upon Monseñor Romero.[52]

Jon Sobrino's recollection of the defining encounter between the worshipping community and the armed soldiers captures the reality in which Romero's devotion to the sacrament of the Eucharist took on flesh in the community. Although by that time Romero had picked up many bodies left behind by the military, starting with his own friend Rutilio Grande in that very church three months before, the encounter on June 19, perhaps for the first time, placed him, his people, and the sacrament of the Eucharistic together as one in the crosshairs of soldiers' rifles. The desecration of the sacrament of the Eucharist that had taken place a month before was on the verge of happening again, and this time its desecration would be inseparable from the desecration of the body of Christ—the *corpus Christi*—that was also the community. Romero's reflections from that prior month—that the church loves by dying with those who are persecuted, that it was the bishop's duty to protect the signs of the church, that the church's beauty was manifest in its fidelity to Christ even unto the cross, that the church had been too comfortable with pious devotions and sacraments that were divorced from concrete historical commitment—all of this was recapitulated in the silent stillness of the moment, when members of the worshipping community cast their gaze upon their pastor. The community could have stayed still, afraid, knowing that too much blood had already been shed in Aguilares, but in lifting higher the sacrament of the Eucharist, in one simple gesture, Romero communicated the presence of the One who journeyed with them—whose journey they were all called to follow. In that crucible, the people of Aguilares and those who had come from other communities came to know firsthand that Romero was indeed their companion and intercessor, and Romero came to know that these were his people, who entrusted him with their lives and for whom he was responsible unto death. He became a refuge for them, a living sanctuary, and they be-

---

[52] María López Vigil, *Monseñor Romero: Piezas para un Retrato* (San Salvador: UCA Editores, 2011), 160–61. Translation my own.

came his sacrament, the *corpus Christi* whose life he had to protect, each supporting the other in the long journey of persecution that lay ahead.

Romero's faith led him to scan the signs of the times constantly for the presence of God in his midst. In his first few months as archbishop, the events in Aguilares and El Paisnal became a sacramental encounter with a poor and persecuted people whose suffering revealed the suffering body of Christ in history. His reflections on the presence of Christ in the sacrament of the Eucharist were increasingly united to the presence of Christ in the poor—the people of God who are also the true and real body of Christ. To protect the poor, to become a sanctuary for the persecuted, was also to become a sanctuary for the body of Christ.

7

Church as Sanctuary

Refuge, Healing, Holiness, and Salvation

The Latin American struggle to become a church that accompanies the poor in their persecution as they attempt to survive in the shadow of multiple forms of institutionalized violence has left an indelible mark upon the universal church's identity. However, while the challenge of becoming a church of the poor becomes ever clearer, it also becomes more complex, for new contours to the category of poverty emerge through the modern world's production of insignificant and disposable subjects who are essentially considered nonpersons. Pope John XXIII's hope for a church of all, but especially a church of the poor, is still in many ways "a dream deferred."[1] Like the poet, one must continue to ask what happens to a dream deferred. Rutilio Grande, Óscar Romero, Maura Clarke, Ita Ford, Dorothy Kazel, Jean Donovan, and countless others were killed for their work of incarnating this dream into reality in El Salvador, and the dream persists as a holy vision for the church in Latin America and across the world.[2]

Cardinal Juan Landázuri's statement at the opening of the 1968 Medellín conference still echoes today as the only credible answer the church can provide: "For a questioning world we have only one answer: we are

---

[1] Langston Hughes, "Harlem," in *Selected Poems of Langston Hughes* (New York: Vintage Books, 1990), 268.

[2] Pope Francis increasingly invites the church to dream and have visions, perhaps most succinctly in his 2021 message for migrants and refugees where he speaks of a new "we" that transforms the borders of the church and the world. See Francis, "Message of His Holiness Pope Francis for the 107th World Day of Migrants and Refugees 2021," September 26, 2021.

witnesses to love."[3] This is the same echo that reverberates at the core of Latin American liberation theology and that gives rise to what Gustavo Gutiérrez calls a "lacerating" question: "How to say to the poor person, to the oppressed person, to the insignificant person, God loves you?"[4] To further specify Gutiérrez's question: How to say to displaced persons who are forced to flee their homes, culture, and legal existence in order to survive and who are then persecuted in other countries that God indeed loves them and desires the fullness of their lives? For the national security state these persons are an illegal and criminal entity, but for the church they are bearers of a fundamental question of faith: "Who do you say that I am?" (Mt 16:15). This is the question Jesus asked his disciples, and this is the question that displaced and persecuted persons also place before the church through their embodied presence. In the United States the challenge of persons who continue to arrive at the country's borders, fleeing violence and seeking life, and those whose unauthorized existence within the country makes them a target for persecution, is one that the church cannot sidestep without becoming complicit in their persecution.

Taking into account all that has been presented in Parts I and II of this book, and bringing together the experience and insights of the 1980s sanctuary ministry, the long history of refuge in the church, the sacramental ecclesiology of Vatican II and Medellín, and theological insights from Latin America, this chapter develops four interrelated categories that mark the church as sanctuary and that can aid in the reconstitution of this ecclesial tradition in our age of forced displacement. To rebuild the church as a sanctuary for the poor and persecuted is to make of it a site of refuge, of healing, of holiness, and of salvation. In our contemporary context, especially in the United States, the practice of *refuge* is a means of resisting violence and overcoming multiple types of distance that undergird lethal processes of othering that prevent the possibility of communion. Refuge gives way to a communal sphere for *healing* the traumatic wounds of displacement and insecurity and the sense of voicelessness inflicted by violence. Theologically, refuge and healing enact *holiness* by bearing witness to the Holy One whose presence dwells

---

[3] Juan Landázuri Ricketts, "Inaugural Address," *The Church in the Present-Day Transformation of Latin America in the Light of the Council*, vol. 1 (Washington, DC: United States Catholic Conference, 1970), 51.

[4] Gustavo Gutiérrez, *The Density of the Present* (Maryknoll, NY: Orbis Books, 1999), 139.

with those whose life is threatened and whom the church is called to accompany in its own journey of conversion. Last, the church embodies its fundamental task of making *salvation* present as a historical reality through the transformation of structures that bring an early death to whole sectors of humanity. These four categories are distilled from the historical practice of sanctuary and from the creative and constructive potential embedded within this tradition that has been tragically marginalized within the church. At its heart, sanctuary is a communal witness to love. In a world dehumanized by violence, sanctuary is a constitutive mark of ecclesial existence. Sanctuary is salvific not only for those whose life is threatened but for the church itself.

Refuge from Violence

The story of persons seeking refuge in their own Roman Catholic Church and being rejected repeats itself across the country. For example, in 2017, as the US government continued to scale up Immigration and Customs Enforcement (ICE) raids within the United States, Carmela Hernandez, a Roman Catholic woman, along with her children, went knocking at dozens of churches seeking refuge.[5] Like thousands of other families, their asylum claims had been denied by the US government, and ICE could "round them up" at any moment. The family left Mexico in 2015 after one relative was decapitated, another shot in the head, and after she and her children became targets of extortion. The Roman Catholic diocese in which they lived did not allow parishes to provide sanctuary, even if the parish discerned that they were being called to do so, but the family finally found refuge at a historically African American Episcopal church and then in a Mennonite church, where she and her four children were protected. The family remained in sanctuary for over three years until their case was no longer a priority for the government's deportation agencies.[6]

---

[5] Alice Speri, "After Going from Church to Church Seeking Help, a Mexican Family Finds Sanctuary in Philadelphia," *The Intercept* online, December 25, 2017.

[6] Jeff Gammage, "Churches Protected Dozens of Families under Trump. Now That They're Leaving, Is Sanctuary Over?," *Philadelphia Inquirer* online, March 15, 2021.

In 2016, when I was conducting research with faith communities in southern Arizona, a Roman Catholic woman, for whom I will use the pseudonym Luz, received an order of deportation and sought refuge in her own parish before ICE could apprehend and deport her. Deportation would have meant that she would have attempted to cross back into the United States through the deadly desert wilderness to reunite with her family. Supplication to her parish leadership for assistance and protection yielded no support. However, she found a mainline Protestant church that was willing to give her refuge, and she remained there for over a year. However, in addition to the toxic stress of living under the constant threat of deportation, Luz was experiencing a profound spiritual displacement while in sanctuary. Since she was not able to leave the property of the church that had given her protection without risking arrest by ICE, Luz was fully immersed and worshipping in a tradition that she felt was not her own. The spiritual formation she had received at her Roman Catholic parish led her to ask me one morning: "Do you think I'm sinning by being here? Is God punishing me?"[7] The piercing simplicity and sincerity of her theological questions raises a plethora of further questions about what is communicated when churches refuse to provide refuge to those seeking protection from government persecution. It is essential to ask whether church leadership and faith communities are sufficiently aware of the lived spiritual agony of families who experience abandonment in times of critical need. The fear of involvement with or indifference to the future of such "unauthorized" persons essentially communicates punishment to those who are already "bowed down," to quote Psalm 146. The communication of such punishment, whether intended or not, makes of these churches an extension of the government's efforts to brand such individuals as criminals and ultimately as nonpersons whose enfleshed existence, but juridical nonexistence, is an aberration to the nation-state's version of law and order that privileges some while disposing of others.

If sanctuary is to be a pillar of ecclesial identity, and more important, a visible sign of the church's sacramental existence that effectively communicates the salvific presence of God in history, the church has no option but to be a community and place of refuge. Those who, for the government, are punishable criminals because they arrived at the borderlands

---

[7] Conversation with author, June 2016.

of the United States seeking life without permission or even manage to make a living in the United States without detection, are, theologically speaking, bearers of God in their existence as poor, displaced, and persecuted persons. Their ecclesial challenge is not simply for more social programs that do not affect the church's very structures, culture, or self-understanding.[8] The church is being invited into a radical transformation, a transfiguration of what it means to be church, and especially a church of the poor in the United States. As Gustavo Gutiérrez has written:

> As a sacramental community the Church should signify in its own internal structure the salvation whose fulfillment it announces. Its organization ought to serve this task. A sign should be clear and understandable. If we conceive of the Church as a sacrament of the salvation of the world, then it has all the more obligation to manifest in its visible structures the message that it bears.[9]

The community of the church must constantly ask itself whether its policies and structures effectively communicate salvation to those seeking refuge from violence and death.

The communal embodiment of refuge is a manifestation of liberation from historical forces of sin. Directly resisting the government's attempts to deport the ten to eleven million unauthorized persons who now live in the United States by providing them sanctuary from their persecution is a means of effectively witnessing against the structural sin that seeks to consume their lives. The sociopolitical and transnational realities that forced vast numbers of Salvadorans and other Central Americans to flee wars and journey north in the 1980s and 1990s were the result of a history of US domination and subjugation of the region, and the effects of that history of violence continue to this day. But if refuge is not to be reduced simply to a political countermeasure, either by supporters or detractors of sanctuary practices, then it is essential to grasp that the

---

[8] In *Evangelii Gaudium* (2013), Pope Francis invites a missionary renewal that that is "capable of transforming everything, so that the Church's customs, ways of doing things, times and schedules, language and structures can be suitably channeled for the evangelization of today's world rather than for her self-preservation" (no. 27).

[9] Gustavo Gutiérrez, *A Theology of Liberation* (Maryknoll, NY: Orbis Books, 1988), 147.

church is always called to be a sign of God's reign in history and that, through the displaced and persecuted "others," comes the presence of the incarnate God, seeking sanctuary.

God is preferentially mediated by "unauthorized" persons seeking refuge, who, through their very presence, recall for the church its own call. Gutiérrez clarifies:

> The church does not authentically attain consciousness of itself except in the perception of [the] total presence of Christ and his Spirit in humanity. The mediation of the consciousness of the "other"—of the world in which this presence occurs—is the indispensable precondition of its own consciousness as a community-sign.[10]

For the church to recognize authentically the depth of its own liberating vocation, it must recognize the depth and density of the other who bears God and who is borne by God in the struggle for life. This entails learning to read the signs of the times in the persons who are literally knocking on the church's doors seeking refuge.[11] The church's own process of coming to know itself passes through the mystery of the other who is a sacrament of God's presence in humanity regardless of whether this person or community has any formal relation to the church. As emphasized in previous chapters, the work of Christ and the Spirit overflows the formal boundaries of the church. In the midst of a suffering humanity the church is called to live its salvific nature and mission. The practice of refuge and sanctuary literally becomes a means for a suffering world, in which God is active, to encounter the church and for the church to be transformed and to come to know itself through the encounter. In reflecting on the church as a sacrament, Gutiérrez adds that "the Church must allow itself to be inhabited and evangelized by the world."[12] The point is not to demarcate one space apart from another in a dualistic manner, but to make historically present the incarnate love of God in particular places through the protection of the life of persons and communities whom the government desires to eliminate from its body

---

[10] Gutiérrez, 147.

[11] *Gaudium et Spes*, nos. 4, 11.

[12] Gutiérrez, *A Theology of Liberation,* 147.

politic.[13] Refuge is an expression of the church's nature and mission in and for the world it inhabits.

The dynamism of the church being inhabited and evangelized by the world that it inhabits bears the potential for overcoming cycles of deadly violence that are perpetuated by enforced distance between peoples. To better understand how distance and killing are intertwined, let me turn to the training that many law-enforcement officers receive in the United States. In his writings focused on the psychological and sociological processes of killing in combat,[14] retired lieutenant colonel Dave Grossman argues that physical and emotional distance, the latter of which is constituted by cultural, moral, and social distance, facilitates the ability to kill.[15] Grossman's "warrior" approach generates controversy, and aspects of his scholarship have been questioned,[16] but his work, nonetheless, has been widely used to train and mentally condition US military and law-enforcement officers.[17] It will become clear that providing refuge can be a means of resisting the very kinds of distance and conditioning upon which societal killing is structured. Unless the church takes an honest assessment of the ways in which it is already being formed to participate in killing, even if indirectly by becoming conditioned to the killing of others, it cannot truly comprehend the transformative power of refuge.

According to Grossman, the greater the physical distance between opponents in combat, the easier it is to deny the humanity of the other. He explains that artillery crews, bomber crews, naval gunners, and those who engage in maximum-range types of killing are protected by physical distance from cognitively seeing those they are killing, which eliminates,

---

[13] For an insightful historical analysis of the metaphor of the body politic conceived as an ideal white body and its relation to non-white immigrant communities who cause indigestion and must be eliminated from the nation-state's borders, see K. C. Councilor, "Feeding the Body Politic: Metaphors of Digestion in Progressive Era US Immigration Discourse," *Communication and Critical/Cultural Studies* 14, no. 2 (2017): 139–57.

[14] Dave Grossman, *On Killing: The Psychological Cost of Learning to Kill in War and Society* (New York: Back Bay Books, 1995).

[15] Grossman. See especially section VIII, "Killing in America: What Are We Doing to Our Children?" 301–36.

[16] Max Hauptman, "'Warrior Mindset' Police Training Proliferated. Then, High-Profile Deaths Put It under Scrutiny," *Washington Post* online, August 12, 2021.

[17] For a soldier's assessment of this kind of conditioning, see Timothy Kudo, "How We Learned to Kill," *New York Times* online, February 27, 2015.

or at least minimizes, the possibility of trauma associated with this kind of killing.[18] It is not simply a matter of not visually seeing the other, but in some sense it is a matter of making the other cognitively nonexistent. This is similar to Bernard Lonergan's notion of bias or scotosis that results in a blind spot, an inability to recognize others or to allow the reality of others to interrupt and question one's understanding or lack thereof.[19] As physical distance is bridged, it becomes more difficult to maintain emotional distance. At mid-range combat, where a soldier can engage in rifle fire without being able to see or hear the wounds and pain of the other, there is a combination of both euphoria and remorse as the soldier attempts to accept, psychologically integrate, or deny the kill.[20] At close range the "undeniable certainty of responsibility on the part of the killer," as Grossman writes, makes emotional distance difficult and can result in psychological trauma and guilt.[21] Denying the humanity of the other, whom one can see and hear at close range, is increasingly difficult. And yet, despite the difficulty, killing is facilitated by constructing cultural, moral, and social distance that permits soldiers or law-enforcement officers to practically deny the humanity of the other.[22]

Cultural distance is built upon key factors such as racial and ethnic differences, which undergird a logic of dehumanization. The "other" is fundamentally framed as inferior in order to generate dissimilarity that overcomes a resistance to killing. Grossman writes, "It is so much

---

[18] Grossman, *On Killing*, 108. With the use of drones to kill, the physical and cognitive distance takes on a new level as these processes mirror videogame play.

[19] See Louis Roy, *Engaging the Thought of Bernard Lonergan* (Montreal: McGill-Queen's University Press, 2016), 218–20; Shawn Copeland, *Enfleshing Freedom: Body, Race, and Being* (Minneapolis: Fortress Press, 2009), 13–15. Merging Lonergan's notion of bias and blindspot with race, Copeland writes: "A white racially bias-induced horizon defines, censors, controls, and segregates different, other, non-white bodies. Ordinarily these bodies are 'invisible' in the processes of historical, cultural, and social creativity and representation, but should these non-white bodies step 'out of place,' they are subordinated literally to surveillance, inspection, discrimination, assessment, and containment."

[20] Grossman, *On Killing*, 112.

[21] Grossman, 114.

[22] Grossman describes the mechanisms that soldiers use to negotiate the humanity of the other at close range. For example, he argues that a hood or blindfold over the victim can protect the psychological health of the executioner, or, that killing from behind so as not to see the face and eyes of the other aids in reconciling oneself with the act of killing. Grossman, 128.

easier to kill someone if they look distinctly different from you."[23] An example of this cultural distance is Grossman's claim that 44 percent of US soldiers in WWII expressed a desire to kill a Japanese soldier, whereas only 6 percent expressed such a desire to kill German soldiers.[24] Within US Border Patrol culture the creation of cultural distance can happen through categorization of those apprehended as either Mexicans or OTM's—"other than Mexicans"—through their official use of the term *alien,* or in use of phrases like "round them up," which construes others as livestock to be corralled. During the administration of Donald Trump, the creation of cultural distance based upon racial, ethnic, and religious difference gave rise to the proliferation of armed vigilante white supremacy hate groups near the US-Mexico border.[25]

Moral distance entails the clearer construction of the other as enemy and the condemnation of the enemy's cause and the legitimation of one's own. Grossman argues that, with moral distance, the enemy is still considered human and "killing him is an act of justice rather than the extermination that is often motivated by cultural distance."[26] The believed superiority of one's position sanctions the punishment or vengeance upon the other (person, community, nation), who is made into a criminal. Grossman explains that this kind of distance is particularly operative in law-enforcement violence (for example, police, Border Patrol) or within civil wars, where it can be more difficult to overcome the similarities between opponents.[27] The criminalization of persons who cross into the United States without authorization and the hyper-militarization of the country's borders can be seen as a manifestation of the construction of moral distance that justifies appropriate punishment in order to safeguard notions of goodness, law, and order. The notion of good citizenship depends on creating moral distance from those others who break the law, who bear guilt, and who both deserve and must be met with violence.

---

[23] Grossman, 161.

[24] Grossman, 162.

[25] For an analysis of the intersection of white supremacy ideology and the US-Mexico border region and Chicana/o communities, see Lee Bebout, *Whiteness on the Border: Mapping the US Racial Imagination in Brown and White* (New York: New York University Press, 2016).

[26] Grossman, *On Killing,* 165.

[27] Grossman, 166.

Lastly, social distance points to the hierarchical and stratified conditions of society that permit emotional dissociation between social classes. Within military and law-enforcement culture, strict hierarchical structures serve as a means of generating obedience so that soldiers can simply carry out orders from superiors. Within broader society, Grossman argues, social distance is the "impact of a lifetime of viewing a particular class as less than human."[28] Combined with cultural and moral distance, it is not difficult to understand how being a poor and displaced person of color, without authorization to be in the country, further generates an identity stripped of humanity, of personhood, or of having a life worthy of protection rather than violence and persecution. In speaking of the growing allure of violence in US society, especially through media, Grossman writes:

> We, as a society, have become systematically desensitized to the pain and suffering of others. . . . We are reaching that stage of desensitization at which the inflicting of pain and suffering has become a source of entertainment: vicarious pleasure rather than revulsion. We are learning to kill, and we are learning to like it.[29]

While there may be truth in such a statement, altering one's behavior requires more than knowing what one is becoming. In fact, having greater clarity about the inner workings of processes of othering has been tragically used to refine society's capacity to kill. Grossman's own workshops to law-enforcement agencies across the country contribute to the ongoing militarization of policing as they internalize distancing mechanisms that allow them to kill with greater ease. Tragically, Grossman's response to what he perceives as society's appetite for killing is to become even better at killing before you are killed. Replicating the cycle of violence that immunizes society to the suffering of others and that justifies killing is, however, one of the most dangerous threats to being human and to humanity.

Based on these insights into the psychological processes that are operative among the military and law-enforcement communities, including Border Patrol and ICE agents, I suggest that the act of providing refuge

---

[28] Grossman, 188.
[29] Grossman, 315.

is a form of resistance to distance-generating mechanisms that aid in the execution of societal violence and killing, especially of persons who are already regarded as "others." Refuge has the capacity to interrupt physical and emotional distance and can allow local communities to grow near to the threatened humanity of displaced and persecuted persons. In order to conceive of refuge as bearing such possibilities, it is important to emphasize that refuge is constituted by a community and that it is not enough simply to open the doors of a church building. Without the people who constitute the church through the practice of witnessing to God's presence as they accompany those whose humanity is threatened, there is no church sanctuary. The provision of refuge itself does not automatically overcome the various types of distancing mechanisms that may already distort the church's own thinking about sanctuary seekers, but the act itself opens unforeseen possibilities. If Gutiérrez is correct that the other mediates for the church its own consciousness as a community sign, that the other is the means for the church to be what it is called to become, then the sanctuary seeker bears the possibility not only of evangelizing the church through the truth of his or her existence, but of unleashing a creative grace that arises in the sustained encounter across difference.

Roman Catholic bishops have not sufficiently considered the power of sanctuary to interrupt the church's own complicity in societal processes of dehumanization that normalize deportation even to war zones. Instead, ecclesiastical leaders have focused on the ways that sanctuary in churches may give false hope to those who take refuge. Cardinal Wuerl, for example, has stated:

> When we use the word *sanctuary*, we have to be very careful that we're not holding out false hope. We wouldn't want to say, "Stay here, we'll protect you," . . . With separation of church and state, the church really does not have the right to say, "You come in this building and the law doesn't apply to you." But we do want to say we'll be a voice for you.[30]

The gift that the church receives from the sanctuary seeker who receives refuge, however, is missing from his assessment: the capacity to come

---

[30] Julie Zauzmer, "Cardinal Wuerl Voices Catholic Support for Immigrants But Urges Caution about Sanctuary Churches," *Washington Post* online, March 2, 2017.

face to face with a world beyond the church's control, which, in its very alterity, can liberate the church from its scotosis, from its incapacity to see beyond the ways it has been conditioned by Anglo-American society to reject who and what is rendered unauthorized and different.

Cardinal Wuerl is correct in pointing out that there is no guarantee that ICE agents will not enter a church building to remove a person who has been given sanctuary by the local community. As shown in Chapter 3, throughout history refuge in a church has never been a permanent or static solution to the underlying conditions that generate the need for refuge, and exactly this dynamic nature of church refuge makes it a powerfully creative response to situations of violence and persecution. As for Cardinal Wuerl's pairing of refuge with false hope, it is best to try to see church sanctuary from the perspective of those who seek it. Persons who have lived in the United States without documents, who must navigate life everyday knowing that others see them as illegal and hunt them down because they are blinded to their fundamental humanity, who bear in their bodies the toxic stress that comes with endless permutations of a sense of impermanence—such persons know very clearly that ICE can come into any church building to drag them out. More important, however, they know in the depths of their being the difference that refuge in a church community can make in their attempt to survive.

Refuge is not false hope. Rather, refuge lays the foundation for hope as persons encounter each other across difference, bridging cultural, moral, and social distance. During the 1980s sanctuary ministry Jim Corbett wrote:

> Hypnotized by the modern state's destructive powers, we often ignore our own empowerment and choose instead to be moralizing bystanders, but no amount of preaching at a superpower will convert it into a Covenant people. . . . Communion with the violated occurs at the person-to-person local community level.[31]

A community of refuge builds capacity for hope and enacts hope in history, aware that the source of such hope always exceeds the bounds

---

[31] Jim Corbett, *The Sanctuary Church* (Wallingford, PA: Pendle Hill Publications, 1986), 14–15.

of history and is a creative response whose ultimate impact cannot be predetermined. Karl Rahner's comments on the church's development and humanitarian work, and the belief that present actions can have a profound effect on an unforeseen future, are fitting in this context:

> Anyone who really has a genuine eschatological hope and wants to realize it can do so only by acquiring a real receptivity for an open future in the present world. . . . Only someone who is prepared here for change and experiment—which, despite all necessary planning, can never be adequately calculated in advance—can be a hoping Christian, whose hope also decides his eternal salvation.[32]

The act and risk of providing refuge sets in motion dynamics that, as Rahner says, cannot be calculated in advance but that open the present to a hoped-for future. That future, while unknown, has a greater possibility of being more humanizing because a community chooses to respond to the mystery of persons who implicitly or explicitly invoke the mercy of God in their attempts to find refuge in the church.[33] Through them, the church itself can receive mercy.

Sanctuary is constructed by each local community that like living stones, lives into the theological conviction of being a people gathered in faith, hope, and love, who cannot become bystanders to the lives of the poor, displaced, and persecuted in their midst. In the late 1980s, when asked to reflect on the US sanctuary movement in relation to El Salvador, Jon Sobrino wrote that "movements such as sanctuary are needed so that the world in its totality may not slip even further down the slope of dehumanization, but take the road to humanization."[34] In the next section, I explore the humanizing possibilities, particularly in

---

[32] Karl Rahner, "Theological Justification of the Church's Development Work," in *Concern for the Church: Theological Investigations XX* (New York: Crossroad, 1981), 72.

[33] As explained in Chapter 3, in the earliest reference to those seeking protection in a church the bishops at the Council of Serdica in the year 343 speak of sanctuary as "the mercy of the church." Canon 8 of this council sets forth the duty of a bishop to intercede for those at risk of banishment, a form of what we now call deportation. See Hamilton Hess, *The Early Development of Canon Law and the Council of Serdica* (Oxford: Oxford University Press, 2002), 204.

[34] Jon Sobrino, "Sanctuary: A Theological Analysis," *CrossCurrents* 38 (1988): 170.

Healing of Wounds

Rev. Dr. Davie Napier, a Hebrew Bible scholar involved in the 1980s sanctuary movement, writes:

> My little paperback Webster's, although published only a few months ago, does not include "our" understanding of sanctuary. Its two-part definition reads "(1) a sacred place, as a church, temple, or mosque; and (2) a place giving refuge or asylum." We know that it is more than a place. We believe sanctuary is a series of related acts, or even only gestures of healing, in a context of incomprehensibly monumental wounds in the corporate body and flesh and mind and spirit of countries and barrios, human communities and families—especially for us now, in Central America.[35]

Refuge for and with persons who have fled violence and who live terrorized by the threat of deportation can transform the church into a sign and instrument of healing in the midst of seemingly incurable violence. As was shown in Part I, sanctuary in the borderlands was conceived as creating the possibility for healing social and ecclesial divisions through diverse communities in the United States and across the American continent, encountering one another and becoming interwoven in communion through solidarity. Healing the body of humanity, and thus the flesh of the church as well, entails learning to attend to the wounds of displaced persons who bear the experience of violence from the place of origin, from the dehumanizing journey north, and from living within a US body politic that seeks to expel them as refuse.

A few years ago, while conducting research at a shelter for deported persons in Nogales, Mexico, I met Pedro (a pseudonym).[36] He was a young man in his late twenties, originally from southern Mexico, who

---

[35] Davie Napier, "Hebraic Concepts of Sanctuary and Law," in *Sanctuary: A Resource Guide for Understanding and Participating in the Central American Refugees' Struggle* (San Francisco: Harper and Row Publishers, 1985), 33.

[36] Conversation with author, May 2016.

had been living in California for many years before he was deported. A few days before I met him, he had attempted to cross back into the United States without success. When I asked him about his experience of crossing the border, he shared a narrative that illuminates the wounds of the journey north. Pedro told me that as he was walking alone through the wilderness of the Sonoran Desert, he saw a teenager lying under a mesquite tree where it was a little shady. He went over, tired and thirsty, and sat there for a few minutes to rest. As he sat, he said "hola" to the teenager. There was no response, so he sat quietly. After a few minutes, Pedro told him that they should get going, and reached over to nudge him to wake up, only to realize that the teenager was already dead. Terrorized, Pedro got up quickly and kept walking. Later that day he came across a second body—a man, bloated from the heat, decomposing, with a stench that filled the air. Not far from there, he encountered the remains of a third person who was only bones, already past decomposition.

As Pedro and I sat quietly that afternoon, surrounded by the memory and the presence of the three *desconocidos*—unknown persons—Pedro added in a solemn tone, "Being so close to death, it does something to you." While Pedro's story reveals the kinds of possibly traumatic events that are encountered by individual persons on the journey, I suggest that, based on the sheer number of such stories one finds at the borderlands, in neighborhoods across the United States, and silently within the church, the "incomprehensibly monumental wounds," to use Rev. Napier's words, that are generated by forced displacement mark us all. We must expand our ecclesial imagination and ask more explicitly how the church can be a means of social and communal healing in an age of forced displacement.

The Casas del Migrante (homes of the migrant) that currently exist from Central America up to the US-Mexico border, which provide physical refuge to displaced persons and a relational and pastoral encounter in what can be a profoundly disorienting journey, are testaments to the creative possibilities of ecclesial communities.[37] Some of these Casas del Migrante began in the 1980s. They worked closely with the sanctuary ministry of the borderlands to develop "evasion services" that could

---

[37] For example, the Casas del Migrante run by the Scalabrini Missionaries extend from El Salvador to Northern Mexico. For more information, see scalabriniani.org.

transport persons from Central America to the US network of church communities practicing sanctuary.

The power of providing refuge for persons seeking protection and the communal encounter that takes place through sanctuary open ways for engaging the traumatic stress that marks the life of millions of unauthorized persons in the United States who live with the constant threat of deportation. Dr. Bessel Van der Kolk, a well-known trauma specialist, writes that "study after study shows that having a good support network constitutes the single most powerful protection against becoming traumatized. . . . Our attachment bonds are our greatest protection against threat."[38] Yet, as ICE continues to apprehend, incarcerate, and deport heads of family, leaving behind children who are US citizens, profound intergenerational wounds are being inflicted upon the health of communities.[39]

National health analyses of the United States have examined the impact that living under such threat has on persons at risk of deportation, especially on children who risk losing their primary support networks. In the midst of such daily uncertainty about the future, it is not uncommon for one neighbor to ask another if it is possible for them temporarily to watch over their left-behind children in case they are suddenly disappeared through deportation. In addition to the toxic stress of parents who fear deportation, children also experience psychosomatic symptoms, which, according to one health analysis of immigrant communities, can include "headaches, stomachaches, nausea, and vomiting . . . anxiety, having panic attacks, displaying symptoms of depression, and/or expressing an overall loss of hope for the future."[40] In Sweden such symptoms brought about by the anxiety of deportation have even led hundreds of

---

[38] Bessel Van der Kolk, *The Body Keeps the Score: Brain, Mind, and Body in the Healing of Trauma* (New York: Penguin Books, 2014), 212. At the core of Van der Kolk's work is the argument that traumatic experiences and toxic stress lodge themselves in the body even when the mind refuses to acknowledge the wounds, and thus that the possibilities for healing also take place through the body in addition to the mind and soul. For insights into how community can be part of the healing process, see chapter 13 of his book.

[39] See Luis H. Zayas, *Forgotten Citizens: Deportation, Children, and the Making of American Exiles and Orphans* (New York: Oxford University Press, 2015).

[40] Samantha Artiga and Petry Ubri, *Living in an Immigrant Family in America: How Fear and Toxic Stress Are Affecting Daily Life, Well-Being, and Health*, Henry J. Kaiser Family Foundation online, December 2017, 12.

refugee children to become unconscious for weeks, months, and years, giving rise to a new medical condition called resignation syndrome.[41] This condition is described as a "depressive onset [that] is followed by gradual withdrawal progressing via stupor into a state that prompts tube feeding and is characterised by failure to respond even to painful stimuli."[42] In the past few years, the syndrome has spread to the island of Nauru—Australia's offshore asylum center—where refugees and asylum seekers may spend years in conditions that have generated a mental health crisis.[43] Comparisons have been made between asylum seekers exhibiting resignation syndrome and concentration camp detainees whose loss of hope for the future also manifested itself in psychosomatic withdrawal.[44] Neurologist Dr. Suzanne O'Sullivan, who studies psychosomatic illnesses, writes with great simplicity: "The cure for resignation syndrome is to offer the child asylum. . . . Resignation syndrome is a language of distress."[45] Without question, living under the threat of deportation adversely affects the health of families, and the effect of the deportation of one person has ripple effects upon whole communities and across generations. In the midst of such wounding contexts the church has a unique potential for developing a response that contributes to a process of rehumanization and healing, especially at an interpersonal communal level.

---

[41] Rachel Aviv, "The Trauma of Facing Deportation," *New Yorker*, April 3, 2017; see also the Oscar-nominated documentary *Life Overtakes Me* (2019), which examines this phenomenon.

[42] Karl Sallin et al., "Resignation Syndrome: Catatonia? Culture Bound?" *Frontiers in Behavioral Neuroscience* 10, no. 7 (2016): 1.

[43] According to a report by *Medecins Sans Frontieres*, 60 percent of refugees and asylum seekers they treated at Nauru had suicidal thoughts and 30 percent had attempted suicide. Medecins Sans Frontieres, *Indefinite Despair: The Tragic Mental Health Consequences of Offshore Processing on Nauru*, Medecins Sans Frontieres online report, December 2, 2018, 5.

[44] See Sandra P. Thomas, "Resignation Syndrome: Is It a New Phenomenon or Is It Catatonia?" *Issues in Mental Health Nursing* 38, no. 7 (2017): 531–32. For more on the term *Muselmann* that was pejoratively used in concentration camps to refer to persons who were living on the border between life and death, see Manuela Consonni, "Primo Levi, Robert Antelme, and the Body of the Muselmann," *Journal of Literature and the History of Ideas* 7, no. 2 (2009): esp. 246–48.

[45] Suzanne O'Sullivan, "The Healthy Child Who Wouldn't Wake Up: The Strange Truth of 'Mystery Illnesses,'" *The Guardian* online, April 12, 2021. See also Suzanne O'Sullivan, *The Sleeping Beauties: And Other Stories of Mystery Illness* (Basingstoke, UK: Picador, 2021).

Before I explore more directly the possibilities for healing embedded within sanctuary practices, I want to return to a paradigmatic event in Óscar Romero's life as archbishop of El Salvador that was presented in the previous chapter, for it captures the humanizing power of entering into communion with the persecuted. There, I narrated the experience of the community of Aguilares, which in 1977 was under military occupation for a month. When Romero was finally allowed to visit the community, his concern for the desecrated body of Christ present in the Eucharist that had been shot and stomped upon by the soldiers was refocused on the desecration of the body of Christ present in the poor of Aguilares, who had been turned into "a humiliated people, sacrificed indignantly."[46] Romero's words provide a keen insight into the social control mechanisms that were operative in the military's actions. The military occupation was a tactic of humiliation that sought to make invisible the humanity of the people to subdue them into obedience.[47] That the military named the occupation Operation Rutilio further highlights the purposeful goal of inverting the conscientization and liberation that Rutilio Grande and the church of Aguilares had been developing years prior.

By shooting at the tabernacle, stepping on the communion hosts, and using the church building as barracks, the military was colonizing

---

[46] Óscar Romero, *Homilías*, vol. 1 (San Salvador: UCA Editores, 2005), June 19, 1977, 149.

[47] In examining the relationship between political theory and humiliation, Paul Saurette provides examples of contemporary tactics of humiliation. For example, when he was sheriff, Joe Arpaio of Arizona forced inmates (many of them immigrants) to wear pink underwear in an attempt to undercut their notions of masculinity. Saurette writes that "Arpaio clearly believes not only that *we can* humiliate people into obedience—but that *we should*." Paul Saurette, *The Kantian Imperative: Humiliation, Common Sense, Politics* (Toronto: University of Toronto Press, 2005), 7; William Ian Miller points out a paradox inherent in acts of humiliation if they are to serve their intended effect: "There is a paradox in the torturer's making someone feel humiliated. He must make sure that the victims continue to retain an image of themselves as worthy of respect, because the feeling of humiliation depends on some part of the self's ability to see things with an un-degraded sensibility." William Ian Miller, *Humiliation: And Other Essays on Honor, Social Discomfort, and Violence* (Ithaca, NY: Cornell University Press, 1993), 166. For other analyses on the role of humiliation in politics and society, see Aviahai Margalit, *The Decent Society* (Cambridge, MA: Harvard University Press, 1996); Evelin Gerda Lindner, "Humiliation and the Human Condition: Mapping a Minefield," *Human Rights Review* 2, no. 2 (2001): 46–63.

and placing under its control the social, cultural, symbolic, and religious structures that had been building hope for a more dignified future in the town. Against this context of communal humiliation as an aspect of processes of dehumanization, the Eucharistic procession in the town plaza served as a means of public resistance to violence and as a practice of rehumanization—of reinscribing humanity and dignity on the social body of Aguilares. If the Eucharistic procession as a whole can be interpreted as a communal means of challenging the military's narrative and performance of domination, the soldiers pointing their rifles to stop the procession can be interpreted as the direct contestation of the people's humanity. At that moment the people turn to Romero and are seen by Romero, and in that seeing, they come to know each other again. Not unlike the biblical story of Jesus and the disciples on the road to Emmaus (Lk 24:13–35), "seeing" and "knowing" each other are bound together in the communion of their shared humanity in the midst of persecution. In Spanish, we would say that they come to *re-conocer* (re-know) each other in their mutually threatened humanity.[48] In Romero's bold gesture of raising higher the monstrance carrying the Eucharist, the defense of the dignity of the poor and persecuted people of Aguilares was made even more public and served as an ecclesial sign against to the humiliation the town had endured.[49] Against processes aimed at invisibilizing dignity, Romero led a public process of rehumanizing the community.

Church communities are uniquely positioned to serve as sites of encounter where those who enjoy state security and those who are victims and survivors of the security state can come to know each other in a process that can begin to heal the adverse impacts of displacement and persecution. In the United States, as ICE becomes a state mechanism for forcing communities into submission by requiring local institutions to hand over information that can lead to apprehensions of persons without legal status—thus conditioning citizens to comply without questioning the ways that legality and criminality are constructed and

---

[48] Etymologically, *reconocer* has roots in *re*—"again," *com*—"together," and *gnoscere*—"to know."

[49] The notion of dignity is generally understood in relation and contradistinction to humiliation. See Paul Saurette, *The Kantian Imperative* (Toronto: University of Toronto Press, 2005), 4, 9.

imposed—sanctuary can be a means of reinscribing humanity into these same communities.[50]

In their work with communities who live in the midst of ongoing violence, John Paul Lederach and Angela Lederach have explored the creative possibilities for healing that exist at the local communal level. They focus particularly on the interpersonal level because, as they say, it "goes beyond individual processes of healing, while at the same time it provides a context of more direct, accessible experience than is commonly experienced in national processes."[51] In the space between the complexities of healing from trauma on a personal level, and the too-often-politicized attempts to address society's brokenness and polarization at the national level (e.g. through "immigration reform"), the interpersonal sphere is a creative site for addressing the multiple forms of violence that tear communities apart. Local communities contain the generative possibility for affecting both individual processes of healing and broader processes of social change.

In their analysis of communities marked by both direct and institutionalized violence, the Lederachs focus on key metaphors through which persons perceive, understand, and structure their world. They write, "Depending on how we use and mobilise the very structure of language and how we use metaphor we shift meaning and, through comparison, the framing of reality."[52] Based on extensive on-the-ground field experience, they identify three fundamental challenges that are tied to healing at the communal level: displacement, insecurity, and voicelessness. Addressing these three challenges by developing the categories of place, safety, and voice becomes the foundation for the possibility of social healing. I elaborate on each of these challenges and then place them in relation to sanctuary to explore the healing potential embedded in this ecclesial tradition.

---

[50] Sanctuary cities technically interrupt government processes that make invisible the humanity of persons without legal status inasmuch as they do not share local community databases with ICE or with other federal agencies that seek to deport them. These noncooperation tactics indirectly protect persons without legal status and are a complement to other sanctuary practices such as church sanctuary.

[51] John Paul Lederach and Angela Lederach, *When Blood and Bones Cry Out* (Oxford: Oxford University Press, 2010), 10.

[52] Lederach and Lederach, 43.

If violence displaces persons and communities at multiple levels, then locating a sense of place, both concretely and conceptually, is an integral part of survival and of healing. The Lederachs write that, in addition to the literal loss of place endured by those forced to flee their town or homeland, at an internal level "'displaced' means a person does not know where they are or what their place is, and they have lost any sense of belonging."[53] Losing one's sense of place is inherently connected to losing one's knowledge of context and of social relations that provide a web for locating one's self vis-à-vis others. In Pedro's story we can recognize that his displacement was marked not only by the literal expulsion from the life he had been living in California and by his further deportation in his attempts to return to the United States, but also by the loss of relational networks of support. Shelters and other Casas del Migrante along the US-Mexico border are some of the few resources that provide a temporary sense of place and belonging through their intentional attempts to build community with and among displaced persons. In the actual journey through the desert wilderness, Pedro's displacement was marked by bodies left behind, decomposing, unknown, and, unless found and identified, forever lost and disappeared to their family and friends. Pedro's insight that being so close to death does something to you was a profound commentary on the impact of seeking life in the midst of death, and, like a mirror, those corpses reflected back the very real possibility that he, too, could be lost in the wilderness and become a desaparecido.

Persons forced to flee contexts that provide a sense of belonging even in the midst of violence have to constantly locate their sense of self, of who they are, and their purpose in the midst of dangerous unknowns. The process of locating both a physical place that affirms their life and an internal place of self and meaning is part of tapping into their own deep well of healing.[54] As the Lederachs suggest, "When people find their place, when they touch, in and out, a sense of location, purpose and

---

[53] Lederach and Lederach, 59.

[54] Perhaps another way of stating this is that social healing has to do with tapping into one's own spirituality forged in the midst of survival. Gustavo Gutiérrez alludes to this when quoting Bernard of Clairvaux; "When it comes to spirituality all people must know how to 'drink from their own well.'" Gustavo Gutiérrez, *We Drink from Our Own Wells* (Maryknoll, NY: Orbis Books, 1984), 5.

meaning, they experience a sense of health."[55] In light of the instability surrounding displaced persons, experiencing a sense of health can be a momentary and fleeting experience made possible by wholesome and, at times, unexpected encounters with places and with persons who provide a sense of belonging.

The violence of living under constant threat, either in the process of displacement or because of the real possibility of deportation, generates profound insecurity in those who long for a sense of safety. For the Lederachs, "to feel insecure means a person no longer has a clear sense of self and often responds to immediate events from internal uncertainty. . . . Insecurity poses a challenge of how to recover a basic sense of trust in the outer social landscape and the inner personal journey."[56] The need always to be on guard in order to survive destroys an internal sense of feeling at home with oneself and others, and even the terms imposed on persons who do not have legal status in the United States generate insecurity. Such persons technically have an "irregular" status that they must conceal as much as possible lest someone report them to the government. The process by which an irregular person can officially stop living under the threat of deportation is *naturalization*, a term laden with ontological implications of what it means to be a person, a whole person, and a natural person in the United States, rather than an aberration in society that must be captured and made to disappear. Persons and communities who live in constant insecurity inhabit and are surrounded by a context akin to a hunt, where they feel perpetually targeted and where they must learn to exist hidden in plain sight. To speak of health and healing in such a context requires addressing the very real threats of both external and internal insecurity.

Health and healing, as the Lederachs propose, are tied to metaphors that take flesh in community: "Security as feeling at home suggests spatial metaphors of feeling comfortably surrounded, having a container in which one feels a sense of belonging and trust. . . . These spatial metaphors point towards a notion of being encircled in the sense of being held, pointing towards notions of container as community and family."[57] Creative communal responses that can respond to a sense of vulnerability,

---

[55] Lederach and Lederach, *When Blood and Bones Cry Out*, 62.
[56] Lederach and Lederach, 63.
[57] Lederach and Lederach, 64.

which prevents persons from feeling at home externally and internally in their everyday "unauthorized" lives, can begin to address the wounds of insecurity. Conceiving of community as a container-like structure that can hold, support, and provide a sense of familial belonging to persons who are persecuted resonates with the concept and practice of sanctuary, for it joins together the concrete structures of church buildings with the protective presence of a people.

In addition to displacement and insecurity, multidimensional violence also marks persons and communities with an experience of voicelessness. On one level, the loss of voice is manifest as "the feeling of *being left out*, creating the experience that solidifies a profound sense of distance and exclusion."[58] Irrespective of how loudly or constantly one may attempt to exercise one's voice, if it is systematically ignored and not taken into account, then the experience is one of speaking into a void. Despite utterances, a sense of not having a voice that matters can lead to the disappearance of one's voice and ultimately of one's sense of self:

> At the deepest, perhaps most complex level, voicelessness means losing touch with a sense of personhood. As metaphor, when a person no longer has a sense of voice they experience a loss of humanity. . . . Voicelessness creates the experience of being numb, without a capacity to feel, to touch or to be in touch. This is in fact the impact of violence. It deadens, numbs and silences life.[59]

The examples provided earlier of refugee children in Sweden who fall into a coma-like state for weeks, months, and even years crystalizes the extreme impacts of existing in a society that does not hear one's clamor for life, that ignores the real fears of what will happen if deported, and that refuses to recognize the communication of one's humanity through multiple attempts to relate one's experiential truth.

When one's life is fundamentally *dictated* by others, one is no longer in tune with one's self. Being a person, on some level, implies the ability to live out of one's voice in relation to others. As the Lederachs and others have pointed out, etymologically, the Latin word for person (*persona*) is related to the meaning of the Latin word *personare*, which can

---

[58] Lederach and Lederach, 65.
[59] Lederach and Lederach, 66.

be defined as "to sound through" (*per* + *sonare*).[60] In Greek and Roman culture, where notions of personhood may have arisen in association with the masks (*prosopon*) worn by performers, it was the sound that would flow through the mask's opening for the mouth that communicated the drama of life and death on the stage.[61] Finding or recovering one's voice has to do with finding one's self even in the midst of the multiple displacements and insecurities caused by violence that may not be visually apparent. Locating voice is a process that is profoundly communal, for one's voice necessitates an encounter with other voices that are close enough to be engaged:

> Voice organises around an aural, sound-based metaphor. . . . It surrounds and can create a sensation of being held. It is based on touch and vibration. When people speak of voice as having connection to change at the community level they use the language of echo: the sensation of feeling sound rise from within and take the form of words that enter a shared space and are received by and touch others. In return, a response comes back and touches the one who spoke. In this process people participate in creating resonance and experience meaningful conversation.[62]

The three key challenges of displacement, insecurity, and voicelessness that erode a sense of self and community, and which can be understood as interrelated social wounds, coalesce around an approach to health and healing that is fundamentally aural. The process of personal and communal rehumanization, of reconstituting humanity in relation to place, safety, and voice, which can happen through the metaphorical dynamics of sound, opens new horizons for discerning the healing potential of sanctuary. In the previous section I argued that providing refuge can serve as a bridge for overcoming lethal mechanisms that keep persons and communities from recognizing each other's humanity. If sanctuary

---

[60] Lederach and Lederach, 96. For Thomas Aquinas's reference to these dramatic origins of *person,* see Thomas Aquinas, *Summa Theologica* I, 29, 3, obj. 2 (New York: Benzinger Brothers, 1948).

[61] See Dmitri Nikulin, *On Dialogue* (Lanham, MD: Lexington Books, 2006), 44–46. For his philosophical insights on how voice presupposes another voice, see his *Dialectic and Dialogue* (Stanford, CA: Stanford University Press, 2010), 76.

[62] Lederach and Lederach, *When Blood and Bones Cry Out*, 67.

provides a physical space for displaced and persecuted persons to locate "place" and "safety" in a literal sense, however temporary this may be, we must inquire further into how this physical dimension of refuge can open a way for an internal journey of mutual healing.

The heart of sanctuary is the community that provides refuge and accompaniment, and this encounter can locate an internal sense of place and safety for those dwelling in sanctuary. When the government's persecution communicates to persons that they do not belong in society, the actions of a sanctuary community interrupt those othering mechanisms and generate a counter discourse that affirms their life and dignity. When an individual or a family takes refuge in a sanctuary, the walls of the building may provide some form of protection, but more important, members of the community typically keep watch within the sanctuary day and night. By being present, the community becomes part of the internal journey that persons in sanctuary are undergoing as they navigate the profound questions of where they are and who they are in relation to a community that has recognized the truth of their existence.

A community's accompaniment is a dynamic presence that, through personal encounter and conversation, has the potential to locate both the community and the persons in sanctuary as they narrate their own fears and hopes and as they reconnect with their sense of meaningful purpose. For example, a church community that responds through sanctuary has generally undergone a process of discernment about its identity, faith commitments, and the risks and challenges that it may have to face for its religious actions. As these elements are repeated over and over through conversations within and beyond the community, the community's communal mission and meaning as sanctuary becomes increasingly rooted and stable as a pillar of its ecclesial identity. These identity-clarifying ecclesial processes also serve to reconnect persons in sanctuary with their own sense of self and belonging as they develop relational networks that can ground them in their attempts to reconcile both the persecution and the embodied companionship they are experiencing simultaneously from different sectors of society.

Imagining sanctuary as a social space or a container-like structure where protection leads to a sense of being at home, where persons encounter and are surrounded by one another's shared voice and stories, invites a reconsideration of the healing power of local communities and the social echo they can cast upon the rest of society. Not unlike the dynamics of sound, where, within a given context, multiple vibrations interact to create resonance and in some cases "natural frequency," as the Lederachs point out in their analysis of how Tibetan bowls "sing,"[63] so too, the repetitive and purposeful daily interactions among persons involved in the practice of church sanctuary have the potential to give rise to a collective voice that includes but is more expansive and deeper than any one person. In the emergence of a collective voice, the individual persons in sanctuary have the capacity to rediscover their own voices, to be heard, to participate in ongoing processes of resistance to violence, to build hope through every encounter that echoes their presence, and to know that their humanity has been seen, heard, and amplified. Social healing arises through such mutual and communal responsibilities for each other. "Social healing," the Lederachs summarize, "represents the capacity of communities and their respective individuals to survive, locate voice and resiliently innovate spaces of interaction that nurture meaningful conversation and purposeful action in the midst and aftermath of escalated and structural violence."[64] The healing of personal and collective wounds through encounter and accompaniment even in the midst of violence and persecution is a mystery into which sanctuary communities enter without a guarantee that a sense of place will be located, that a sense of safety will not be violated, or that their individual and collective voice will not be silenced. However, in the creative act of communally risking place, security, and voice for another, mutual humanity is touched and processes of rehumanization begin their collective journey.

The creative exploration of social healing developed by the Lederachs has an affinity to the theological and ecclesial notions of communion explored in previous chapters. Persons who seek sanctuary and those communities that respond to their invocation of this tradition echo each other. The process of approximating each other, of having a common purpose and hope for the future, reflects an aspect of becoming one mystical, true, and real body in shared vulnerability. As shown in Chapter 2, during the 1980s sanctuary ministry and movement Jim Corbett wrote that "through the corporate practice of love and service,

---

[63] See Lederach and Lederach, 89–110.

[64] Lederach and Lederach, 208.

we are to enter into the full community with the violated that heals humanity into one body."[65] There, he was echoing the biblical affirmation found in Isaiah 58 that, where the bonds of injustice are loosened, where the homeless poor are brought into homes, where one does not hide oneself from one's kin, there healing shall arise (vv. 6–8). Social healing and communion find resonance in each other, and, theologically speaking, they represent the social and historical incarnation of love whose echo each ecclesial community can amplify as it binds its fate with their kin whose humanity has no borders. It is also fitting to recall Henri de Lubac's description of the Eucharistic sacrament of communion as the body of Christ "engaged in a mystical action, a ritual echo, endlessly reverberating in time and space, of the unique action from which it takes its sense"[66]—the life, death, and resurrection of Jesus. To become a sanctuary from violence *is* to become a clear echo through time and space of the Word who touches and heals all that is wounded and broken. Sanctuary is an effective sign and instrument of love and communion for healing humanity.[67]

Dwelling in Holiness

Traditionally, the concept of sanctuary has been defined in relation to refuge and holiness. Although the US government recognizes some places as set apart from its ordinary domain of enforcement, it would be inaccurate to claim that the government recognizes "holy" places as places of refuge. The closest the government comes to acknowledging the uniqueness of certain places in relation to immigration enforcement is what it calls "sensitive locations." An ICE memo from 2011 advises its officers that enforcement actions should not ordinarily occur at "sensitive

---

[65] Corbett, *The Sanctuary Church*, 12.

[66] Henri de Lubac, *Corpus Mysticum* (Notre Dame, IN: University of Notre Dame Press, 2007), 62. For more on the sacramental logics that are foundational for church sanctuary, see chap. 5.

[67] The Lederachs end their insights into social healing by turning to the mystery of love. They write: "Key to our inquiry is the awareness that rises from the simple recognition that, although not visible, love has a tangible impact, and that love may in fact move in spatial and aural modalities." Lederach and Lederach, *When Blood and Bones Cry Out*, 232.

locations" such as "churches, synagogues, mosques, or other institutions of worship."[68] In addition to places of worship, ICE also lists sites of public religious ceremonies, schools, hospitals, and public demonstrations as sensitive locations. While this notion of sensitive locations has helped some communities in their discernment to become a church that provides sanctuary, theoretically because it gives them some sense of protection, realistically there is no guarantee that ICE will not enter places of worship to apprehend those taking refuge.

The practice of sanctuary is not a privilege vested upon the church in the modern nation state but an ecclesial responsibility it bears by its faith. The possibility of the church providing refuge does not reside in a notion of the church as a holy place; rather, through the act of providing refuge, the church can live into holiness as it witnesses to the Holy One of whom it is called to be a sign. Sanctuary transcends lingering traditional notions of sacred and profane, for that which appears to be incidental or beyond the holy is, in fact, what bears holiness. To grasp holiness not as a static, fulfilled reality but as constitutively bound to making present the presence of God in history liberates the church to become a sanctuary for life regardless of whether it is considered a sensitive location or holy place, and regardless of the persecution that may become its fate.

The presence of God is holiness itself. Throughout history there has been a creative tension in localizing this presence. However, from the perspective of the history of God's revelation, the trajectory has been that of God increasingly dwelling with and within humanity.[69] In the

---

[68] US Immigration and Customs Enforcement (ICE), "Enforcement Actions at or Focused on Sensitive Locations," ice.gov, October 24, 2011; see also "FAQs: Sensitive Locations and Courthouse Arrests," ice.gov.

[69] The Hebrew word *shakan* means, "to dwell" or "inhabit," and is the root for *mishkan,* which can be translated as "dwelling place." *Shakan* is also the root for *Shekinah*—the Holy presence and dwelling of the transcendent God who journeyed with the people in the desert. The Hebrew word *kadosh,* which means holy, is the root for the word *mikdash,* which can be translated as "sanctuary." Dwelling and sanctuary go together in scripture as in Exodus 25:8 ("and have them make me a sanctuary, so that I may dwell among them"). See Yves Congar, *The Mystery of the Temple* (Westminster, UK: The Newman Press, 1962), 7–19. Also, for an analysis of these terms in light of the Holy Spirit's indwelling as understood in the New Testament and the Christian tradition, see Yves Congar, "God Has Sent the Spirit of His Son into Our Hearts," in *I Believe in the Holy Spirit,* vol. 2 (New York: Herder and Herder, 2015), 79–99. Mikdash is also the name for the Jewish sanctuary

words of Yves Congar, "The story of God's relations with his creation and especially with man is none other than the story of his ever more generous, ever deeper Presence among his creatures."[70] From God's dwelling in the cloud that shaded the Hebrew people by day and in the pillar of fire that gave them light by night as they traveled in the wilderness (Ex 13:21), to the dwelling above the mercy seat in the ark of the covenant and in the tent where Moses consulted God's will (Ex 25:33), the presence of God has been one on the move. Even when King David desired to construct a temple where God could dwell, the prophecy of Nathan recalled that God is not contained by any temple, for God desires to dwell among God's people wherever they are. "The truth is that where his people is, there is Yahweh" (2 Sam 7).[71] In the development of the understanding of God's presence, the prophecy to Nathan clarified that humans would not provide a shelter for God but God would build a house—a permanent presence—among God's people.[72] For Christians, Nathan's prophecy to King David became radically present in the incarnation. Jesus became the dwelling of God, became enfleshed holiness itself, and became "the starting point of the communication of every form of holiness."[73] Through the Spirit, the primary place of God's dwelling becomes human persons. To speak of holy places, then, is primarily to speak of persons and communities who make present the holy presence of God through their life.

The binding of God's presence or holiness to human persons requires that, regardless of whether notions of holy places as places of refuge are present in society, communities of faith are bound to serve as a living temple where God and neighbor can dwell.[74] Enfleshing sanctuary, where life is protected and holiness enacted, extends beyond the boundaries of any conception of church. In speaking of the church as a spiritual temple—as a temple linked to the work of the Holy Spirit in history—

---

movement in the United States. See T'ruah: The Rabbinic Call for Human Rights online.

[70] Congar, *The Mystery of the Temple*, ix.

[71] See also Congar, *Mystery of the Temple*, 15.

[72] The Hebrew word *bait* (Greek *Oikos*) is used in the prophecy in a double meaning that points to lineage or family as well as to a dwelling place. See Congar, *The Mystery of the Temple*, 27–28.

[73] Congar, 138.

[74] "For the prophets, God was present where he reigned." Congar, 228.

Congar reminds us that "many constitute the temple, but invisibly."[75] To bear the presence of God is to witness to love and to love what God loves. In a society and world where persons are forcibly displaced and then persecuted and deported to their possible death, to become a sanctuary that protects life is also to encounter the mystery of the presence of God seeking life.

The temptation to separate holiness from the transformation of structures that deny life to those rendered poor and insignificant is a constant struggle in the life of the church. The words from the Medellín conference are still a challenge for the global church: "We must avoid the dualism that separates temporal tasks from sanctification."[76] As church, our ecclesial imaginary is still too segregated between holy work and temporal work, between worship of God and service to neighbor, between sanctified church space and a profane world beyond church structures. One of the most powerful possibilities embedded in the concept and practice of church sanctuary is that it can radically challenge these dualisms that are profoundly unchristian, for they do not sufficiently account for the impact of the incarnation and the reality that there is one history where the mystery of the Holy One and all that is human converge.

In its historically traditional form, sanctuary entails persons taking refuge and living within the church until they are forcefully removed or until a resolution is found for their persecution. Given this, there is a very real convergence of what some would call worldly, or extra-ecclesial concerns, with the sphere of worship. Worship becomes inseparable from the accompaniment and protection of persons who are dwelling within or in the vicinity of the spaces used for formal and communal praise.

---

[75] Congar, 198. In addition to affirming that many constitute the temple invisibly, Congar also speaks of degrees of incorporation: "The movement of conversion to God is to be fulfilled in a bodily sacrament. So too our incorporation into the structure of the temple is to be fulfilled in the concrete community by our participation in his sacrifice of his body and blood." However, Congar also goes on to speak of all creation as the temple of God: "Christ's sovereign power as source of the new spiritual creation is also applied to the universe and is to include it in his work of salvation and transfiguration. It will make the universe too, in its way, the temple of God. Not of course, a purely cosmic temple, but an essential element, and therefore one dimension of the spiritual temple" (198–201).

[76] Medellín, *Justice*, no. 5. See Latin American Episcopal Council (CELAM), *The Church in the Present-Day Transformation of Latin America in the Light of the Council*, vol. 2 (Washington, DC: United States Catholic Conference, 1970).

Rather than engaging with the church's mission outside the space where formal liturgy happens, the mission becomes one with what the church celebrates.[77] For a church community, the convergence of "temporal tasks" and "sanctification" that occurs through the practice of sanctuary has the potential to transform an understanding of holiness away from dualisms that separate God and human history. The church in the United States needs a deeper theology of incarnation that recognizes that God dwells in the poor, displaced, and persecuted of this world, and that God's partiality for those whose life is threatened means that the church—in all its dimensions—is their genuine dwelling place. The dwelling of God in the poor and the poor in the church becomes the ground for the rest of the community to celebrate its own dwelling with the Holy.

In this inversion and transformation of traditional understandings of guest and host, the church can begin to move from being a community that assists the persecuted to becoming one where they are at home. Such a cognitive and spiritual conversion is essential if sanctuary is going to be grasped as more than an ethical response that the church provides to a world in need. Persons who enter sanctuary become a catalyst for the church to rethink holiness amid the conflictual politics of the United States.

The constitutive relationship between holiness and sanctuary reframes the horizon of this religious tradition, whose theological, ecclesiological, and sacramental dimensions are too easily and strategically disappeared. Returning to the 1968 Medellín document is helpful for clarifying how sanctuary helps concretize a church of the poor in the United States. The document distinguishes between real poverty as the deprivation of what is necessary for life, spiritual poverty as the openness to God's will, and poverty as commitment, which leads the church to struggle against the evil of real poverty.[78] A church of the poor, I showed, is one that follows the logic of the incarnation by making itself present among structures of injustice, violence, and, ultimately, death in order to witness to love and the God of life. Essentially, it is a church that follows

---

[77] For insightful essays on the need for historical verification of what the church celebrates in liturgy, see Philippe Bordeyne and Bruce Morrill, eds., *Sacraments: Revelation of the Humanity of God* (Collegeville, MN: Pueblo Books, 2008), 115–52.

[78] Medellín, *Poverty of the Church*, no. 5. See, Latin American Episcopal Council (CELAM), *The Church in the Present-Day Transformation of Latin America in the Light of the Council*.

Jesus—holiness itself present through the Spirit—into new contexts of death to struggle in communion and solidarity against that which kills God's creation. For the church in the United States the contemporary challenge of forced human displacement and the need for sanctuary is a way of effectively becoming a church of the poor and of making real this unfulfilled ecclesial vision of Vatican II, Medellín, and the very heart of scripture. Below, I weave sanctuary into Medellín's three understandings of poverty to clarify further the nature of holiness in our times.

Like the violence of real poverty, structures that forcefully displace persons are evil, for they threaten life. Too often, the narrative imposed upon displaced persons to justify their deportation is that they choose to migrate and that they are simply seeking a better life. What such phrases conceal is that persons are forced to leave their homes to find life itself and that deportation, historically, has been and continues to be a form of killing.[79] Even those who leave because of dire economic realities are fleeing for life because poverty will otherwise be the slow death to which they are condemned. The world of persons who have been displaced to the United States and who live in persecution because of their lack of legal status is a manifestation of the world of the poor, and the church community enters this world to the degree that displaced persons find life in the church. Tragically and too often, legality rather than faith becomes the primary lens for reading the world of the displaced and persecuted poor. Legality and illegality have been mapped upon life and death, and for some church communities, witnessing to legality supersedes witnessing against death. Despite appearances, the tension is not primarily one of church against state or of civil law versus God's law. Rather, at the core of the tension is how holiness is misapprehended. At this point, entering into Medellín's second understanding of poverty is critical.

Spiritual poverty is the way for the church in the United States to grasp the holiness of sanctuary. Medellín speaks of spiritual poverty as "spiritual childhood," as the "attitude of opening up to God, the ready disposition of one who hopes for everything from the Lord."[80] Unless church communities have faith that God leads them and will journey

---

[79] For an example of how deportation can lead to death, see Sarah Stillman, "When Deportation Is a Death Sentence," *New Yorker* online, January 15, 2018; see also, Human Rights Watch, *Deported to Danger: United States Deportation Policies Expose Salvadorans to Death and Abuse*, online report, February 5, 2020.

[80] Medellín, *Poverty of the Church*, nos. 4–5.

with them regardless of the legal, social, or financial consequences of their actions, they will remain turned in upon themselves, seeking first their own security. As Gutiérrez argues, "Spiritual childhood alone makes possible an authentic commitment to the poor and oppressed."[81] The clarity of his conviction points to the freedom that is found when persons and communities, like the prophets of scripture, surrender to the mystery of the Holy One in whom the church finds its meaning. Spiritual childhood implies a kenotic process, a conversion by which communities empty themselves of their attachments to security, privilege, and to a guaranteed predictable future, to live into the holy uncertainty that comes with following Jesus. In speaking of an authentic conversion to the poor, Gutiérrez adds that "to be converted is to know and experience the fact that, contrary to the laws of physics, we can stand straight, according to the gospel, only when our center of gravity is outside ourselves."[82] A church turned in upon itself and its own security loses its grounding in God. Only by risking its very self in the protection of the life of others does the church find its true self in the presence of God. The process of spiritual childhood, the ongoing conversion to God and neighbor, is nothing less than the full immersion in and surrender to the mystery of an unknown future and the possibility that the church's identity can and will be transformed. Capturing the depth of what constitutes an authentic ecclesial conversion, Gutiérrez writes:

> Our conversion process is affected by the socio-economic, political, cultural, and human environment in which it occurs. Without a change in these structures, there is no authentic conversion. We have to break with our mental categories, with the way we relate to others, with our way of identifying with the Lord, with our cultural milieu, with our social class, in other words, with all that can stand in the way of a real, profound solidarity with those who suffer, in the first place, from misery and injustice.[83]

Without spiritual poverty, without a surrender to the mystery of God and trust in God's merciful presence in the poor, who seek the sanctuary

---

[81] Gutiérrez, *We Drink from Our Own Wells*, 127.
[82] Gutiérrez, *A Theology of Liberation*, 118.
[83] Gutiérrez, 118.

the church can provide, church communities are more likely to surrender to and trust in the very structures that persecute and kill the poor.

A church that lives in spiritual poverty is one whose mark of holiness is inseparable from its commitment to the life and love of the displaced and persecuted poor. In the history of the church, holiness is the first mark attributed to this community, though the New Testament does not in fact speak of the church as holy.[84] Discourse of the church's holiness exists always in relation to its responsibility to communicate and make concrete the love of God. As Jon Sobrino states, "Simple though it may sound, the Church of the poor is the church that restores the fundamental gospel truth: no one has greater love than those who give their life for the brethren. All love and holiness is to be understood by analogy with this supreme giving."[85] Standing upright in the struggle for the life of communities who are systematically targeted, persecuted, and expelled for their attempts to flee from forces of death is holy. This witness to love may divide the church at multiple levels, and it will certainly place it in conflict with those who desire the elimination of millions of "unauthorized" persons residing in the country and others in the process of arriving. The church's credible response, however, is offering its life for others. In witnessing in love and to love, the church dwells in holiness. Sobrino clarifies: "If this holiness is lacking, the Church is not only not true, it is not a church at all. Holiness serves to distinguish not so much between true Churches and false Churches as between various degrees of realization of the Church."[86] To be church is to live out of God's holiness, and doing so always requires that the church offer its life in love.

The undying struggle and desire for life of persons forced to leave their homes reflects what Sobrino has termed "a primordial holiness," for they echo the God of life who wills their life.[87] For the church to dismiss their hopes by cooperating with deadly structures that work for

---

[84] Yves Congar, "The Spirit Is the Principle of the Church's Holiness," in *I Believe in the Holy Spirit,* 52.

[85] Jon Sobrino, *The True Church and the Poor* (Maryknoll, NY: Orbis Books, 1984), 109.

[86] Sobrino, 110.

[87] For Jon Sobrino's use of "santidad primordial" (primordial holiness or primordial saintliness), see Jon Sobrino, *Terremoto, terrorismo, barbarie y utopia* (San Salvador: UCA Editores, 2003), 35–36, 127–71. For the English translation, see *Where Is God?* (Maryknoll, NY: Orbis Books, 2004), 5–6, 71–102.

their expulsion from the United States is for the church to place trust in the state before trust in God's partiality for the poor. The refusal to protect the lives of displaced and persecuted communities effectively constitutes a refusal of the holy presence of God. The words spoken by Pope Paul VI before the Medellín conference, that the poor are a sacrament of Christ akin to the Eucharist, are an invitation to bishops who prevent parishes from providing sanctuary to reconsider how sanctuary seekers are a fundamental aspect of the church's own source and summit.[88] To reject the poor who seek refuge in the church is for the church to reject itself and its mission as a bearer of good news.

Mutual Salvation

"Eventually, we no longer stayed in our homes because of the threats. We slept in the hills. At about 10:00 pm one night, fifteen days or so before I left the country, we saw a car approaching the village. We knew that we had been under observation since about 7:00 pm. We saw that men were knocking on doors of several houses, and became frightened. About twenty minutes later we heard shots. The following morning when I went toward the city I found three of my friends . . . dead. I thought they might have been killed by the three shots we heard, but apparently they had been killed with machetes; their arms were cut off. They had been left on the side of the street."[89]

This horrific scene of bodies left on the side of the road in El Salvador resonates decades later with the fear that persons at risk of deportation experience while attempting to survive in the United States. Persons like Carmela Hernandez, whose story I mentioned earlier, are forced to leave their US homes in search of sanctuary because they are afraid that ICE will knock on their doors at any moment, incarcerate them

---

[88] See *Lumen Gentium*, no. 11.

[89] Excerpt from a July 18, 1981, interview with Juan, a 24–year-old Salvadoran who was a Roman Catholic catechist in El Salvador. He was interviewed in Tucson, Arizona, after church communities bailed him out from the Border Patrol Detention Center. "Conversations with Refugees from El Salvador, 1982," University of Arizona Special Collections, MS 362, Box 30, Folder 24.

in a detention center, then deport them. While the violence inflicted upon this unauthorized population in the United States is not that of machetes, there is a dismembering that takes place when parents are torn from their children or when youth are sent back to countries that are no longer or never were home, and where they will face persecution from criminal organizations or from the police itself. When whole communities in a society are hunted, it is not imprudent for the church to live with urgency, or as Óscar Romero said, "in a state of emergency,"[90] locating itself like the Good Samaritan alongside those left to die.[91] It is, in fact, necessary.

The church's actions or lack thereof are a matter of sin or grace, death or life, condemnation or salvation. Marked by his experience of the church in El Salvador, Ignacio Ellacuría wrote that "for the oppressed believers in Latin America injustice and whatever brings death and denies dignity to the children of God are not merely historical effects, nor even a legal failing; they are sin in a formal sense, something that formally has to do with God."[92] Forcibly returning people to contexts of violence and death from which they have been forced to flee in order to survive is sin. Sanctuary makes real the historical dimensions of salvation, not only for displaced and persecuted persons, but for all who, through sanctuary, come to participate in processes of healing and of encountering the mystery of holiness that is present where communities enter into communion with one another. As Pope Francis emphatically argues, "We can only be saved together."[93]

Persons who are forced to seek refuge in the church are seeking historical salvation in a society that condemns them to multiple forms of death for the false crime of seeking life. By the very logic of the incarnation the

---

[90] Óscar Romero, *Homilías*, vol. 6 (San Salvador: UCA Editores, 2009), February 17, 1980, 290.

[91] The power over life and death, and its management, is in fact how state sovereignty is exercised in modernity, as Michel Foucault, Achille Mbembe, and other theorists have argued. For an analysis of sovereignty and its relation to biopower and necropolitics over migrants attempting to arrive in Europe, see Mareike Gebhardt, "To Make Live and Let Die: On Sovereignty and Vulnerability in the EU Migration Regime," *Redescriptions: Political Thought, Conceptual History, and Feminist Theory* 23, no. 2 (2020): 120–37.

[92] Ignacio Ellacuría, "The Historicity of Christian Salvation," *Mysterium Liberationis* (Maryknoll, NY: Orbis Books, 1993), 276.

[93] Pope Francis, *Fratelli Tutti*, nos. 32, 137.

church must enter their reality, and their reality must enter the church. This is the redemptive logic expressed in the iconic opening words of *Gaudium et Spes*: "The joys and hopes, the grief and anguish of the people of our time, especially of those who are poor or afflicted, are the joys and hopes, the grief and anguish of the followers of Christ as well." This is the redemptive logic that undergirds the documents of Medellín, and it is the redemptive logic and reason for the church's sacramental nature. The church struggles against the reality of sin and the death it produces by making present, as institution and community, the salvific presence of God in history.

Forced human displacement is an overwhelmingly universal sign of political violence and economic oppression that kills,[94] and the inability of the church to live into sanctuary with communities who are displaced and persecuted risks making of the local and the universal church a counter sign, a scandal where God's gift of self—salvation—appears absent. Sacramental theologian Louis-Marie Chauvet asks:

> Is the concrete community the living sign of what it celebrates? If it is not a reconciling force in the world, is it not in contradiction to the sacrament of reconciliation it celebrates in the midst of the world? If it is not concerned about the fate of immigrants . . . what is the meaning of the welcome it extends to the children of these same immigrants when it baptizes them?[95]

The church's sacramental nature cannot be separated from the ongoing enfleshment of salvation in concrete forms, according to the real hopes of God's beloved and suffering people.

Vatican II's affirmation that the church is a sacrament of salvation in and for the world continues to serve as one of the most capacious ecclesiological insights for understanding church as sanctuary. In previous chapters I focused on the sacramentality of the church and the sacramentality of the poor, and the way in which the one is present in

---

[94] In a similar manner, Archbishop Óscar Romero spoke of hunger in El Salvador as a sign of oppression and death, and of bread as a sign of liberation and life. See Romero, *Homilías,* August 5, 1979, vol. 5 (San Salvador: UCA Editores, 2008), 173–80.

[95] Louis-Marie Chauvet, *Symbol and Sacrament* (Collegeville, MN: Liturgical Press, 1995), 414.

the other, because both participate in a unique manner in the body of Christ. The church is a sacrament, for it is a community led by the Spirit whose faith carries on the historical life and mission of Jesus Christ. The poor are a sacrament, for they bear God's preferential presence in their threatened existence. The Latin American bishops' Puebla document (1979) reminds us, in their face is encountered the suffering face of Christ.[96] Ignacio Ellacuría explains the sacramentality of the historical body of Christ present in the church and the poor in the following way:

> One can say that the true historical body of Christ, and therefore the preeminent locus of his embodiment and his incorporation is not only the church, but the poor and the oppressed of the world, so that the church alone is not the historical body of Christ, and it is possible to speak of a true body of Christ outside the church.[97]

Both the church and the poor can manifest the body of Christ in history, but, as a community of faith, the church sacramentally embodies its true historical nature when it becomes a church of the poor. By embodiment, Ellacuría refers to the act of God becoming corporeally present—the Word of God taking on flesh.[98] By incorporation, he refers to the process of this embodiment being incorporated into the one body of history. As a living community in the Spirit, the perennial task of the church is to incorporate Christ into history and to recognize in the poor the

---

[96] Puebla Final Document, nos. 31–39. For the official English translation, see *Puebla and Beyond*, ed. John Eagleson and Philip Scharper (Maryknoll, NY: Orbis Books, 1979), 128–29.

[97] Ignacio Ellacuría, "The Church of the Poor, Historical Sacrament of Liberation," in *Mysterium Liberationis,* 546.

[98] Louis-Marie Chauvet makes a similar point on the need for faith and the Word to become corporeally present in history: "The fact that there are sacraments leads us to say that *corporality is the very mediation where faith takes on flesh* and makes real the truth that inhabits it. It says this to us with all the pragmatic force of a ritual expression that speaks by its actions and works through the word, the word-as-body. It tells us that the body, which is the whole word of humankind, is the unavoidable mediation where the Word of a God involved in the most human dimension of our humanity demands to be inscribed in order to make itself understood. Thus, it tells us that faith requires a *consent to the body*, to history, to the world which makes it a fully human reality." Chauvet, *Symbol and Sacrament,* 376.

embodiment of Christ struggling to survive. In speaking of the church as the continuation of the historical body of Christ, Ellacuría does not set it against notions of the mystical body of Christ. Rather, he emphasizes that the mystery of the body of Christ whose presence exceeds history must continue to become historical—made present—in the work of the church. Because of the embodiment and incorporation of God in history, Ellacuría can say that "it is impossible to speak of salvation except in terms of concrete situations."[99] To claim that the church is a sacrament of salvation is to speak of the church's responsibility to tend to the concrete wounds and wounded of history.

In its willingness to suffer and die in the struggle for the life of the poor, the church serves as an effective historical sacrament of salvation. Ellacuría warns that "the church faces few temptations more serious than that of considering itself an end in itself, and of evaluating each of its actions in terms of whether they are convenient or inconvenient for its survival or its grandeur."[100] As a sacrament, the church's horizon is the reign of God and the in-*corpor*-ation of this presence—giving body to this presence—in history. This constitutes its fundamental reason for existence. To sacrifice this task for the sake of self-preservation is for the church to make itself an idol, a pseudo-reign of God, and to make of worldly powers its preferential friend and companion. "Only by emptying itself, in self-giving to the neediest people, unto death and death on the cross," writes Ellacuría, "can the church claim to be an historical sacrament of the salvation of Christ."[101] The self-emptying, the offering of its own corporality as a people and institution, is shaped by the demands of the concrete historical situation of sin. Ellacuría clarifies that "salvation takes different shapes in different historical moments, and that is why [the] history of salvation must be embodied and incorporated in history by assuming the nature of a salvation that is also historical."[102] Without the historicization of salvation, whose correlate is the transformation of sin and all the ways in which sin becomes embedded in structures of violence and death, salvation loses its meaning and no longer communicates

---

[99] Ellacuría, "The Church of the Poor, Historical Sacrament of Liberation," 544.
[100] Ellacuría, 548.
[101] Ellacuría, 549.
[102] Ellacuría, 550.

a God who became human to heal humanity. Despite a preponderance of juridical images surrounding the mystery of salvation, at its deepest root, salvation is always in relation to the mystery of healing humanity, of making it whole in communion and peace beyond violence. The fullness of salvation always transcends history, but it is in the here-and-now that it becomes fully human.

In the 1980s, Jon Sobrino argued that church sanctuary was a means of reparation for the evils carried out by the United States on Central American people: "Reparation is necessary for actions past and present, for so many evils inflicted. . . . The sanctuary movement is an expression of this reparation because of its program: helping Central Americans who are basically victims of US policies."[103] No reparation can ever be complete, because the loss of life and of whole generations will remain a living memory. And yet, like a salvation that always exceeds history, the repairing of the breach of humanity to which reparation points must begin anew at every moment, by every person and community who still hope.[104] Sobrino added that "the risks and sufferings of the sanctuary movement, the deprivations which some US citizens are undergoing so that there may be life in Central America, must also be viewed, objectively, as expiation for the secular sin of oppression."[105] This theological insight, however, did not resonate with most ecclesiastical leaders in the 1980s, since most Roman Catholic bishops in the United States did not support sanctuary.[106] The temptation to this day is to reduce the ecclesial tradition of sanctuary to secular politics rather than to recognize the theological implications of its practice and the historical effects of its omission.

---

[103] Jon Sobrino, "Sanctuary," 169–70.

[104] In Isaiah 58 we find this capacious vision of rehumanization, of a community that is called "the repairer of the breach" (v. 12).

[105] Sobrino, "Sanctuary," 170.

[106] Some of the bishops who in the 1980s did publicly give support for sanctuary included John Quinn of San Francisco, Rembert Weakland of Milwaukee, John Fitzpatrick of Brownsville, Texas, and Raymond Hunthausen of Seattle. See Lawrence J. McAndrews, *Refuge in the Lord: Catholics, Presidents, and the Politics of Immigration, 1981–2013* (Washington, DC: CUA Press, 2015), 40ff. Also, Gary MacEoin, ed., *Sanctuary: A Resource Guide for Understanding the Participating in the Central American Refugee Struggle* (San Francisco: Harper and Row Publishers, 1985), 26–27.

Archbishop Romero points the way for a church who takes upon itself reparation for state violence. Romero's 1977 response to the military's actions in Aguilares and across El Salvador, where the body of Christ was being desecrated and humiliated, was a way of taking responsibility in a context where the government was radically failing in its responsibility. Romero could not have forced the government of El Salvador to make reparation for its atrocities, and neither can the church in the United States force its government to do so. However, in both cases the church as a community and institution can make reparation through its constructive practices such as church sanctuary, which is a critical form of resisting the violence of the state in an age of forced displacement.

Sanctuary contributes to the rehumanization of displaced and persecuted persons and communities, and the church itself is rehumanized as it incorporates—makes present—the life of Jesus within the church. Reflecting on the church of the poor, Ellacuría argued that "the historical shape of the church, as a salvific and liberating response to this universal cry [of oppressed peoples], presupposes first its permanent conversion to the truth and the life of the historical Jesus; and second, its historical participation in the salvation of a world that can only be saved by following the way of Jesus."[107] In doing as Jesus did, the church becomes what it already is as a sacrament of salvation. In the previous section on healing I showed how getting in touch with one's voice is an essential dimension of locating one's self and place in the world. For the church, its own process of rehumanization is tied to becoming the echo of the voice of Jesus, who preached the reign of God to all, and especially among the poor who sought God's presence, healing, and mercy. The universal cry of oppressed peoples—the cry of Jesus in the flesh of the poor—must resonate in every corner of the church's body until it encounters and is encountered by the voice of Jesus embodied in the church. The rehumanization of the church—the healing of the church itself—happens when the church's presence is not dictated by worldly powers or by fear, but by the Word become flesh in history. When Jesus's words and the church's words interact meaningfully and reach what was earlier referred to as a "natural frequency,"[108] then the church will be in tune with its deepest self as a sacrament of salvation in and for the world. Being in

---

[107] Ellacuría, "The Church of the Poor, Historical Sacrament of Liberation," 556.
[108] Lederach and Lederach, *When Blood and Bones Cry Out*, 206.

tune with the voice of Jesus always demands being in tune with the cry of the oppressed in whom Jesus speaks to the church and to whom the church must answer in historical commitment. The force that is released when the poor and the church echo each other in Jesus is nothing less than what is required for the transformation of a history of oppression into a history of salvation.

A church that embodies the historical salvation to which it is called by the cries of the displaced and persecuted is a church that will be displaced and persecuted as well. In the 1980s, government agents infiltrated communities who provided sanctuary and threatened them with arrest, eventually charging some persons with federal crimes and sending them to prison. But as Rabbi Marshall Meyer wrote in the mid-1980s: "[Sanctuary] exists not only to fight against the powers of evil and idolatry but to celebrate the sanctity of life and to help people to live in spite of persecution. . . . Let us be brothers and sisters, responsible for one another, and let us celebrate life and its sanctuary and its sanctity, and if needs be, we will celebrate in prison."[109] Even in displacement and persecution, or perhaps especially under such circumstances, the church cannot do otherwise than witness to making salvation historical by protecting and celebrating life. A world where the poor are persecuted but the church is not, is a world in which the church is not sufficiently present with the poor.

Ellacuría reminds us that "while not all persecution is a sign and miracle proving the authenticity of faith, the absence of persecution by those who hold power in a situation of injustice is a sign, irrefutable in the long range, that the proclamation of [the church's] message lacks evangelical courage.[110] While the church may be spared for a lack of courage, the life of the poor will not be spared. With Louie-Marie Chauvet we may ask again: "Is the concrete community the living sign of what it celebrates?"[111] The celebration of the life of Jesus and the remembrance of his death becomes a living sign—takes on flesh—in the celebration of the life of the poor for which it struggles, and in the remembrance of their death, for which it shares responsibility. Like Jesus, a living sign

---

[109] Marshall Meyer, "The international Struggle for Human Rights," in MacEoin, *Sanctuary,* 135–36.

[110] Ellacuría, "The Church of the Poor, Historical Sacrament of Liberation," 560.

[111] Chauvet, *Symbol and Sacrament,* 414.

and instrument of salvation will inevitably face persecution and will be displaced unto a cross. But, as Romero proclaimed, "Christ invites us not to be afraid of persecution, because believe it brothers and sisters, those who commit to the poor must meet the same fate as the poor, and in El Salvador we know what the destiny of the poor signifies: to be disappeared, to be tortured, to be captured, to be found dead."[112] This is still the reality for persons in El Salvador, throughout Central America, and in countless places around the world to which the United States continues to forcibly deport.

A community that responds to the displaced and persecuted who are forced to flee to the church will become a church community configured by mercy. In Chapter 3 I explained that the earliest reference to church sanctuary is found in the Council of Serdica's canons from the year 343, canons in which bishops formally established that the church was to intercede before the Roman government for the poor and oppressed, widows and orphans, and all who "flee to the mercy of the church" (*ad misericordiam ecclesiae confugiant*).[113] Mercy, Jon Sobrino says, is a "re-action to someone else's suffering, now interiorized within oneself," a particular kind of love that "is in the absolute beginning of the history of salvation" and that "abides as a constant in God's salvific process."[114] Mercy moves God to act on behalf of the cries of the oppressed, and, by way of mercy, the church follows God's salvific actions in history. Etymologically speaking, at the root of mercy is the poor (*miseri*) and the heart (*cor*), and, as Gustavo Gutiérrez among others has said, to have mercy is to have the heart of the poor, of the insignificant, of the nonpersons of our time, and thus the heart of God.[115] We can expand this to say that the poor are the heart of the church who always belong in the heart of the church. When the displaced and persecuted poor seek sanctuary in the church, they are not trespassing or seeking entrance into buildings and communities to which they have no relation. Formally speaking, from

---

[112] Romero, *Homilías*, February 17, 1980; 6:284–85.

[113] Hess, *The Early Development of Canon Law and the Council of Serdica*, 203–4.

[114] Jon Sobrino, *The Principle of Mercy* (Maryknoll, NY: Orbis Books, 1994), 16–17.

[115] Gustavo Gutiérrez, "Misericordia y Justicia," *Páginas* 41, no. 244 (2016): 6–9. Also, Walter Kasper, *Mercy: The Essence of the Gospel and the Key to Christian Life* (New York: Paulist Press, 2013), 21–22.

the perspective of God's partiality for the poor, they are simply living into an existential truth that they have always belonged in the church, even when the church has forgotten, ignored, or rejected their presence.

At stake are not simply works of mercy, but a whole transformation of the church into a church fundamentally defined by this kind of love. The love of mercy impels the church to risk itself for the protection of others as the Good Samaritan exemplifies in the Gospel. Sobrino explains, "In this world works of mercy are applauded or tolerated, but what is not tolerated is a church configured by the principle of mercy, which leads the church to denounce robbers who produce victims, to unmask the lie with which they conceal oppression, and to support victims in their liberation from them."[116] When the contemporary equivalent to robbers is ICE and other government agents, mercy becomes a work of justice and of the transformation of social, political, and economic structures that inflict violence and death. Unmasking the lies with which legalized violence is justified is a required element of mercy, and it will certainly turn the government's forces upon the church. In the midst of these conflicts, the church must remain close to the wounded ones who are forced to take refuge in the church while they journey toward their own freedom. "The re-action of mercy," Sobrino adds, "is what verifies if the church has de-centered itself, and to what extent it has done so."[117] A church whose center is outside itself is a church who has found itself.

During Romero's time as archbishop, groups of poor campesinos would sometimes occupy and take refuge in the cathedral because it was the only place from which they could denounce the government's repression without being immediately killed. Romero understood that he and the community had a responsibility to protect them. About a month before he was killed in 1980, he made the following statement:

> Over at the Cathedral one is moved with pity. Some only judge from outside the occupation of the temple, and certainly it is an inconvenience. But when you see inside the masses of poor people

---

[116] Sobrino, *El Principio Misericordia* (San Salvador: UCA Editores, 2012), 42. Translation my own. For published English version, see Sobrino, *The Principle of Mercy*, 23.

[117] Sobrino, *El Principio Misericordia*, 40, translation my own; I have chosen to translate *herido* as "wounded" for greater accuracy to the Spanish original. For published English version, see Sobrino, *The Principle of Mercy*, 22.

who have come fleeing from their villages, to which they cannot return because they will be persecuted, and that if they cannot take refuge in a temple they will have to flee to the hills, then we understand that the church, truly, must always live in a state of emergency.[118]

The reality of the poor who had been displaced and persecuted and who sought the protection of the church was a living reminder of what is structurally required of the church at all times. Romero does not say simply that an emergency response was needed, rather, that the church "must always live in a state of emergency." In El Salvador, this meant risking the institutional resources of the church itself in terms of buildings, priests and religious, lay catechists, parish leaders, and the life of the bishop himself, whose commitment to the poor and persecuted included living and dying as their sanctuary. The church incarnates sanctuary when it seeks in mercy those who are forced to flee to the church. The encounter will transform the church into a refuge where God and the poor can dwell in each other's holy presence, and where salvation is made historically present through the gratuitous mercy of God.

"How does God's love abide in anyone who has the world's goods and sees a brother or sister in need and yet refuses help?" (1 Jn 3:17) This question was at the root of the sanctuary ministry in the 1980s, and it is a question to which the church always has to respond. In the story of the Good Samaritan, the person who was attacked and left for dead is taken to the inn, where the wounds—the *traumata* from which we get the word *trauma*—begin to heal.[119] In the early church the inn—the *pandocheion* in Greek,[120] which means the place where all are received or welcome—was allegorically interpreted as a symbol of the church itself.[121] In our global state of violence-induced

---

[118] Romero, *Homilías*, February 17, 1980; 6:284–85.
[119] *Traumata* appears only once as a noun in the New Testament, in the story of the Good Samaritan in Luke 10:34.
[120] *Pandocheion* (inn) is a compound of *pas* (all, every) and *dechomai* (receive, welcome).
[121] See Robert H. Stein, "The Interpretation of the Parable of the Good Samaritan," in *Scripture, Tradition, and Interpretation: Essays Presented to Everett F. Harrison* (Grand Rapids, MI: Eerdmans, 1978), 279–80. For further analysis of early

displacement, the church is literally, not simply allegorically, called to become a sanctuary where persecuted communities may find refuge, where wounds may be attended, where holiness is encountered, and where salvation becomes historical in the enfleshment of good news to the poor. Church as sanctuary is an act of worship that invokes the creative Spirit, who makes present the presence of the crucified and risen Jesus in whose transformed wounds the church ultimately finds its own refuge, healing, holiness, and salvation.

Christian places of refuge for strangers, pilgrims, the sick, and the poor, see Olivia Remie Constable, *Housing the Stranger in the Mediterranean World* (Cambridge: Cambridge University Press, 2004).

Conclusion

In the past four to five weeks I have seen the burnt hillsides of El Salvador, refugee camps and bombed-out villages, nights pocked by bombs, blackouts and hideous cries, two weeks of wandering in Mexico City, endless and exasperating waiting for help near the frontier, and even smuggling Salvadorans across the Sonoran desert into Arizona and finally into California. It has been a time of dashed plans, constantly shifting ground, and little or no certainty about states of affairs or the possibility of success. I've met people who have been without homes for seven years, I've visited the sites of martyrdoms and the graves of martyrs, I've been compelled to accept the charity and good will of others with resources that I didn't have, I've shared in the fear and occasional desperation of people who are on the run for their lives, and one night I even slept on the sidewalk in a vain hope that help would come. I've met literally scores of good people who have sacrificed much and jeopardized all for the sake of human rights, including dedicated Jesuits who have totally embraced the poverty necessary to carry on such work, and prophetically brave Americans in Tucson who have been tried and convicted for their work on behalf of the oppressed.

I've been running on adrenalin for four weeks, have lost weight, and feel exhausted. I still feel the fear level that kept us aware and awake the whole time as we evaded detection by Federales in Mexico and the migra in the US. Suddenly, even normal people in crowds have come to look suspicious, and I have learned the refugees' wariness of the telephone.

More important than all of these experiences and aftereffects, I feel that I've been changed. Something has happened, the full implications of which I am still figuring out. This experience has touched me at the core of my being. It has forced me, as few other experiences have, to take possession of my own personhood, perhaps because these weeks have been partly concerned with saving the life of another person. The experience of these weeks has expanded my North American horizon to include an entire continent and its suffering people. Furthermore, these weeks have forced me to confront and accept the grace and love of God in ways that I never could have anticipated or planned. It has been a trial and a blessing.[1]

—PAUL CROWLEY, SJ

In the spring of 1988 Jesuit priest and theologian Paul Crowley journeyed to El Salvador. While there, fellow Jesuits asked him if he would be willing to accompany a Salvadoran man named Vicente who needed to flee El Salvador and find refuge in the United States. Although Paul and Vicente made it to Mexico without incident, from the brief excerpt of his narrative one can glimpse the uncertainty and shared vulnerability that marked the rest of their trip to the US-Mexico border. By the time the logistics for crossing into the United States were finally arranged, Paul was accompanying not only Vicente but also five Salvadoran women and children who had been waiting on the Mexican side of the border for an opportunity to cross. With assistance from the underground network developed by Jim Corbett in the early 1980s, they eventually crossed the desert into Tucson and, from there, Paul accompanied Vicente to his destination at Casa Rutilio Grande in Los Angeles, a sanctuary house for persons who had fled the violence and war in Central America.

Accompanying Central Americans who were forced to seek sanctuary required that Paul enter the dangerous world of persecution without a guarantee that they would find refuge, and it changed his life. In Paul's words, it forced him to "take possession of my own personhood." The journey north with Vicente and the other Salvadorans was a journey of maturation in faith, of growth in consciousness, and of surrender to the mystery of God who also journeys with each person seeking life.

This book has sought to provide theological scaffolding around the central concept and practice of sanctuary that is still not a permanent pillar of the church, but which is urgently needed for the church's own

---

[1] Paul Crowley, "May 4, 1988," in *The Sanctuary Experience: Voices of the Community* (San Diego: Aventine Press, 2004), 259–60.

legitimacy as bearer of good news to displaced and persecuted persons and for the sake of the countless lives who continue to be disappeared by the exclusionary and violent structures of societies, especially in the global North. All scaffolding is meant to assist in the process of rebuilding, repairing, or restoring a structure, and the edifice I have worked upon is the church—a living sanctuary that, in a world of forced displacement, must follow Jesus by convoking community beyond deadly borders. The hope of this book has been to remember the tradition of church sanctuary that is already part of our too easily forgotten history, and, more important, it has been a hope for the present transformation of a church in the United States whose future is indelibly bound with persons arriving at the borders of the country and at the borders of the church. In the conclusion to *A Theology of Liberation*, Gustavo Gutiérrez reminds us of the following:

> If theological reflection does not vitalize the action of the Christian community in the world by making its commitment to charity fuller and more radical, if—more concretely—in Latin America it does not lead the Church to be on the side of the oppressed classes and dominated peoples, clearly and without qualifications, then this theological reflection will have been of little value. Worse yet, it will have served only to justify half-measures and ineffective approaches and to rationalize a departure from the Gospel.[2]

The theological analysis of the previous chapters provided lenses for understanding church sanctuary as a genuine expression of the Christian tradition, and more particularly, of what it means to be a church that accompanies the poor in their own journey of resisting forces that threaten their life. Christian communities and ecclesiastical leaders who dismiss church sanctuary as mere politics end up, unwittingly perhaps, justifying social and legal structures that, in the final analysis, kill.

The sanctuary ministry of the 1980s that grew into a national movement is a reminder of what is possible when communities commit to

---

[2] Gustavo Gutiérrez, *A Theology of Liberation* (Maryknoll, NY: Orbis Books, 1988), 174.

respond to the institutionalization of violence with nonviolence and to the lies of political interests with the truth of their witness. To the systemic humiliation and dehumanization carried out by military forces in El Salvador that extended to the United States through the actions of the Immigration and Naturalization Service, the actions of sanctuary churches became an enfleshed counter-narrative whose truth was manifest in their willingness to suffer. Sanctuary churches were like truth commissions across the nation, resisting lies through noncooperation with the forces of deportation. The Gandhian insights presented in Chapter 2 illustrated that, although the actions of a few church communities may not seem like a great contribution to the transformation of society, through the depth of conviction of each witnessing community, society is reconstructed, and what was previously unimaginable becomes a possibility and a historical reality. As forced human displacement becomes an ever deeper wound of modernity, sanctuary actions become an instrument of peace and a sign of nonviolence for healing society and the church itself.

Changes in the church's self-understanding—its core identity—happen slowly and are never unambiguous, as Part II showed. However, the church's ongoing task is to discern the times in which it lives and the presence of the Spirit who is already at work in history with and for humanity. Conflict is inevitable because to remain uninvolved with situations that dehumanize others is to be complicit, but there is grace in recognizing the conflict in which the church already finds itself, for only then can it begin to accept the responsibility that it bears by its faith. Óscar Romero and other martyrs killed for their love of the poor and persecuted have shown what a church in the midst of institutionalized violence must do to remain faithful to the mystery of the incarnate God. In a conflictual and polarized reality, the poor show the way the church must travel. In an age of forced displacement, persons who are forced to seek refuge and who are branded illegal and unauthorized reveal the church's true nature and mission as a sanctuary of and for life.

Acknowledgments

The seeds for this project emerged over a decade ago, when I worked in Tucson, Arizona. Thank you to Bill Remmel, Bishop Kicanas, John Fife, Alison Harrington, Randy Mayer, Noel Andersen, Samaritans, No More Deaths, and all who struggle in the borderlands for the life of migrants. At the University of Notre Dame I was nourished in both the theology department and in the Kroc Institute for International Peace Studies, and Sr. Mary Catherine Hilkert, Timothy Matovina, John Paul Lederach, Kraig Beyerlein, and Gustavo Gutiérrez guided my vision with profound generosity. To my Kroc cohort and to all who drew out of me what I could not see—gracias! At Fordham University my colleagues have encouraged and supported me since I arrived. Their wisdom is woven into this book. I am grateful for the support of the Louisville Institute, the Hispanic Theological Initiative, and the Institute for Advanced Catholic Studies at USC for investing in my research through grants and fellowships, and to Orbis Books, especially Robert Ellsberg and Thomas Hermans-Webster, for editorial guidance. Last, my deepest gracias to the De La Salle Christian Brothers of the San Francisco district for standing with undocumented students; to my mother Rosa Guardado, who twice made the journey to the United States during the war in El Salvador, bringing me with her the second time—*muchísimas gracias mamá por la vida y el amor;* to Thomas X. Davis, abbot emeritus of the Trappist Abbey of New Clairvaux—thank you for your companionship and prayers over decades of friendship. And to Duane L. Sisson, a friend of God and compañero who was part of this project from the beginning and who now lives on the other side, across the border, in the boundless sanctuary—you taught me with great tenderness how to trust the light.

Index

Ambrose of Milan, 79–81, 86
American Baptist Churches (ABC) v. Thornburgh, 58–59
Aquinas, Thomas, 95
Arius of Alexandria, 72
asylum, 6, 9, 29, 196
    Australia, asylum-seekers in, 59, 199
    cities of refuge and asylum, 64–71, 92
    ecclesiastical right of asylum, 64, 85–92
    legal asylum proceedings, 8, 9
    norms of asylum in nation-states, 37
    political asylum, 4, 10, 19
    US failure to grant asylum, 39–40, 185
Athanasius of Alexandria, 72–73
Basil of Caesarea, 77–79, 125–26
Benedictine order, 91–92
Bondurant, Joan, 44, 46, 48, 56
borderlands, 14, 28, 31
    biblical wilderness, comparing to, 36
    civil initiative in the borderlands, 38, 53–55
    desert borderlands, 29, 33
    ecclesial identity of border crossers, 186–87
    healing of wounds at the border, 196–97
    sanctuary communities of, 56, 58–59, 63
    sanctuary ministry in the borderlands, 6, 93, 163
Border Patrol, 5, 191, 192–93
Casa Óscar Romero, 32

Casa Rutilio Grande, 230
Casas del Migrante, 197, 203
Central America, 11, 14, 164
    Casas del Migrante in, 197
    Central American refugees, 9–10, 18, 34, 102, 231
    Chicago Religious Task Force on Central America, 20–28, 42, 55
    church on the move from, 35–36
    deportation of asylum seekers from, 9–11, 18, 22, 40, 43, 225
    evasion services for transport of migrants, 197–98
    human rights violations in, 58
    root cause of oppression in, 26
    sanctuary for the displaced of, 17, 19, 30, 31, 33, 36, 163, 230
    United States policy on, 8, 57, 222
    US Central American peace movement, 24, 88, 196
    violence in Central America, 8, 63
    wars, asylum seekers fleeing, 63, 187
    See also El Salvador
Chathanatt, John, 45–46
Chauvet, Louis-Marie, 219, 224
Chenu, Marie-Dominique, 93, 94–100, 102, 113
Chrysostom, John, 81–84, 90–91
church sanctuary, 22, 57, 184, 219, 228
    civil initiative, enacting, 38–44
    counter-narrative of sanctuary churches, 232
    healing, church as a site of, 196–209
    holiness, dwelling in, 209–17
    public sanctuary churches, 16–20

reconstruction of, 59, 94, 115, 127–28
refuge from violence, church as, 185–96
reparation, sanctuary as a form of, 222
salvation, in relation to, 217–28
theological horizon of, 30–37, 63
civil initiative, 18, 38–44, 52, 53–54
Clarke, Maura, 5, 183
Code of Canon Law, 64, 85–87
Colombia, 127, 129, 140
Congar, Yves, 109, 111, 112, 211, 212
Conquest of Violence (Bondurant), 44
conscientization, 140, 166, 200
Corbett, James A., 9, 17, 29, 52, 59, 60, 93, 194
   on the ABC agreement, 58–59
   Bondurant, as influenced by, 44
   on the church on the move, 35–36
   on civil initiative, 18, 38–43, 53–54
   CRTFCA and, 20, 23, 24, 55
   "Dear Friends" letters, 10, 12, 15, 22, 30
   discernment process of, 12–14, 102
   Freedom Seder, describing, 32–33
   Mexico, Corbett in, 22, 229
   nonviolence, practicing, 56–57
   post-Constantinian vision of, 34–35
   as a Quaker, 9, 10, 27–28
   sanctuary ministry, as a founder of, 11, 31
   social healing, writing on, 208–9
   static sanctuary, defining, 37
   underground network, developing, 19–20, 230
   See also Tucson
corpus Christi, 165, 173–76, 177, 179–82
corpus mysticum, 150–54
Cortright, David, 47
Coughlin, John, 86
Council of Serdica, 63, 72, 74–78, 81, 86, 122, 225
Coutin, Susan Bibler, 25–26
Cowan, Margo, 17

Cresconius of Milan, 79–81
Crittenden, Ann, 25
Crowley, Paul, 230–31
Cunningham, Hilary, 26–27
Cupich, Blase, 89–90
David, King, 211
De Lubac, Henri, 128, 153
   corpus mysticum, discussing, 150–52, 154, 157
   sacramental insights, 155, 158, 209
   Susan Wood on ecclesiology of De Lubac, 156–57
desconocidos (unknown persons), 197
Dominican order, 94
Donovan, Jean, 5, 183
Ducloux, Anne, 75–76, 78
East Bay Sanctuary Covenant, 25–26
El Centro detention center, 3–4, 8, 9, 38
Elder, Jack, 32
Elford, Ricardo, 7, 9, 11, 33
Ellacuría, Ignacio, 218, 220, 223–24
El Salvador, 14, 35, 39, 40, 178, 187, 218, 225
   Aguilares, town of, 164, 167
      Corpus Christi, persecuted citizens as, 177–78
      El Señor de las Misericordias parish, 165–66
      Eucharistic procession in, 176, 179–81, 201
      military occupation of, 170, 171–75, 200, 223
      mission team murder in, 168–69, 170
      sacramental encounter with the poor in, 182
   the borderlands, Salvadorans in, 4–5, 28, 54, 56
   Corbett as assisting Salvadoran migrants, 12, 30, 230
   deportation of Salvadorans, 3–4, 8–11, 19–20, 40
   El Paisnal village, 165, 168, 171, 176, 182

Freedom Seder caravan, refugees protected by, 32–33
network for displaced Salvadorans, 11–12, 22
persecuted Salvadorans, accompanying, 16, 231
Salvadoran immigrants, sanctuary for, 23, 25, 26
Salvadoran soldiers, Romero appealing to, 15–16
sanctuary movement in relation to, 195, 232
temporary protection for asylum seekers, 58, 230–31
United States, Salvadoran migrants in, 30, 42
universal church concretized in the church of, 173
violence in, 4, 6, 7, 18, 21, 164, 183, 217, 229
See also Romero, Óscar
Episcopal Church, 91
Eucharist
Aguilares, Eucharistic procession in, 179–81, 201
De Lubac on mystery of the Eucharist, 153–57, 209
desecration of the Eucharist, 171–77, 181, 200, 223
Paul VI on mystical correspondence of, 127–28
presence of Christ in, 130–31, 149, 150–51, 157–59, 165, 174, 182, 200
Eutropius, Emperor, 81–82, 83, 90
evangelical poverty, 147–48
evasion services, 19, 40, 197–98
Fife, John, 7, 9, 12, 18, 20
Ford, Ita, 5, 183
Francis, Pope, 102, 103, 109, 118, 127, 218
Freedom Seder, 32–33
Gandhi, Mahatma, 29, 32
on civil initiative as method for social change, 43, 53–55

constructive program of, 49–53
Gandhian sanctuary, 57, 232
as faithful response to dehumanizing violence, 43–44
in framework for social change, 28, 44–53, 56
nonviolent alternatives, offering, 140–41
Satyagraha movement and, 45–49
Gaudium et Spes, 95, 116, 122
key elements of, 94, 115
as last document of Vatican council, 103, 112–13
missionary spirit of, 105, 117–20, 121, 133
as the most human conciliar document, 126
opening words of, 120, 219
the poor, identifying the church with, 13, 89, 113
schemas of early draft, 113–14
violence and the church, discussing, 124–25
Golden, Renny, 21
Grande García, Rutilio, 165, 167–69, 170–71, 181, 183, 200
Greenberg, Moshe, 66
Gregory of Nazianzus, 77–79, 125
Grossman, Dave, 189–92
Guatemala, 8, 33, 35
borderlands, displaced Guatemalans in, 28
deportation of Guatemalan refugees, 19–20, 40, 54
indigenous migrants from, 23, 25
protecting fleeing immigrants, 22, 32, 58
Salvadoran refugees, deportation to Guatemala border, 4, 11
sanctuary for Guatemalan refugees, 26, 56
Gutiérrez, Gustavo, 94, 105, 187, 193, 215
on evangelization of the church by the world, 188

Latin American church and, 184, 231

on mercy as having the heart of the poor, 225

Hernandez, Carmela, 185, 217

Heschel, Abraham Joshua, 32

Hess, Hamilton, 73–74

Honduras, 4

Humanae Salutis apostolic constitution, 100–101

Immigration and Customs Enforcement (ICE), 185, 217, 226

church, protection from ICE in, 186, 194, 209–10

intergenerational wounds, creating, 198

psychological insights into ICE agents, 192–93

sanctuary as an act of resistance against ICE, 201–2

Immigration and Naturalization Service (INS), 7, 8–10, 17, 39, 40, 58, 232

International Eucharistic Congress, 129

Jesuit order, 165, 171, 180, 229, 230

Jesus Christ, 98, 101, 109, 137, 170, 211, 225, 231

Basil, comparing to, 78–79

body of Christ, 133, 156, 177

desecration of, 181, 220, 223

in the Eucharist, 150, 154, 165, 209

historical body of Christ, 151, 154–55, 157, 158–59, 164, 220–21

mystical body of Christ, 128, 151, 153–55, 156, 221

in the poor, 131, 149, 150, 165, 182

sanctuary for, 157–60, 182

crucified Jesus, 177–78, 228

disciples and followers, 110–11, 120, 134, 148, 184, 201, 215

in the Eucharistic mystery, 129–31, 150, 154, 156, 157

in *Gaudium et Spes,* 13, 113

good news of, 105, 153

historic Jesus, 133, 151, 153–54, 156, 157–59, 220–21

imitation of Christ, 104, 106–8, 117, 131, 136, 149, 175, 213–14, 223

mission of Christ, 106, 118, 126, 220

Peter, Jesus's promise to, 82–83

prophetic spirit of, 99–100

reparations to Christ, 173, 174

resurrection of, 147, 153, 157, 209

salvific work of, 120, 146

in the theandric mystery, 104, 106

See also poverty and the poor

John Paul II, Pope, 86

John the Baptist, 134

John XXIII, Pope, 113

church of the poor, vision of, 131, 146, 183

Constantinian captivity, calling for liberation from, 35

hopes for Vatican II, 101–2, 108, 122–23

tone for Vatican II, setting, 93, 100

Kasper, Walter, 106–7, 108

Kazel, Dorothy, 5, 183

King, Martin Luther, Jr., 32

Landázuri Ricketts, Juan, 132, 133–34, 159, 183–84

Larraín, Manuel, 128

Latin America, 13, 14, 24, 26, 127, 163, 218

ecclesial base communities of, 12

Gutiérrez and the Latin American church, 184, 231

listening to the poor in, 128–34, 135

Medellín document on the poor of, 128, 137, 142–48

the poor, Latin American church accompanying, 183

religious awakening in, 35–36

salvation for the people of, 135, 164

spiritual poverty in, 45–46

violence in, 68, 138–39

Latin American Bishops Conference (CELAM), 128, 132, 163

Index

Lederach, John Paul and Angela, 202–5, 208

Leffel, Gregory, 26

Lemus, Nelson, 168

Lercaro, Giacomo, 123, 150

Le Saulchoir (Chenu), 96

Levinas, Emmanuel, 68–71, 83, 92, 123–24

Life of Saint Ambrose (Paulinus), 79–80

living sanctuary, 92, 127, 165, 179–82, 231

Lonergan, Bernard, 190

Love Makes a Way organization, 59

Lumen Gentium, 89, 94, 103, 109, 112, 124

    affirmation of love for the afflicted, 130

    on church as a sacrament for salvation, 106–8

    ecclesiological framework expressed in, 120–21

    on the followers of Christ, 110–11

    light of Christ, on the church reflecting, 104–5

    on the total environment of the world, 115

magisterium, 101, 165

martyrdom, 27, 35–36, 229, 232

McConnell, Michael, 21

McGrath, Mark, 113–14

Medellín conference, 36, 133, 212

    as clarifying different meanings of poverty, 144–49, 213–16

    justice, document on, 128, 137–38, 150

    Landázuri's opening statement, 132–34, 159, 183–84

    love, understanding of, 135–36

    Paul VI's vision for, 128–29

    peace, document on, 128, 138–39, 150

    poverty, document on, 128, 141–43, 158

    redemptive logic undergirding documents of, 219

    religious formation inspired by, 165–66

Romero on the luminous documents of, 163–64

    sacramental insights on the poor, 127, 131, 217

    violence, conference position on, 139–41

mercy, 37, 38, 81, 146, 211

    clerical duty to practice mercy, 74, 77–79, 83, 89, 125–26

    mercy of the church, the poor fleeing to, 74, 102, 122, 123

    refuge seekers, mercy upon, 73–76, 82, 195

    salvation as historically present via mercy, 227

    Sobrino on the principle of mercy, 226

"Message to Humanity" address, 100, 102

Mexico, 10, 19, 20, 185

    Mexico-Guatemala border, 4, 11, 22

    Sonoran Desert, 33, 197, 229

    US-Mexico border, 11, 22, 63, 163, 191, 197, 203, 230

Meyer, Marshall, 224

Moses, 64, 211

mutual salvation, 217–28

Napier, Davie, 196, 197

Nathan, prophet, 211

Nicene Creed, 72

nonviolence, 28, 30, 32

    ahimsa theme, 46, 47, 48, 49

    civil disobedience and, 51

    civil initiative and, 39, 41, 53–54

    Gandhi's philosophy of, 44, 46–48, 140–41

    mercy as doing justice nonviolently, 37

    sanctuary as nonviolent means and ends, 55–60

    of sanctuary churches, 63, 232

    Satyagraha, as a pillar of, 45, 49–50, 52

    theological aspirations to, 125

Noriega, Arnie, 11

Nuremberg principles, 38–39, 43, 54

Nuremberg Trials, 10, 38
Oblate Sisters of the Sacred Heart of Jesus, 180
Operation Rutilio, 171, 200
Organ Pipe Cactus National Monument, 4, 25
Ortega, Jose Luis, 171
O'Sullivan, Suzanne, 199
Our Lady of Fatima, 175
pandocheion (inn) as a symbol of the church, 277
Paulinus of Milan, 79–80
Paul VI, Pope, 86, 134
  body of Christ, binding with the poor, 150, 158–59
  Bogotá, homily in, 129–30
  end of Vatican council, presiding over, 94
  Latin America, first pope to visit, 128–29
  Medellín conference, homily prior to, 127, 131
  on the poor as a sacrament of Christ, 127, 217
  violence, quoted by bishops on, 139–40
Philibert, Paul, 96
Pima Friends Meeting House, 33
Pironio, Bishop, 131
Potworowski, Christophe, 99
poverty and the poor, 164, 229
  Aguilares, living with the poor in, 165–69
  body of Christ in the poor, 149, 150, 165, 182
  church of the poor, 138, 158, 160, 187, 216
    historical nature of the church and, 220, 223
    John XXIII's vision of, 131, 146, 183
    Lercaro as promoting concept of, 123, 150
    Medellín conference as clarifying, 128, 141–49, 150, 213–14

commitment, poverty as, 145, 147, 149, 213
learning to listen to the poor, 128–34
Medellín document on poverty, 141–49, 158, 213–16
mercy, the poor fleeing to, 74, 102, 122, 123, 223
sacrament of Christ, the poor as a, 127, 128, 149, 150, 158–59, 217
Puebla document, 220
Quakers, 9, 10, 21, 27–28, 32, 33
Quiñones, Ramon, 11
Rahner, Karl, 115–16, 195
real poverty, 145, 213–14
recombinant church, 31, 33–34
redemption, 97–99, 148, 154, 158, 219
refuge
  biblical understanding of, 29, 31, 211
  church, refuge in, 17, 35–36, 64, 71–85, 86, 88–92, 125, 163, 184, 210
  cities of refuge, 64–71, 76, 83, 92, 123
  ecclesial practice of, 93–94, 102, 122
  healing as a category of refuge, 196–99, 206–7
  holiness as a category of refuge, 209–11
  network of communities providing refuge, 12–13, 19–20, 22, 23
  Romero as refuge of the oppressed, 165, 181
  violence, refuge from, 90, 124, 185–96
refugees, 22, 39, 55
  1980 Refugee Act, 18, 39
  borderlands, refugees in, 28, 54, 59
  civil initiative and sanctuary for refugees, 39, 41–42
  communion with refugees, 13, 63
  CRTFCA as working with refugees, 21, 22–26
  deportation of Central American refugees, 9–11, 18, 22, 40, 43

El Salvador, refugees from, 3–6, 8, 10, 14, 30, 42, 170
Freedom Seder, refugees participating in, 32–33
in *Gaudium et Spes,* 118
refugee children, 199, 205
Romero, Óscar, 33, 163, 218, 223
  Aguilares occupation, homilies given during, 176–79
  assassination, commemoration of, 17, 21
  blessed sacrament, duty to protect, 171–72, 200
  Corpus Christi, reflections on the feast of, 173–76
  Eucharistic procession, taking part in, 179–82, 201
  first year as archbishop, 164–65
  as a martyr, 5, 27, 183, 232
  nonviolence, advocating, 15–16, 18
  persecution, on Christians not fearing, 225
  the poor, living in the company of, 165–69
  Rutilio Grande, on the death of, 170
  state of emergency, on the church living in, 218, 227
  static sanctuary, on Cathedral as, 226–27
salvation, 83, 94, 133
  church as sacrament of, 123, 135, 158, 187, 219, 221–23
  economy of salvation, divine work in, 137–38
  in *Gaudium et Spes,* 117, 119
  Jesus as an instrument of, 149, 224–25, 228
  Latin America, salvation for the people of, 135, 164
  in *Lumen Gentium,* 104–8
  mercy of God, role in salvation, 227
  the poor as participating in the work of, 147
  Rahner on hoping for eternal salvation, 195

refugees as seeking, 184, 185, 218–19
Yves Congar on salvation, 111, 112
sanctuary ministry, 35, 63, 232
  community of refuge, building, 184–85, 194–95
  conflicting visions of sanctuary, 20–23
  discernment of sanctuary, 6–7, 11–16, 16–20, 28, 102, 207, 210
  evasion services, developing, 197–98
  foundation for ministry of sanctuary, 7–11
  nature and purpose of sanctuary, 24–28, 227–28
  Romero as patron saint of, 163–64
  social healing and communion of, 208–9
  transformation of society as goal of ministry, 29–30, 93
San Jose de las Mosquera, 129, 158
Santuario de Nuestra Señora de Guadalupe, 11
Satyagraha (nonviolence), 43–44, 44–53, 54
Second Vatican Council. *See* Vatican II
signs of the times, 116, 178, 188
  Chenu, helping to discern, 93, 94, 96–98
  Jesus on distinguishing the signs of the times, 100–101
  Medellín conference, discernment at, 133
  prophetic charism, reading through, 99–100
  Romero as constantly scanning, 182
sin, 97, 125, 144, 154
  Chrysostom on, 83, 91
  church's struggles against the reality of, 218–19, 221
  misery, sin as generating, 136
  original sin as reaching maturity, 96
  poverty in relation to, 145, 146
  as rejection of love of neighbor, 135
  reparations for sins, 175

salvation not overcome by, 137
secular sin of oppression, 222
structural sin, 138, 187
violence and sin, 158, 164
Smith, Christian, 24
Sobrino, Jon, 34, 180, 181, 195, 216, 222, 225, 226
Solorzano, Manuel, 168
Southside Presbyterian Church, 7, 12, 16–18, 25, 27, 32
spiritual poverty, 145, 146–47, 149, 213–16
Stern, Craig, 65
St. Mark's Presbyterian Church, 7
Suenens, Leo Joseph, 121
Task Force on Central America (TECTF), 8, 9
Tellis, Allwyn, 50
Theology of Liberation (Gutiérrez), 231
Thürmer, Mechthild, 91–92
Timbal, Pierre, 85
Trump, Donald, 90, 191
Tucson, 3, 9, 10, 39, 230
  borderland experiences in, 55, 93
  CRTFCA, comparing to Tucson community, 22–23, 24–28
  ongoing discernment in, 7–8, 11
  prophetic bravery exhibited in, 229
  Quaker houses of, 32, 33
  Salvadorans, transporting into, 17
  sanctuary ministry in, 12, 18, 20, 26–27, 33, 44, 56, 63
  theoretical frameworks for sanctuary, 6–7, 43, 57
Tucson Ecumenical Council (TEC), 4, 7–8, 17, 22, 27
Tucson refugee support group (Trsg), 22
underground network, 19, 22, 23, 230
United Nations High Commissioner for Refugees, 22
United Nations Refugee Agency (UN-HCR), 39–40

United Nations Refugee Protocol, 39
Van der Kolk, Bessel, 198
Vatican II, 109, 121, 150, 166
  Chenu's contributions to, 94–100
  on church as a sacrament of salvation, 219
  church sanctuary tradition and, 85, 103, 123
  Code of Canon Law, revisions due to, 86, 89
  Constantinian captivity, role in freedom from, 35
  humanizing vision of, 93–94, 114, 125
  John XXIII's hopes for, 108, 122–23
  Latin American church, calling for renewal of, 128
  mission of the church, new sense of, 118, 126, 127
  modern mind, dialoguing with world of, 115–16
  Paul VI's closing speech, referencing, 134
  post-council conferences, 129, 163
  sacramental ecclesiology of, 106–7, 155–56, 157, 184
  unfulfilled ecclesial vision of church of the poor, 214
  See also Gaudium et Spes; *Lumen Gentium*
Veronica (biblical figure), 175
Vides, Ricardo, 171
Vietnam War, sanctuary for opponents of, 88
Walker, William, 12
Waskow, Arthur, 32
Wellington Avenue United Church of Christ, 20
Wood, Susan, 156
World Day of the Poor, 127
Wuerl, Cardinal, 194